In the Phoenix Company, an unspoken, solemn vow was lived: Americans were on the ground; the Phoenix would come to get them!

As they came on short final (one-fourth mile out), the fire grew heavier. Then Mayberry slammed the Huey down amid the exploding mortar rounds, while six heavily laden soldiers rushed for the helicopter. A mortar round hit in front of the soldiers and another simultaneously just behind them. Flattened like bowling pins, the group was thrown to the ground, all badly wounded. Mayberry shouted to the crew chief, Sp5. John Ackerman, and the door gunner, Sp4. Wayne Wasilk, "Get them!" The two young Minnesotans rushed twenty yards through the mortar fire, helped four of the men up, and shouldered them to the helicopter. The firing continued, landing all around them, and Rayburn felt AK-47 rounds and mortar fragments peppering his Huey as if the Huey's skin were his own.

Mayberry looked over his right shoulder, through the cargo bay door to his right rear. Mortars were being walked up the mountainside toward him as he watched. He held his breath, waiting for the next round. . . .

# THE PRICE OF EXIT

# OF EXIT

## Tom Marshall

IVY BOOKS • NEW YORK

An Ivy Book
Published by The Ballantine Publishing Group
Copyright © 1998 by Tom Marshall

http://www.randomhouse.com

Library of Congress Catalog Card Number: 97-95366

ISBN 0-8041-1715-2

Manufactured in the United States of America

First Edition: June 1998

10  9  8  7  6  5  4  3  2  1

To those who remembered their birthdays,

for those who'd come . . . when you were downed,

ABOVE THE BEST!

Stoop, Angels, hither from the skies
        There is no holier spot of ground
        Than here where defeated valor lies
        By mourning beauty crowned
                        —HENRY TIMROD

# Contents

# Preface

In 1994, President Bill Clinton, who had refused his country's call to service during the Vietnam era, signed a law permitting business and trade with the people of Vietnam. By year's end, one-fourth of tourists to the country were American college students. One-half of the businessmen visiting were Americans.

President Clinton, however, was not alone in his opposition to the war. During Clinton's college years, he'd worked for Arkansas Senator J. William Fulbright, a longtime opponent of the war. Fulbright's 1966 book, *The Arrogance of Power*, influenced the antiwar movement. In it Fulbright stated, "In a democracy, dissent is an act of faith, to criticize one's country to do it a service. . . . It is an act of patriotism."

Some Americans sought college deferment from the military draft. A few moved to foreign lands, renouncing American citizenship. Others, sunshine patriots, joined local reserve or national guard units, knowing that call-up for service in Vietnam was unlikely. Personnel slots in those units evolved into such sought-after commodities by 1968 that they became subject to political favoritism as politicians offered help to distressed parents of draft-age sons. Parents with financial or political ability, desperate to avoid risking their sons' lives in a foreign land, fueled the inequities of the selective service system.

One-third of the male population would honor the selective service draft or volunteer for military service. The

Vietnam era conflict was the major sideshow of the Cold War. Only 12 percent of the total eligible male population served in Vietnam. According to military sources, a very small number, less than 3 percent of the male population, served as combatants. However, those who served in country understood that all were subject to 122mm rocket and 82mm mortar raids, even in the supposedly secure rear areas of noncombatants.

This is the story of many who served in army helicopters. The last two major actions in I Corps were the major events of 1970 and 1971. No one wanted to be the last man killed there, yet they served proudly, winning personal battles and enduring hardships despite a declining war effort. Army aviation traditions were born and strengthened in the actions of Firebase Ripcord, Landing Zone Lolo, and Pickup Zone Brown.

There had been five years of American buildup before the time of Hamburger Hill, in May 1969, which would symbolize the tragic, downward spiral that ended with the American exit. It would take the United States three years to exit the battlefields of South Vietnam. More men would die after the decision to leave was made than during the preceding five years.

After Hamburger Hill, those who served, merely following orders and performing their duties, were patriots in the most difficult of times. While others ran, protested, and evaded, those who were drafted and those who volunteered truly earned their rights as veterans . . . and patriots.

As the war effort waned, the demands on the helicopter crews did not diminish. The enemy added new and more powerful antiaircraft weapons, claiming more and more helicopters until the very end. The helicopter crews were all volunteers called upon to support a much less capable Army of South Vietnam while American troops departed the combat zone. As the American departure accelerated, it was the helicopter pilots, crew chiefs, and gunners who paid the heavy price of withdrawal.

When an army helicopter was shot down, another helicopter crew instantly dived to save the downed crew. Others continued the mission with resolve and, most importantly, absolute faith in their brother fliers.

Some pilots were labeled cowboys, some anointed paladins. But all were volunteers. They championed an unpopular American war effort, flying just above the trees, on warhorses of magnesium, aluminum, and fiberglass.

When the time came to pay the toll for American exit, the price of exit could only be paid in warrior souls.

This book would not be possible had I not met through the Vietnam Helicopter Pilots Association former Phoenix pilots Ken Mayberry and Jack Glennon, together with Mike Sloniker, Lt. Col., U.S.A. Retired, who also served in the army during that period. Their importance is explained in the story.

This story began as my autobiography, covering the time I served as a warrant officer aviator in the period August 19, 1970, through August 18, 1971. As I began the research and writing it evolved into something very different. In order to understand the horrors of the Laotian invasion and the experiences of the helicopter crews, one had to understand the Firebase Ripcord story.

I entered the war in August 1970 at An Khe in the Central Highlands of II Corps. When the 4th Infantry Division departed, I transferred to an assault helicopter company, C Company, 158th Aviation Battalion, 101st Airborne Division, which had the call sign Phoenix. The Phoenix was one of the most highly decorated assault helicopter units in I ("eye") Corps. The consequence of being a Phoenix and working the worst AO (area of operations) was the loss of thirty-four pilots and crewmen in twenty-four months. The number of Phoenix aircraft damaged and destroyed was also heavy. Only nine of the original twenty Hueys shipped to South Vietnam returned home. Even those sustained major combat damage.

I have solicited advice and recommendations from those who also served when I did. Where possible, individuals described in the story have participated in the review process. All involved agree that personal perspectives vary. The heat of battle, compounded by mission responsibilities, frequently leaves even well-trained minds in a sensory overload. Each of us remembered pieces of the puzzle differently. The bibliography lists published sources that I referred to while writing. Where possible, real names have been used, but some names have been changed to protect the privacy of individuals.

My personal story is a small part of the larger story of those I crossed paths with. It has been my personal journey to understanding, to sort some meaning from experiences, some of which remain as vivid as yesterday.

I now understand that having served in that time and place, the experience is forever a part of me. I can never leave it . . . neither can I go back.

In 1991, a Vietnam-era draft dodger, serving as the Republican secretary of defense, prosecuted the most successful war in American history.

In 1994, another Vietnam-era draft dodger, the president, legalized trade with the people of Vietnam.

As readers peruse this book, they should keep in mind the following words. Before the Vietnam War, Chairman Mao Tse-tung, borrowing from the ancient words of Suntzu, set the strategy for his students:

> The enemy advances: we retreat
> The enemy halts: we harass
> The enemy tires: we attack
> The enemy retreats: we pursue

During the Vietnam War, a student of Mao, Ho Chi Minh, leader of North Vietnam, proclaimed:

You will kill ten of our men, and we will kill one of yours, and in the end it will be you who tire of it.

Years later we learned:

The Communist North Vietnamese lost 1,100,000 killed during the 21 years of the Vietnam War.
                                        —Associated Press, April 4, 1995

*Coda*

The Wall in Washington, D.C., is a fallen V for victory; descendent of the symbolic peace sign of the Vietnam War era. It is engraved with over 58,200 names. For the families of those named on the Wall, as well as the men and women who served with them, it is akin to the mysterious monolith seen in *2001: A Space Odyssey*. Not just a black granite memorial, it is another dimension of the American experience, filled with rich personal stories and sacrifices for the American way of life. Families and friends of those lost make pilgrimages to Washington, D.C., to *touch* individual names. As they face the Wall and reach out, they close their eyes, remembering individual faces and stories in a tragic episode of our national history. By reverently fixing those memories in a place of honor, removed from the rage and disgust over their loss, the healing begins.

If you visit the Wall before dawn, you may have the blessing to chance upon a compassionate guide, a warrior, scholar, and humanitarian. An army veteran with two tours of duty in the Nam. He is often found, honoring their memories at sunrise.

                                        Tom Marshall
                                        1998

# Map 1. Republic of Vietnam

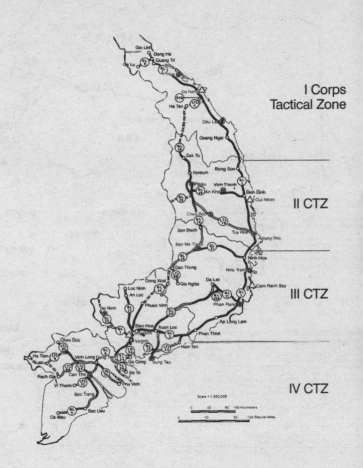

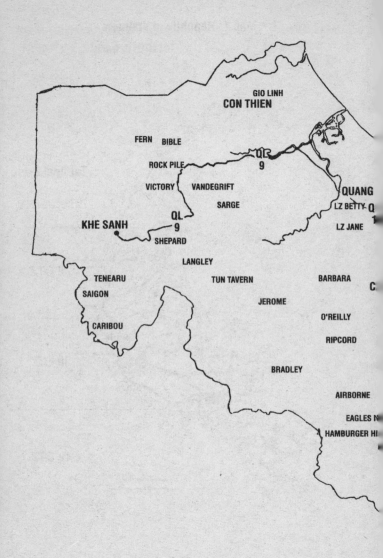

# Map 2. Firebases and LZs in Northern South Vietnam

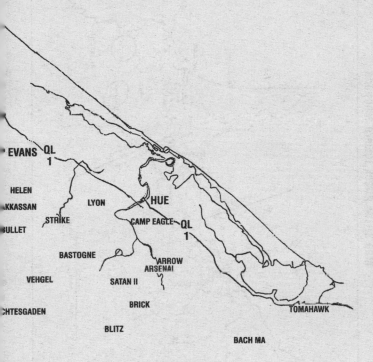

Map 3. The Attack Toward Tchepone

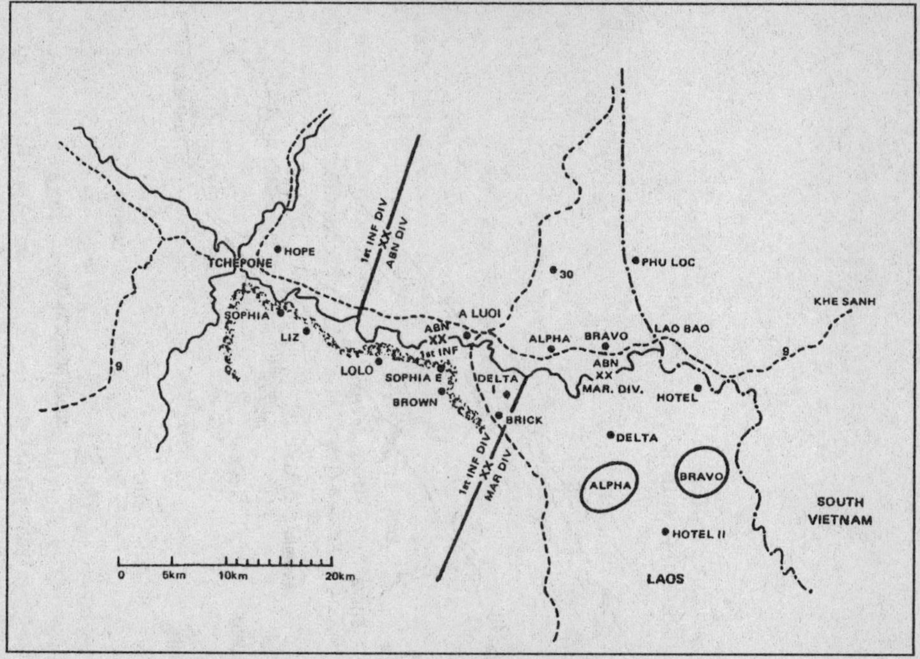

# Prologue

The "Phoenix" was Company C (Assault Helicopter),
158th Aviation Battalion, 101st Airborne Division (Airmobile). It was based at Camp Evans, midway between
Hue (pronounced "way") to the south and the demilitarized zone separating North and South Vietnam.

The morning of September 20, 1970, started like any
other mission day. Rising before dawn, they departed the
Phoenix Nest at oh-dark-thirty, to fly another combat assault. They would be carrying army Rangers, supporting
troops of the 1st Brigade of the 5th Mechanized Infantry
Division. The 1/5 was dispersed along the northern border with the enemy, North Vietnam. The intended landing
zone was on the north side of the demilitarized zone,
where the North Vietnamese troops (NVA) didn't expect
them. The Huey helicopter departed the Phoenix Nest at
Camp Evans and proceeded north to Quang Tri (QT).

At the 1/5 Mechanized Infantry pad, Papa Company
Rangers assembled. Killer Team 1-8 boarded the Phoenix
Huey. Sgt. Harold Sides, from Dallas, Texas, was the team
leader. With him were Sp4. Raymond Apellido, the assistant team leader, of Bakersfield, California. Sp4. Dale
Gray and another Ranger also took their positions, sitting in the door of the Huey's cargo bay, with their feet
dangling over the helicopter skids. Team members Sp4.

1

Anthony Gallina of Maplewood, Missouri, and PFC Glenn Ritchie of Mount Pleasant, North Carolina, also assumed their positions. They were well trained and highly experienced. They were to spend six days setting ambushes and booby traps near the center of the demilitarized zone (DMZ), an eight-mile-wide swath stretching from the South China Sea to the Laotian border.

With the Rangers loaded, the Huey departed QT, climbing to an altitude of only one hundred feet. Across the panoramic landscape of Quang Tri Province, the South China Sea was visible two miles to the east. The beautiful but deadly mountains of North Vietnam and Laos filled a distant horizon to the northwest. Flying high above them was the command-and-control Huey. It was accompanied by a Cobra gunship light-fire team, two Cobras ready to dive at the slightest provocation to the Huey.

It was a classic assault helicopter operation—inserting Rangers behind enemy lines. The Rangers' intent was to place mines and booby traps, perhaps capture a prisoner. Then to kill as many enemy as possible—creating havoc and fear, disrupting the enemy's daily routine on his home turf.

Passing west of Dong Ha, the last South Vietnamese village and military base, they descended to twenty or so feet above the ground, below the enemy radar horizon. Continuing northwest, they passed just west of Con Thien, the site of major battles between U.S. Marines and the NVA during the mid 1960s.

First Lieutenant Al Finn, the Phoenix 1st Platoon leader, was the aircraft commander. He was flying with a young warrant officer as his copilot. Passing west of Outpost Charlie-Two, which overlooked the demilitarized zone, they descended to five or ten feet above the ground. Accelerating to one hundred knots airspeed, the Huey entered the DMZ at an altitude of less than ten feet, with a speed approaching 120 miles per hour. It was a demanding ground-level sprint across the barren mudscape. The view was reminiscent of a World War I no-man's-land. The exit would also be as fast and as low as the Huey could go; North Vietnamese (NVA) bunkers with .51-caliber anti-aircraft machine guns were dispersed throughout the area. Flying even fifty feet above ground level would assure death at the hands of NVA .51s.

For the young Rangers, the Huey helicopter was a magic-carpet ride. With their feet dangling above the skids, they looked into the onrushing air, intently observing their objective. Flying at 120 miles per hour a few feet above the ground was quite a rush.

The Huey was coming loud and mean. The *whopping* of the rotor blades in normal flight was casual compared to sounds of the assaulting Huey. Its speed did not compare to that of an airplane. But in the three-mile-an-hour world of an infantryman, 120 miles per hour at five or ten feet above the ground was awesome.

The North Vietnamese could hear the helicopter coming two miles away, less than a minute's flight time, but the sound from ground-level flight was diffused enough to mask the Huey's exact location and direction. An NVA gunner alert enough to hear it coming would have to be quick and lucky to get a killing shot at the Americans.

The crew chief, Sp4. Dan Felts, and gunner, Sp4. William Dotson, scanned the onrushing landscape. They were flexing their M-60 machine guns, cleared hot, ready to suppress enemy fire.

The mission risk was high, but it was accepted as their duty. The aircrew, as well as the Rangers, believed it would be a routine killer-team insertion. The Phoenix had done it successfully many, many times before. Just another day in the saddle.

Suddenly, the Huey nosed into the ground, flipping tail over nose into a flaming mass. In an instant, four helicopter crew members and five Rangers died. Badly injured, one Ranger was thrown from the aircraft.

Instantaneous calls passed between the control bird

and the gunships following high above. One Cobra pilot thought he'd witnessed the Huey taking .51-caliber fire, on the right side, head-on in the aircraft commander's windshield. The other thought the cause might have been pilot error, flaring too sharply, contacting the ground. Whichever, the Huey had impacted the ground, flipping over, in an area occupied by the enemy.

To the surviving Phoenix pilots and crewmen, it didn't matter how or why. The final enemy, Death, had claimed two more pilots and two crewmen. The brotherhood of warriors in Company C had lost four brethren.

That evening back at Camp Evans, pilots gathered in the officers club. Adorning the small club stage was a carved wooden emblem of the Phoenix, resurrected in flames. Low voices, absent the young warrant officers' usual bravado, offered somber toasts, interspersed with blasphemous epithets. As the night wore on, war's reality settled in. The awareness of combat risk and one's very personal mortality settled to the forefront of their minds.

The combat-experienced aircraft commanders and first pilots studied the new mens' eyes. Seeking an intuitive answer . . . to the most serious but unspoken question: "If I go down, are you gonna come get me? . . . No matter what!"

Words could not matter. The answer was in the young men's eyes: unspoken, intuitive acceptance of duty, enduring whatever burden accompanied it. For the young men, duty performed with honor, despite a declining American war effort, required that they have faith in each other. There was a very real prospect of being shot down, and the fear of being left behind was the heart of darkness. The pilots shared a deeply personal desire: to avoid capture, torture, and death. An unmarked grave in a foreign jungle, in a war we were simply leaving, departing without victory.

The young pilots and crewmen would complete their duties and, so doing, pay the price of America's exit. The political decision to exit the conflict had been made by the U.S. Senate four months earlier, in June 1970. The toll would be paid in lives and body parts. It would also take a toll in the memories of those who returned, remembering friends lost.

Among the young pilots and crewmen, that intensely personal understanding, assured in unspoken personal bonds, helped to sustain personal calm in the most depressing of circumstances. It empowered the pilots and crewmen to go out the next day . . . and do it all over again.

# 1

# Fire Support Base Ripcord

## I Corps, Republic of Vietnam

Firebase Ripcord had been reopened on April 1, 1970, when Company B, 2d Battalion, 506th Infantry, 101st Airborne Division, air assaulted onto the hill. The hill served as a firebase, part of the interlocking firebase network along the eastern perimeter of the A Shau Valley. It had been operated by the 101st Airborne Division in 1969, then closed when monsoons prevented resupply. Marines had operated from it in 1967 and 1968.

Firebase Ripcord was established as a major combat base in I Corps. As an operating base, infantry patrols would walk out into their assigned AO (area of operations) to block the North Vietnamese (NVA) divisions positioned to move on Hue.

Hue had been overrun by the North Vietnamese Army during the 1968 Tet Offensive. NVA had held the city for over twenty days. It was the largest population center north of Da Nang, and, more importantly, a provincial capital. The battle for Hue City by Marines and soldiers was widely covered by TV reporters. A clear military victory for U.S. and South Vietnamese (ARVN) forces, the 1968 Tet offensive soon became the most misinterpreted action of the war, convoluted by reporters into an NVA political victory.

Unknown to us at the time, Firebase Ripcord was very important to the commander of U.S. Forces Military Assistance Command, Vietnam (COMUSMACV), Gen. Creighton Abrams.

American military leaders were faced with managing a withdrawal from an ongoing war. The 9th Infantry Division, which had been based near Saigon, was already gone, as well as the 25th Infantry, the "Tropic Lightning," which had returned to Hawaii. The 1st Infantry Division, the "Big Red 1," had also gone. The 4th Infantry Division at An Khe would be next. With dramatic American troop reductions under way, some offensive moves had to disrupt any offensive intentions the North Vietnamese Army had.

Ripcord was part of General Creighton Abrams's overall plan that would culminate with an invasion into the heart of the enemy forces in Laos. I Corps, home of the 101st Airborne Division, was nearest the North Vietnamese Army homeland and subject to the greatest military threat. It was widely considered the worst area of operations (AO). The Cambodian invasion of May 1970 was one of the critical offensive moves designed to buy time for the overall withdrawal, hitting the enemy as hard as possible where he least expected it.

On April 1, 1970, Sp. John Mihalko was serving as a member of the Reconnaissance (Recon) Platoon, Company E, 2d Battalion, 506th Infantry, 101st Airborne Division, at Camp Evans. The recon platoon members were a mix of well-trained veterans blended with new guys who fit in well. The men were a proud and diverse group who worked well together. Their confidence was based upon successful combat experience. They were concerned that their platoon leader, a lieutenant, had DEROSed (Date Expected Return from Overseas) and been replaced with another. The familiar questions ran through Mihalko's mind. Is the new lieutenant gung ho? Does he have his shit together?

Reports were coming in over the radio, describing continuous enemy fire. The April Fool's Day CA (combat assault) insertion on top of Ripcord was not going well.

The combat assault onto the mountaintop was "hot, very, very hot."

Everything bad that could happen was happening. The enemy they'd searched for in March was now there in abundance. Uncharacteristically, the NVA were slugging it out, not disappearing into the jungle.

Mihalko and his platoon headed out to the helicopter pad in silence. The situation was bad and getting worse. Reinforcements were having an extremely difficult time getting into Ripcord. The choppers were delayed getting there and took heavy fire when they did make it in. Casualties were mounting, and the North Vietnamese Army still showed no sign of their characteristic flight from the battle once surprise had been lost. After interminable waiting, the helicopters arrived at the PZ (pickup zone), and the men mounted up.

The recon platoon had been trained to work silently, stalking through the jungle in search of an elusive enemy. They were highly effective because they worked in small groups, and they usually had the element of surprise on their side. Their tactics were to hit hard in swift and deadly ambushes. But this time the recon platoon was ordered to conduct a combat assault: no element of surprise, a hot landing zone. No stealth in the jungle shadows, only fire and maneuver in the open to assault enemy bunkers!

A few Huey helicopters (slicks) had been shot down earlier in the day, raising the anxiety level of later passengers. Mihalko looked at the helicopter crews without envy, knowing they would have to go out to Ripcord repeatedly, totally exposed to antiaircraft fire while going in and mortar fire while on the pads. The aircrews, however, were equally reluctant to think of spending the night on Ripcord.

Mortar fire prevented the helicopters from landing immediately, so they circled in daisy chains just out of range. During one of the turns, Mihalko glanced down and got his first glimpse of Ripcord. It didn't look like much from that altitude, simply a bald mountaintop surrounded by lush green jungle. As they began the approach, mortar rounds were hitting the hill. Then Mihalko saw a Huey lying in the jungle below the mountaintop where it had been shot down. They circled, still descending. Finally the crew chief shouted above the roar of the rotor blades and engine, "We're going in, get ready!"

A mile out, on extended final approach, the door gunner shouted into his microphone, "Taking fire." He began laughing as he opened up with his M-60 machine gun. Mihalko watched Cobras working out beside them. Then the crew chief and door gunner were both firing. Mortar rounds were impacting where they were supposed to land.

With mortal combat under way below them, the door gunner shouted to him, "Isn't this neat?" Mihalko thought the door gunner was either the most gung ho soldier he'd ever seen or simply crazy! On final, the mortar rounds came in like hail. The landscape ahead spewed into the sky in front of them. The helicopter was shuddering as it lost airspeed. With mortars impacting the landing zone in front of him, the pilot initiated a go-around. Breaking off the approach, he pulled in maximum power, accelerating away from the fire without touching down.

The second and third tries were equally unsuccessful. After the fourth, the Huey was running low on fuel. Just as the Rangers relaxed, thinking they wouldn't have to return to Ripcord that day, the pilot said, "We're just gonna refuel at Camp Evans and try it all over again." It was just another day for the air crews. They would keep trying until the combat assault was successfully completed. Luckily for Mihalko, his CA was called off. Only part of his platoon made it onto the mountaintop.

On April 3, it was rumored that Ripcord was going to be evacuated and that the recon platoon members were coming in. It was true, but Mihalko's teammates looked as if they had been through a meat grinder. Their fatigues were spattered with blood. The legs of one man were exposed from his thighs to his knees, dripping in blood from wounds that he didn't even seem to notice. People were glad to simply be alive. The only fatal casualty his platoon had suffered was the new lieutenant, killed in action.

Then the "Word" spread: "We're staying on Ripcord." At that point, Mihalko realized the Ripcord area of operations was going to be the recon platoon's home for a long time to come. There were one hell of a lot of bad guys out there, and they could mount a real attack any time they chose. After several months in country, the events of April 1 left him with his first bitter feelings: he began to question decisions of those above him.

The April Fool's Day assault shook Mihalko up. Like other combat veterans, he came to realize that simply being good was not enough to survive in close combat. Luck had a big say in the matter. Of course, the combat assault into Ripcord was a "piece of cake," compared to the extraction under artillery siege that would occur on July 23.

Ripcord was quickly expanded by combat engineers to house four hundred men, and it became the starting point for many foot patrols into the surrounding hills and valleys. Infantry patrols would walk the hills below the twenty-eight-hundred-foot mountaintop, searching for the enemy. The presence of the Screaming Eagles at Ripcord blocked North Vietnamese Army divisions from moving into the Hue area, the provincial capital and largest population center north of Da Nang.

On April 28, Company B, 2d Battalion, 502d Infantry, while patrolling a valley floor below Ripcord, discovered an occupied North Vietnamese Army position. They successfully assaulted and killed fifteen NVA. Among the weaponry captured, they were startled to find U.S. equipment, including an M-60 machine gun, an M-79 grenade launcher, and most important, a PRC-25 FM radio. It was obvious that the North Vietnamese Army units in the field were monitoring American radio transmissions.

On May 17, the North Vietnamese Army stepped up activity across I Corps, and a Chinook helicopter in the mountains west of Firebase Nancy was shot down. The entire crew was lost.

A Phoenix Huey on a resupply mission took fire coming out of the mountain ridgelines. Capt. Randy House was surprised to take hits over a usually safe area. With flames leaping into his cargo bay, he immediately dived to the lowland plain. It took one hundred knots airspeed to beat the flames back. His copilot, WO Don Mears, called out critical instruments as they completed the forced landing safely. Near Ripcord, other aircraft were taking heavy antiaircraft fire while resupplying ARVN Firebase O'Reilley. The pilots were taking fire at places they generally considered safe. Something was up with the North Vietnamese Army.

The next day, just south of Fire Support Base O'Reilley, a Phoenix Huey supporting combat engineers was shot down in flames. Three crew members and two passengers were killed in the crash. For the second miraculous time in two months, Phoenix crew chief, Specialist Fourth Class Easterling, jumped from the helicopter an instant before it crashed into the ground. He was knocked unconscious, but walked out of the jungle two days later. To have survived jumping from a crashing helicopter that killed all remaining on board was a trial of survival instincts and reflexes matched, amazingly, by four other Phoenix crew members.

Crew Chief Specialist Mike Amos had jumped from his Huey before it impacted the mountain lowlands on December 21, 1969. After recuperating on the hospital ship *Repose*, Mike returned to the Phoenix. He'd shown no reluctance to get back in the saddle.

Fate, however, placed him in another Phoenix Huey late in the afternoon of January 29, 1970. Three Phoenix Hueys were in loose trail formation east of the A Shau Valley. Their mission was to pick up a team of combat engineers who had been inserted that morning to cut a new landing zone out of the jungle. The lead aircraft, piloted by Capt. Don Swanson and WO Phillipe Las Hermes, touched down in landing zone Z. As the ground troops scrambled aboard, an explosion rocked the Huey.

WO Jack Glennon was in the second aircraft, on long final for the landing zone. Glennon watched in disbelief as a rocket-propelled grenade impacted the Huey's fuel cell and flames engulfed the aircraft.

Whether by instinct or as a reflexive effort to clear the landing zone, preventing further injuries to the ground troops, Swanson and Las Hermes lifted the doomed Huey out of the landing zone. It flew a hundred yards, fluttered, then fell toward the jungle-covered mountain foothills. Aboard the tumbling aircraft, determined to survive, Mike Amos unclasped his safety harness, and jumped from his seat at eighty feet above the ground. The flaming Huey fell through the jungle canopy, exploding, ultimately killing all three aboard. Two died instantly. One crew member would die from fatal pneumonia. Desperately trying to escape the burning wreckage, he'd breathed flames of the crash, and death. It would take two torturous weeks in a hospital, in Japan, to end his struggle.

Amos was rescued the next day by a medical evacuation (medevac) Huey. This time he was transferred to the hospital ship *Sanctuary*. He would go home to heal a broken leg. Amos's story was strangely similar to Easterling's two jumps. Their stories gave little hope or comfort to other crewmen, who were aware of just how many had died.

Also on May 18, Rangers operating southwest of Tun Tavern destroyed two NVA trucks, one a small 2 1/2-ton truck and one a larger five-ton model. Both were carrying supplies toward O'Reilley and Ripcord. The sequence of these events proved the North Vietnamese were successfully inserting not only men but weapons and supplies on a scale not publicly acknowledged in Saigon or Washington, D.C.

On June 12, warrant officers Tom Tindor and John Wilson were on a routine day of ash-and-trash resupply. While flying over the mountain jungle, a single AK-47 round hit the aircraft. In the Huey's normally loud turbine engine hum, with vibration of the rotor system and wind whipping through the cockpit at ninety miles per hour, the bullet was not heard. Nor was it felt . . . except by Wilson.

The 7.62mm slug ripped upward through the Huey's belly. It passed between the pilot's collective and armor seat plate, missing each by millimeters. It entered John Wilson's abdomen, tumbling upward into his heart. Tragically, mercifully, killing him instantly.

Tindor was stunned to see his copilot slump, as if asleep, without a word, even a sigh. It took Tindor a few seconds to comprehend Wilson's death. There simply was nothing he or anyone else could do. Even so he later experienced survivor's guilt and personal disgust. Tindor thought he'd taken too long to comprehend Wilson's death and was sickened at his inability to help! Why had it happened to Wilson, why not himself?

A few days later, Tindor was called Stateside on emergency leave. He would not return to the Phoenix.

## Camp Eagle

On June 23, Col. Benjamin Harrison assumed command of the 3d Brigade, 101st Airborne Division, "Currahee." His initial orders were to set up a forward command post near the demilitarized zone, and a plan was worked up to reopen Firebase Shepard, which overlooked the abandoned Khe Sanh airfield to its west. There had been armed "contact" by the 2d Troop of the 17th Air Cavalry Squadron, and North Vietnamese regular forces were openly moving through Khe Sanh, the Da Krong, and the A Shau Valley areas. The level of NVA activity increased around Khe Sanh and the A Shau. The harassment of ARVN firebases O'Reilly and Barnett was soon overshadowed by intense contact in the Firebase Ripcord area of operations.

Vo Nguyen Giap, the North Vietnamese General, had apparently commenced a major offensive to extract a high price in American casualties, an attempt to humiliate American troops in the eyes of the international press. Giap knew the offensive would cost high casualties, but Giap understood that American casualties would fuel antiwar protests, possibly encouraging further troop withdrawals.

## Washington, D.C.

While the festivities were under way on and around Firebase Ripcord, a heated political debate culminated in Washington, D.C. The United States Senate voted to repeal the Gulf of Tonkin Resolution, the political and legal basis for U.S. military operations in Indochina. Political decisions were being made that would dramatically affect our nation's history. A few days later, on June 30, 1970, the Senate passed the Cooper-Church Amendment, which barred funds for support of United States ground troops in Cambodia and Laos without prior congressional approval.

In a rare moment of truth and consequences, the political decision forced the military command decision to withdraw.

## Firebase Ripcord

Enemy contact generally subsided at the mountaintop firebase until July 1, 1970. Things dramatically changed when infantrymen of the 803d NVA regiment used assault rifles, rocket-propelled grenades, and satchel charges to attack night defensive positions of the battalion spread on the valley floor.

On July 2, Firebase Ripcord came under sustained recoilless rifle fire for the first time. Ripcord was being pounded from Hill 1000, the first high ground to its west. Ground assaults conducted by Charlie and Delta companies, 2/506th, were disappointing. The reluctance of the company commander to lead the men up the hill in the face of obviously horrendous odds was angrily observed by the upper ranks. There had been several friendly casualties, and most units were operating at 60 percent of assigned strength. Realistically, only so much could be asked of them.

That evening, Ripcord began receiving 120mm mortar attacks. It was the first use of the 120s south of the DMZ. The very large mortars showed a major logistic success by the enemy. It was now obvious to all they were being supplied by trucks or tracked vehicles, which were necessary to transport the very heavy mortars, their base plates, and ammunition. The 122mm rocket was well known by all those serving in Vietnam. It was, however, an indiscriminate, inaccurate weapon. The 120mm mortar, however, was different: it could be sighted and walked carefully across specific targets. Ripcord was then under an NVA artillery siege.

On the night of July 3, the Ripcord perimeter began receiving probing ground attacks. They would occur nightly for the following week. An infantry company, D Company, 2d Battalion, 501st Infantry (2/501st), at the base of Hill 805, in the valley below Ripcord, had heavy ground attacks four nights in a row. The surrounded company, in its night-defensive position, required a continuous stream of combat air support flights and helicopter flare ships and gunships. Air force forward air controllers remained overhead to save them from being overrun. All available in-range artillery, including 105mm, 175mm, and eight-inch guns, was employed in defending the ground troops in the field. After four nights of continuous pounding by the enemy, D Company was ordered extracted from Hill 805.

While waiting for helicopters in the pickup zone, Capt. Chris Straub's Kit Carson Scout (a North Vietnamese prisoner of war who volunteered to serve as a scout for U.S. troops) pulled a pin on a hand grenade, killing himself, seriously wounding Straub and two others standing nearby. The former NVA simply couldn't live with the fact that they were killing so many North Vietnamese that he'd helped find.

On the evening of July 4, the North Vietnamese Army celebrated the American holiday by massing to attack the command post and 1st and 2d platoons of Company C, 2d Battalion, 506th Infantry, in the valley below Ripcord.

At midnight, NVA sappers (combat engineers carrying very destructive explosive charges called satchel charges) crawled through the night defensive perimeter. Once in place, the charges were blown in a coordinated attack while B-40 rockets and rocket-propelled grenades flashed into the American positions. Then NVA infantrymen swarmed through the positions, shooting, grenading, and bayoneting. In the surreal nightscape of trip flares, explosions, tracers, automatic-weapons fire, and screams, the company commander and seven other GIs died. Six others were wounded in action. One man was missing, believed captured. The NVA left fifteen bodies. Several more were believed killed or wounded.

The platoon medic, who survived the onslaught, reorganized the defensive perimeter with the survivors and called for artillery and gunships. Jets also came to their aid.

On the afternoon of July 5, Sgt. Robert Granberry was informed his recon team of E Company, 2/506th, would search Hill 1000. Granberry was raised hunting and fishing in the woods of northwest Florida; he was comfortable in the "bush." His father had been a decorated navy corpsman (Medic), serving in the South Pacific in World War II. Granberry and his men were an experienced, very successful recon team, and Granberry was over the hump of his tour. He had developed the "sixth sense," awareness of danger and enemy threats. Even so, he and his team had once been bombed by two F-4 Phantoms directed by a "visually impaired" air force forward air controller (FAC). The bombs had been close, but not close enough. And once a Cobra gunship had also dived on them. Luckily, recognizing them as friendlies, he broke off at the last second.

As Granberry and the five other team members were listening to the reports of the line companies below Ripcord, the news was bad and kept getting worse. Hill 1000, the recon team's next-day objective, was the apparent source of enemy attacks and mortar fire.

The team members sat together at lunch, overlooking the hilltop saddle, a narrow ridge that connected Hill 1000 and Ripcord. The next day they would cross it in daylight and search for the North Vietnamese Army positions. The situation reports from line companies on patrol worried them. In an attempt to lighten the tension, men began joking about the need for a "sky pilot," a chaplain.

Granberry recognized the underlying concerns imbedded in the words. Each man was dependable and experienced. Recognizing the seriousness of the situation, Granberry polled his team members. They all agreed. Later that afternoon there was a short, somber, offering of prayers officiated by a chaplain on behalf of the recon platoon. Afterward, grim jokes continued about their "last rites."

After a restless night punctuated by NVA harassment of the firebase and the troops below, morning came. The recon team moved across the hilltop ridge toward Hill 1000.

By midafternoon, they'd entered the base of Hill 1000 and begun hearing the metallic sounds of North Vietnamese Army troops moving munitions and mortar pieces. Granberry knew the North Vietnamese Army protected their artillery pieces; they carried them too far to risk them casually. There was probably a company defending them, if not more.

He radioed his observation to a second lieutenant atop Ripcord. A few minutes later, he was told to "engage the enemy position." Granberry couldn't believe it. Including himself, there were a radioman, a medic, and four soldiers. Astonished, he informed the lieutenant they were only a recon team and asked him to reconsider. The lieutenant, obviously obeying a superior, repeated, "This is a direct, lawful order. Engage the enemy!"

Granberry informed his team members of the order. With his men, he carefully reviewed the options: Refuse the order and face a court-martial or attack the position and get killed or wounded (if very lucky).

They angrily agreed to go on with the attack. Without even the cover of darkness, the six men silently moved forward, up the hill, utilizing as much natural cover as possible. The sounds became louder, mixed with NVA voices. Close, they still could not see the enemy defensive positions. Then three rocket-propelled grenades (RPGs) exploded above them, and shrapnel showered from above, badly wounding the six men.

The PRC-25 radio on the back of Dixie Gaskins disintegrated in the explosion, saving his life. Granberry awoke in pain to the moans of others. Shrapnel had hit all over his back and legs. His M-16, useless, was melted into the shape of a C. He drew his .45 and awaited the NVA charge to finish them off. Thankfully, it never came. Instead, a soldier from Company D led the rescue from behind them. They were carried out of the fire zone and medevacked.

They had followed orders that they knew were simply stupid. Considering the options given them, the outcome had been "as well as could be expected," a familiar line in many letters home!

After artillery bombardment, unsuccessful company-size assaults began the following day. What had been unsuccessfully attempted by a six-man team, was twice repeated by an understrength eighty-man company. None of the assaults was successful. All suffered casualties.

On July 8, Companies B and C of the 2d Battalion, 506th Infantry, again assaulted Hill 1000, losing two KIA and four wounded without dislodging the NVA. The NVA had not only maintained, but improved their defensive position since April. There was obviously a lot more to the North Vietnamese Army fortifications than met the eye. There had to be a large complex, mostly underground and well manned.

On July 10, eight artillery attacks fell on Ripcord, killing two and wounding seventeen. From July 11 through 16, ground action below Ripcord claimed another ten Americans killed and fifty-two wounded. Only twelve NVA were confirmed killed in the same period. Artillery attacks on Ripcord would continue.

On July 18, 1970, a Chinook helicopter carrying a sling load of 105mm howitzer ammunition onto Ripcord was shot down by 12.7mm antiaircraft fire. Mortar fire after the crash started a fire and a huge plume of smoke. The flaming wreckage touched off a series of explosions in the ammunition storage area where it crashed. Six 105mm howitzers from B Battery, 2d Battalion/319th Field Artillery, were destroyed, and thousands of shells exploded in the fire. Two recoilless rifles and countermortar radar were lost as well. According to Colonel Harrison, "It looked as if the entire mountaintop were erupting."

This was the second loss of a 2/319th Artillery battery in the same region. Beginning at 3:00 A.M., May 13, 1969, C Battery, 2d Battalion/319th Field Artillery, was overrun at Firebase Airborne while firing support for the fighting at Dong Ap Bia (Hamburger Hill). North Vietnamese Army sappers claimed twenty-two U.S. killed from a battery of approximately sixty artillerymen. The guns were destroyed and the battery rendered combat ineffective.

The destruction of the Chinook helicopter on top of Ripcord's 105mm howitzer battery was a disaster; the defensive capabilities of Ripcord were greatly diminished. The howitzers were necessary because they were capable of close and continuous, easily adjusted fire support with a high rate of fire. The larger 155mm howitzer battery was designed to back up the direct-support 105mm units. With Ripcord's 105mm artillery destroyed, the base was incapable of close-in artillery support. The beginning of the end of Ripcord had begun.

Colonel Harrison then requested Brig. Gen. Sid Berry to immediately reopen Firebase Gladiator to position a battery of 105mm howitzers in support of the troops in the Ripcord area. That evening, an engineer mine and booby-trap element was dispatched from Camp Evans with a recon platoon for security. They were flown to commence the mine clearance of Firebase Gladiator. The following morning, a 105mm howitzer battery was operating at Gladiator. By nightfall, the battery was providing direct support to troops in the field around Ripcord.

On the evening of the nineteenth, Colonel Harrison realized he had five of eight total infantry battalions in the division under his operational control. All five had some elements in firefights and hot contact with the enemy troops. It was becoming clear that Ripcord was a major battle brewing, with NVA forces massed in the vicinity. Elements of the 66th North Vietnamese Army Regiment were confirmed north and west of Ripcord. The 29th and 803d North Vietnamese Army Regiments were now located southeast of Ripcord. Harrison realized that with the extraction of some troops in the field, those remaining became more dependent upon fire support.

That evening, he sent for his air liaison officer (ALO), Major Brown (USAF). Colonel Harrison was to spend the night on Ripcord and asked Major Brown to get his gear together. Major Brown responded that he could do a much more effective job coordinating air support from his aircraft *above* Ripcord. Colonel Harrison angrily told him he expected continuous airborne FAC with relief on station. If at any time he could not talk instantly with a FAC in the air, he would send a helicopter to pick up Major Brown and have him report to a bunker at Ripcord. With this encouragement, Major Brown and other forward air controllers provided some of the most effective and intense air support witnessed in the entire Vietnam war. The forward air controllers benefited from the experience of Colonel Harrison, who was also an army aviator who had commanded an aviation battalion on a previous tour. The colonel had the knowledge of the ground situation and understood aviation terminology. He would have many direct conversations with the aircrews involved and would request the most specific types of missions for critical tactical needs.

Capt. Chuck Hawkins was commander of the battered infantry of Alpha Company, 2d Battalion, 506th Infantry. The following day he reported that a tap on an NVA landline (wire) between a division headquarters and an artillery regiment on the valley floor below Ripcord had revealed that four NVA regiments with up to twelve thousand men had surrounded Ripcord. Colonel Harrison immediately ordered his staff to develop plans to counter the enemy regiments, and they worked up a plan requiring six additional U.S. battalions. In the middle of the night, Colonel Harrison realized the severity of the situation for Alpha Company and immediately ordered it extracted. The company was successfully extracted under fire at first light.

General Berry realized that with a division headquarters on the valley floor below Ripcord, the North Vietnamese were there to stay, between eight thousand and twelve thousand soldiers. A force that large was adequate to initiate an attack against Hue, no less to attack Firebase Ripcord and the patrols surrounding it.

Early the next morning (July 21), General Berry told Colonel Harrison, "We're closing Ripcord. What do you need in the way of support?" Colonel Harrison was surprised; it had never occurred to him to withdraw. Berry was able to see that the battle forming would claim a large number of lives, and he knew that the firebase was already scheduled to be closed due to monsoons in October. Rather than continuing daily losses, General Berry concluded it was time to withdraw the troops. After the closing, they would pound the enemy with artillery and tactical air. Harrison had been entirely too close to the situation in terms of the tactical operations and had not observed the strategic picture. Of course, for some of the infantrymen around Ripcord, the withdrawal was a little late. One platoon had been reported overrun by NVA, and a company was in danger of being overrun.

General Berry had asked Colonel Harrison what was needed for the extraction and evacuation. Colonel Harrison immediately told him he needed an air cavalry squadron, an aerial rocket artillery battalion, and unlimited close-air support, all planned well in advance. On the following day, July 22, the major commanders met at Camp Evans. This included the Marine air wing general from Marble Mountain and air force and navy carrier air wing representatives. Harrison told the marine general that he needed four sets of air support every hour, for twelve continuous hours, starting at 0600 hours on July 23. The Marine general said it would be impossible to designate and control that many strikes—forty-eight sets of two to four aircraft each. Colonel Harrison's air liaison officer with the air force, Major Brown, assured the general he could do it; he had no intention of spending nights on Ripcord. The S-3 Air, Captain Stalls on Colonel Harrison's staff, would spend his daylight hours in a light observation helicopter (LOH, pronounced "loach") controlling a number of the air strikes. They set in motion forty-two sets of Marine, navy, and air force aircraft, bombing carefully selected targets in the perimeter and foothills surrounding Ripcord.

# 2

# Exit from Ripcord

On the morning of July 21, fresh troops were inserted to strengthen A Company, 2d of the 506th, just prior to extraction, which was involved in a running battle with large numbers of NVA. The birds of the 158th Aviation Battalion and 101st Aviation Battalion were bringing in new troops with water and ammunition. Some exhausted troops were being rotated back to Camp Evans. The LZs were hover holes, just large enough for one Huey to lower into. During landings, all aircraft were under fire from NVA 12.7mm machine guns and large numbers of AK-47s.

WO Don Mears and his peter pilot were in a string of Phoenix Hueys assigned to extract troops via the hover holes in the jungle valley below Ripcord, which required bringing the Huey to a 150-foot hover above the ground. The tricky part was a slow vertical descent, rotor blades mere inches from overhanging trees, to the troops below. The pilots relied upon the crew chief and door gunner to guide them down, sometimes having to hover backward, clear of trees. The time required by the maneuver rendered the Huey a very easy target.

Flying through green antiaircraft tracers, Mears piloted the aircraft to a hover hole landing zone in a valley southeast of Ripcord. But green 12.7mm rounds were visible in all sectors of the operation, not merely against his Phoenix Huey. The Huey hovered with one skid touching a fallen log, and six heavily laden infantrymen scrambled aboard amid the cacophony of incoming and outgoing fire. With outgoing troops aboard, the crew chief shouted on the intercom, "Clear!"

Mears pulled in the collective power, and the over-loaded Phoenix Huey ascended through the same anti-aircraft fire it found on the way in. The copilot was reading out critical instruments for Mears, who had to keep his eyes on the rotor blades and the encircling trees, warning him, "You're gonna overtorque . . . redline, redline—there it goes!"

Mears replied, "Fuck it, we gotta get out!" The ascent continued, carrying very thankful troops to safety. The flight of his Phoenix Huey was repeated countless times that day. It wasn't surprising that a very popular chorus in the Phoenix officers club was an Animals song with the refrain, "We gotta get outta this place!"

On the morning of July 22, after the TAC air strikes (fighter-bomber jets) and artillery bombardment, the Huey helicopters returned to extract other troops below Ripcord while Cobra gunships shot up the area.

During the night of July 22 and the early morning of July 23, over 2,200 artillery rounds pounded the area. Commencing at first light on July 23, navy, air force, and Marine fighter-bombers flew continuous strikes.

At first light, on July 23, fourteen Chinook helicopters dashed in to begin lifting out the 2d Battalion, 506th Infantry, from the top of Ripcord. They could carry thirty to forty men per trip. Everything was going smoothly until 7:40 A.M., when antiaircraft fire destroyed a Chinook. It crashed in flames on the lower pad, preventing the other Chinook helicopters from lifting out the rest of the men, artillery, and heavy equipment. The infantry would have to be pulled out by Huey helicopters, which could carry only six men at a time. All available Hueys in the 101st Airborne were put to the task, and they would line up in sight of Ripcord before darting in, one by one, to extract soldiers—all the while under continuous antiaircraft fire and flying through artillery bombardment.

While action on the twenty-eight-hundred-foot mountaintop was taking a drastic turn for the worse, Huey helicopters of the Phoenix were combat assaulting troops of D Company, 2/506, to reinforce A Company on the valley floor. With those reinforcements, the American infantrymen were successful in beating back North Vietnamese attackers. Then, while Cobra gunships and jets kept the enemy at bay, the infantry would be extracted after operations on the mountaintop above them were completed.

After the crash of the Chinook, the Hueys were refueled and assembled for the largest "hot" extraction of U.S. forces in South Vietnam. Sixty UH-1 Hueys from the companies of the 158th Aviation Battalion at Camp Evans would be joined by sixty Hueys from the 101st Aviation Battalion at Camp Eagle. The Redskins of the 158th Aviation Battalion (Cobra gunships), the Hawks (Cobra gunships) from the 101st Aviation Battalion, and (4/77) Griffins (aerial rocket artillery) of the battalion formed up with the lift birds and the other Cobras from Camp Eagle.

Normally, either aviation battalion would have had the aircraft lift capability to perform the extraction alone, but antiaircraft fire had damaged so many Hueys that some companies could only provide sixteen or eighteen of their normal twenty Hueys. The two aviation battalions of Camp Evans and Camp Eagle would work together.

Capt. Randy House, platoon leader from C Company, 158th Aviation Battalion, correctly observed it was time to get on with the mission, but he'd had no contact with Colonel Harrison in the command-and-control ship flying high above because the North Vietnamese Army and some highly qualified Communist Chinese advisers were blocking the radio frequencies normally used as alternate frequencies one, two, and three with voices, or the enemy's keyed mikes. The enemy effort was aided by electrical gremlins in the command-and-control bird. After boring doughnut holes in the sky for twenty minutes, Captain House, the Phoenix lead, departed his flight to overfly Ripcord. With no further communication from Colonel Harrison, House realized a cluster fuck was in the making. Positive steps had to be taken, quickly—120 Hueys were airborne, awaiting instructions to commence the extraction.

House saw that the upper pad by the 155mm howitzers was taking much less mortar fire than the lower pad, which was under continuous shelling and still partially blocked by the wreckage of the burning Chinook, so he made contact with a pathfinder on Ripcord and told him he was ready to continue the extraction. The pathfinder, sitting in the middle of the barrage, briefed House with specific landing recommendations.

House ordered the Phoenix birds to commence the extraction, coming inbound along a riverbed, turning over the mountain waterfalls, and continuing to Ripcord. Hueys from both aviation battalions would follow. House then instructed the Phoenix birds to commence approaching the pads with thirty-second intervals between Hueys. As the mission proceeded, the pathfinders on Ripcord instructed some birds to use different pads. The NVA, however, were listening to the pathfinders' radio frequency. So, if a Huey was directed to pad 1, mortars fired on pad 1. Hearing the mortar shells fired, the pathfinders would then divert the Huey to another pad at the last second. Soldiers would scramble aboard, and the Huey would depart, just prior to impact of the next round of mortars.

One by one, the Huey helicopters of the Phoenix touched down. The small pads were just big enough for one Huey to land, pick up five or six passengers, and depart while under continuous .51-caliber antiaircraft fire, and that of hundreds of AK-47s. The main pad was also under continuous fire from 120mm and 82mm mortars. For some reason, the NVA had not targeted one of the upper pads as closely. Light 82mm fire and 75mm recoilless rifle fire were being received there, but it was intermittent, not the persistent, continuous fire being received at the lower pad level.

The only hopes of salvation for soldiers on that mountaintop were birds of the Phoenix and other 101st Airborne Division units—the olive-drab line of Hueys. The pilots and crewmen in the other units calmly waited their turns. Despite seeing what was happening to the Phoenix, undeterred, they would follow.

As the final evacuation of Firebase Ripcord commenced, WO Ken Mayberry was flying as a Phoenix Company aircraft commander (AC) with WO David Rayburn as copilot. As they approached, they observed small groups of men waiting on the mountaintop. Artillery bombardment continued in the form of 120mm mortars, 82mm mortars, and recoilless rifle fire. Luckily, the heavier stuff had tapered off somewhat, but the mortar fire was continuous. A single mortar shell could easily destroy a Huey, killing all on board. As they approached the landing zone, Rayburn was dismayed by the ferocity of the mortar fire. Both pilots were combat veterans and had taken hits on many prior occasions so the action was familiar to them. But the intensity was far greater than Rayburn had ever encountered.

The scene reminded Mayberry of another very hot landing zone near LZ Kelley, southwest of Ripcord. A few weeks earlier, Mayberry had flown through a wall of tracers and was rocked by an airburst that nearly nosed his helicopter into the mountain. Whether it was a satchel charge placed in the trees or a fused RPG-7 didn't matter. It had been terrifyingly close. Of twenty Phoenix Hueys in that operation, only four aircraft remained flyable after the troop extraction. Despite having the experience to understand what was unfolding, Mayberry continued the approach.

As they neared the landing pad, Mayberry counted nine mortar shells exploding around the pad. He also saw six GIs standing in the open, waiting for him. Someone radioed, "Go around!" but Mayberry replied, "We're going in."

Rayburn looked over at Mayberry and said, "Ken, you sure you want to do this?"

Mayberry kept looking forward, flying the aircraft and watching the landing zone. He responded, "We're their only way out, and if we don't get them . . ."

In the Phoenix Company, an unspoken, solemn vow was lived: Americans were on the ground; the Phoenix would come to get them!

As they came on short final (one-fourth mile out), the fire grew heavier. Then Mayberry slammed the Huey down amid the exploding mortar rounds, while six heavily laden soldiers rushed for the helicopter. A mortar round hit in front of the soldiers and another simultaneously just behind them. Flattened like bowling pins, the group was thrown to the ground, all badly wounded. Mayberry shouted to the crew chief, Sp5. John Ackerman, and the door gunner, Sp4. Wayne Wasilk, "Get them!" The two young Minnesotans rushed twenty yards through the mortar fire, helped four of the men up, and shouldered them to the helicopter. The firing continued, landing all around them, and Rayburn felt AK-47 rounds and mortar fragments peppering his Huey as if the Huey's skin were his own.

Mayberry looked over his right shoulder, through the cargo bay door to his right rear. Mortars were being walked up the mountainside toward him as he watched. He held his breath, waiting for the next round.

The crew chief and door gunner struggled to get the last of the men into the cargo bay, then the crew chief shouted, "Go! Go!" and Mayberry lifted off through black-gray clouds of fragmentation, dirt, and smoke. Moments later, a second Phoenix bird, piloted by WO Dave Wolfe,

picked up another group of six. Wolfe and his crew thought
they'd suffered amazingly minor damage—no wounds to
the crew or the passengers. Wolfe departed Ripcord under fire and joined the departing string of Hueys behind
Mayberry.

Still ten miles west of Camp Evans, in the Annamite
mountain range, Wolfe, ignoring normal radio procedures,
radioed Mayberry, "Ken, you're smoking. I don't see flames,
but there is smoke everywhere. You're losing fuel. There
are pieces falling off everywhere. I think you better put
that thing down now."

Mayberry came on the radio. "I've got a little vibration.
I might be losing some instruments. All my pax (passengers) are badly wounded, so I'm going direct to Charlie
Med pad (187th Mobile Army Surgical Hospital), we'll
check it out there."

Sp5. Larry Frazier, Wolfe's crew chief, watched Mayberry's limping Huey, amazed it was still flying, relieved
his bird wasn't in the same condition. Wolfe, awestruck
by Mayberry's combat damage, hadn't yet observed the
damage to his own aircraft.

The mobile army surgical hospital was adjacent to the
Phoenix officers' quarters. There Mayberry brought his
limping bird to a careful landing off to the side of the
pad, out of the way of normal traffic, shut it down. With
the engine shut down, the caution lights shut off, and no
apparent fire, he sat there, shaken, but mission accomplished! People were already attending the wounded. Rayburn climbed out and walked around to help Mayberry
out. Only then did Mayberry realize he had a bloody boot.
He'd been wounded in the lower calf by mortar fragmentation. Medics offered aid for Mayberry's wound, but he patiently waved them to his seriously wounded passengers.

After Rayburn helped Mayberry down to the ground,
they hobbled around the aircraft, then stood in stunned
amazement at the battle damage. Rayburn grimly said,

"Well, Ken, this one's DEROSing."* They were physically fatigued and emotionally drained. They also shared an incredible sense of awareness of their being alive. Rayburn had now endured the worst; for Mayberry, it had just been one more hot PZ (pickup zone). The Huey had effectively been destroyed by enemy bullets and mortar fragmentation.

After the wounded had been removed, Mayberry and Rayburn very carefully hovered the bird a hundred yards back to the Phoenix Nest. There they counted over forty holes from enemy fire. Then they got a replacement aircraft and rejoined the extraction of troops from hover holes below the mountaintop.

While atop Ripcord, Sp5. Larry Frazier, the crew chief on Wolfe's Phoenix Huey, had helped six infantrymen scramble aboard under fire. Shortly after they lifted off to the relative safety of "only antiaircraft fire," a rifleman motioned to Frazier. He handed Frazier a piece of paper from his chest pocket. Frazier read it and handed it to the pilots. It read, "Thanks for saving our asses." Frazier was impressed that the GI had written it under artillery bombardment, before being picked up on top of Ripcord. Even before being extracted, the GI had faith that the birds would get them out, no matter what!

After operations ended that day, Wolfe flew back to refuel at Camp Evans. Frazier hopped down from his crew chief's well, walked forward to open Wolfe's door, and moved his sliding armored plate back. As he reached for the pilot's door handle, he was startled to see Wolfe's

---

*i.e., "Going home to the U.S.A." From the abbreviation DEROS, "Date Eligible for Return from Overseas Service," most GIs' favorite date. Rayburn believed it was shot up beyond repair. As it turned out, the Huey was dismantled and returned to the States. Aviation maintenance depots Stateside would take five or six shot-up Hueys and use them to rebuild three or four good ones.

"air-conditioning." The lower part of the pilot's door had been blown away by rounds passing through the nose radio compartment and exiting under Wolfe's legs through the left pilot's door. They also found several holes in the fuselage under the door gunner's seat. Frazier later joked about Wolfe's reaction: "If he hadn't been sitting, he might've collapsed." Wolfe had been so distracted by Mayberry's damage he'd not noticed his own.

Captain House, Phoenix Lead, still circling above Ripcord, continued the extraction with the other lift companies. The Ghostriders and other helicopter companies had been circling, in clear view of the action, waiting their turns. House had watched as his Phoenix birds were getting shot to hell and he was painfully aware of his responsibility to the troops still on Ripcord. House also knew he had to continue his role of impromptu air mission commander. The sooner they were finished and gone, the better.

House called to Ghostrider Lead, "Rider One-six, Phoenix One-six."

Ghostrider One-six responded, "Go!"

"This is Phoenix Lead, the other briefers are not up. It's pretty strong (antiaircraft fire) west of Ripcord. I hate to be the one to keep this damn thing going . . . but give me your poz (position)."

Ghostrider Lead responded, "Between Phong Dien, blueline by Jack (west of Camp Evans combat base, over the river)."

House then gave instructions on the best approach direction and separation. Ghostrider Lead then briefed the other birds in his flight, all of whom could see the continuous bombardment under way. Ghostrider Lead continued, "I'm not gonna order you into that stuff, but if you think you can get onto the pad, do it!"

The essence of the Phoenix vow was a requisite for Ghostrider aircraft commanders as well. All of the riders in the sky would continue the extraction. The Huey helicopters would come, as long as there were Americans on the ground.

One by one the pilots and crews commenced their approaches, and the radios came alive with pilots' commentary on the evolving tactical situation. "Pretty white stuff on top," called a Ghostrider as he approached the upper landing zone amid a flurry of mortar shells.

"It's CS," one calmly remarked. Tear gas.

Another asked, "Are we using CS (tear gas)?"

"No," responded a pilot, "they are."

Not only would the pilots fly through walls of .51-caliber antiaircraft tracers to land amid exploding mortar bombs, they'd have to endure clouds of tear gas, which could temporarily blind them!

Sitting on Ripcord, Ghostrider One-six called, "Mortar fire hitting all areas of pad, five to ten meters of pad, all the way down the hill!"

Another Ghostrider, also touching down on Ripcord, called, "Go in top pad, one more hit just right beside me!"

Another, "On short final—going around!"

The pathfinder atop Ripcord called, "Did a slick just get shot down?"

Comanchero One-one (A Company/101st Avn Btn), "No, a mortar hit him sitting on the ground."

Ghostrider Chalk Seven, "Taking small-arms fire one hundred meters out of LZ. They're leading it onto the pad."

Lead called, "Abort, Chalk Seven!"

Chalk Seven, "No, I've aborted three times already, I'll just continue in!"

Ghostrider Lead, "I'll leave it up to you, go in if you can!"

Another bird called, "POL (fuel storage) just went up, took a mortar, right beside me."

The Ghostriders, Lancers, Comancheros, Black Widows, and Kingsmen continued the procession, just as the

Phoenix had. Many were taking hits, suffering wounded crewmen.

The smoke of fires, streams of green and gold enemy tracers, the sight of jets swooping low, laying down napalm, with Cobras attacking lines of enemy troops, overwhelmed the senses. But the Hueys kept coming. When one was shot down, another dove down to retrieve the crew.

As long as soldiers remained on Ripcord, the Hueys would come.

By noon, only eighteen fighting men remained atop Ripcord of an original force of nearly four hundred. Driven from their secure positions by 155mm ammunition exploding from flames, they ran to the other end of the firebase to form a defensive perimeter. They saw North Vietnamese Army soldiers swarming up the mountainside like ants, breaching the lower perimeter wires, less than a hundred yards away. Most of the GIs were lugging M-60 machine guns, spraying the enemy.

Rambo would have been proud of the way they moved from one position to another—firing M-60 machine guns from the hip, on the move, feeding their own ammunition! They simply wanted off the godforsaken mountain, alive. PFC Daniel Biggs watched as a Huey approached the pad. Two mortar shells hit directly on the pad. The pilot continued his landing to the exact spot within three seconds. Biggs later told a *Stars and Stripes* correspondent, "He came right in, didn't turn away or nothin'!"

Above Ripcord, another flight was concluding the mountaintop evacuation of troops. WO1 Jim Saunders, a navy admiral's son, was copiloting a Huey in. On short final, the bird was shot out of the sky by 12.7mm heavy machine guns, crashing downhill of the lower landing pad in the midst of North Vietnamese soldiers. As the Huey slid down the mountain slope through the lower barbed wire of the perimeter, North Vietnamese were assaulting the firebase all around them.

The crew escaped from the burning wreckage, immediately running up the steep hill, discarding chicken-plate armor as they ran to another pickup zone, one under less heavy fire, so another Huey could pick them up. While running, Saunders glanced over his shoulder at North Vietnamese crawling through the concertina wire at the perimeter. They were less than twenty-five yards away. Entangled in the razor wire, they were so busy, they hadn't tried to shoot him.

They made it up to the top of the next hill. On the other side of the hill were more North Vietnamese! As Hueys circled with machine guns firing, one crew chief waved them toward another pad at a lower level. So they began running, downhill this time, between two more columns of North Vietnamese, who were tangled in concertina wire so close that they didn't fire for fear of hitting one another! Saunders and his crew made it onto another Huey and escaped in a hail of small-arms fire.

A short while later, the last helicopter off Ripcord sustained major damage and heavy casualties. Troop withdrawals from the valley floor would end two hours later.

Thus ended the Firebase Ripcord saga. All the army helicopter pilots earned Distinguished Flying Crosses. The crew chiefs and door gunners received Air Medals with *V* for valor.

By early afternoon, all known living soldiers on Ripcord had been carried back to Camp Evans. Tragically, several shell-shocked men, hiding in their bunkers, would not run the gauntlet of mortars to the Hueys. They even hid from the men searching bunkers to insure that everyone got out. They died that evening by flamethrower or were bayoneted in their bunkers. NVA swarmed through Ripcord until air strikes ended their celebration. The severed heads of several American soldiers would be found six weeks later by a recovery team flown in by the Phoenix.

\* \* \*

The last fighting men off the mountain were members of B Company, 2d Battalion, 506th Infantry. They'd also been the first ones to go in there in April.

That evening, after the flow of Mayberry's adrenaline had ebbed, he hobbled over to the flight surgeon's hootch, where a medic removed the shrapnel from his calf. He wouldn't receive his Purple Heart medal orders until nineteen years later at an Arlington memorial ceremony for another Phoenix crew.

Ripcord was not the first nor the last firebase to close under enemy contact. Ripcord was, however, the only U.S. firebase closed in a "retrograde" operation without breaking contact with the enemy. There was continuous action, beginning days before the withdrawal and continuing up to the moment the last soldier was removed. North Vietnamese General Giap, who'd masterminded the attack on Ripcord, had also masterminded the defeat of the French at Dien Bien Phu in May 1954. At that battle, the defensive troops of the French totaled 14,000. Offensive troops surrounding them were 40,000. The attackers outnumbered the defenders 2.9 to 1.

During the siege of U.S. Marines at Khe Sanh, defensive troops were 6,600 with 20,000 offensive North Vietnamese Army troops attacking. The attacker/defender ratio was 3:1. The Khe Sanh siege was widely but erroneously described by newswriters as a Dien Bien Phu repeat. The Marines had taken casualties on a daily basis for occupying the ground. The press reports were distortions of fact in the light of the Tet Offensive. The Marines were never in danger of being overrun, but they paid a steep price in casualties to maintain that position. The NVA were, however, shelling them from the relative safety of tunneled gun emplacements in Laos and North Vietnam, just as they'd done to the French at Dong Khe and Dien Bien Phu.

At Ripcord, there had been astounding odds against

the U.S. troops: eight hundred defensive troops versus a minimum of eight thousand offensive troops. An attacker/defender ratio of 10:1. The same odds Davy Crockett had faced at the Alamo! There were 406 casualties on Ripcord, including killed and wounded, out of 800 at the beginning of the operation.

Ripcord was a highly successful fighting withdrawal. It left the enemy in control of the jungle, but nothing else. Their offensive threat to Hue and the lowlands ended for two years. The NVA were then pounded continuously with B-52s and tactical air fighter-bombers. Helicopters, including gunships and lift ships, were crucial to Ripcord. The withdrawal could not have been made without the courage and daring of Huey pilots and crewmen braving direct mortar fire, recoilless rifle fire, walls of .51-caliber antiaircraft fire, and heavy volumes of AK-47 fire.

Beginning April 1 and continuing through July 31, 1970, 135 UH-1H Hueys from an inventory of 120 took serious antiaircraft damage, rendering them unflyable. The vast majority of the division pilots and crew members had survived combat damage to their aircraft. Ten AH-1G Cobras and three Loaches (OH-6A) also sustained serious hits. Only two of the six Huey lift companies did not lose a crew killed in action. Even in the usually safe missions of the larger twin-rotor Chinook, thirty-eight sustained serious damage and three crews were killed.

The pilots among the companies of the 101st Airborne Division agreed that Ripcord was about as bad as it could get. But those remaining in country would learn that Ripcord was just a training mission; the sum of all damage and casualties in four months of the Ripcord operations would be exceeded in one day on the following March 3, 1971. And again on March 20.

The day after Ripcord was evacuated, on the twenty-fourth, Colonel Harrison conducted a press conference at Camp Evans. Between twenty-five and thirty members of the media, mostly from Saigon news offices, showed up to hear the story of Ripcord. Some newsmen were obviously disappointed that it hadn't been a major U.S. disaster. They couldn't know that Captain House's decisive action had forestalled disaster when the enemy had jammed Colonel Harrison's communicating with the Phoenix Hueys.

Colonel Harrison extolled the virtues of the Chinook pilots who'd worked the mountaintop under continuous fire until one was shot down blocking the largest landing pad. They deserved the praise they received. But virtually no mention was made of the Phoenix, Ghostriders, Lancers, Kingsmen, Comancheros, and Black Widows. The Chinooks flew from 6:00 A.M. to 7:40 A.M. The slicks flew from 6:00 A.M. until after 2:00 P.M. It had been a nightmare for all.

Military historians would later conclude that the evacuation of Ripcord was one of the most complex and brilliantly executed airmobile operations ever conducted. The flight lead, assumed by Capt. Randy House, Phoenix One-six, had been absolutely superb. He'd maintained a continuous stream of aircraft to pick up troops. Captain House extended his tour to command a rifle company, Company C, 2d Battalion, 506th Infantry Brigade, 101st Airborne Division. There he crossed paths with a Lt. Col. John Shalikashvili. Both were destined to become generals and fight a highly successful war twenty-one years later.

Standing off to the side of the news briefing was Lt. Col. George Stenehjem. The 158th Aviation Battalion Commander was dealing with the loss of his personal friend, Lt. Col. Andre Lucas. They had been West Point classmates. Lucas had died atop Ripcord during a 120mm mortar bombardment. Stenehjem had visited Lucas the day the first Chinook had been shot down. Together, they'd dodged a torrent of burning fuel. The past four months

had seen demanding combat, but Stenehjem had simultaneously endured a division command inspection by the
inspector general, while incorporating a new IBM maintenance record system. War was hell, and then some.

Sgt. Robert Granberry, who'd led the near fatal assault
on Hill 1000 back on July 5, was lying in a hotel bed on
his stomach, slowly sipping whiskey, in Honolulu, Hawaii.
He was on R & R leave. The whiskey eased the pain as his
fiancée changed the many bandages of his rocket-propelled-
grenade (RPG) wounds. Watching the TV news coverage
of Ripcord, he had a clear understanding of the event not
conveyed in the evening news; he still had five months to
finish in his tour of duty, in the worst area of operations.

# 3

# Flight School:
# Warrant Officer Rotary Wing
# Aviator Class 70-5

The thing is, helicopters are different from planes. An airplane, by its nature, wants to fly, and if not interfered with too strongly by unusual events or by deliberately incompetent pilots, it will fly.

A helicopter does not want to fly.

It is maintained in the air by a variety of forces and controls working in opposition to each other, and if there is any disturbance in this delicate balance, the helicopter stops flying, immediately and disastrously.

There is no such thing as a gliding helicopter. This is why being a helicopter pilot is so different from being an airplane pilot, and why, in general, airplane pilots are open, clear-eyed, buoyant extroverts, and helicopter pilots are brooders, introspective anticipators of trouble. They know if something bad has not happened, it is about to.

—HARRY REASONER, July 1977

**Candidate Marshall's Pink Slip:**
**February 13, 1970, Fort Rucker, Alabama**

As a warrant officer candidate in the initial contact flying with the UH-1 Huey, I'd encountered my first failing flight grade. I had my pink slip pulled the preceding day for mishandling an electrical malfunction. A pink slip was the most serious warning a student pilot could receive. Two pink slips could result in a student being sent back to the class following his. Under some circumstances, you could be ejected from the flight program and become an infantryman. My pink slip was earned for mishandling an electrical malfunction that, if not understood, could lead to an emergency landing that might not be necessary.

Our training was nearly 70 percent complete. I'd successfully completed the initial contact flying in the Hughes TH-55 at Fort Wolters, Texas. It had a canopy like the eye of a praying mantis mounted on a spindly airframe. We sometimes called it the Mattel Messerschmitt because of its toylike appearance and mosquitolike agility.

I'd also successfully completed instrument training in the Bell H-13T (Model H-47G) at Hanchey Army Heliport at Fort Rucker, Alabama. It was the original helicopter workhorse, first introduced in the Korean War. By 1970, it was relegated to serving as a flying instrument platform for student pilots.

My training had progressed to the workhorse of the Vietnam War, the Huey (UH-1D). It was powered by a Lycoming gas turbine (jet) engine, which drove the overhead rotor system and synchronized antitorque tail-rotor system. The Huey was a joy to fly. It pulsated with the hum of a jet engine and the physically encompassing vibration of the main rotors overhead, beating the air into submission. The *whopping* sound it made came to symbolize the helicopter war.

After several hours training in the jet-turbine-powered Huey, I had not correctly handled the proper emergency procedures for an electrical malfunction involving the inverter. All electrical instrumentation was powered by the inverter, which had a three-position switch: on, off, and spare. Now I was facing a very serious standardization check ride. The instructor was a retired army major, flying as a civilian instructor, Mr. Baldwin. He oversaw all instructors in the department. If I failed the ride, that would mean a second pink slip—I'd be sent back to the preceding class. Or placed in enlisted ranks, then shipped on to advanced infantry training and a ground tour in Vietnam.

Army helicopter training featured repetitive training in emergency procedures. The most serious emergency, a loss of engine power, involved autorotation (a powerless descent) to a full stop on the ground. It wasn't called a glide, because you went nearly straight down. The idea was to land without damage to the aircraft or your passengers. There were no parachutes for helicopter crew members, nor were there ejection seats; you couldn't escape the overhead rotor blades.

Successful autorotations were possible if the pilot immediately recognized the loss of power. He would have to reduce the collective (rotor blade pitch and engine power) to flat (bottom), allowing the upward (reverse) flow of air through the rotor blades. The pinwheel effect caused by the falling helicopter's moving through the air would spin the blades, allowing one terminal pull upward of the collective, cushioning the aircraft from a two-thousand-feet-per-minute descent to a soft landing. If the pilot pulled (raised) the collective too early, the helicopter would flutter to a stop too early, roll upside down, and kill those aboard. If the pilot pulled the collective too late, the helicopter would smash into the ground.

Autorotations are simply a helicopter pilot's last chance at survival. One pull of the collective at the precise aircraft altitude, speed, and attitude meant the difference between life and death! A day rarely went by without practicing three straight-in and a couple of 180-degree autorotations, which reversed directions in the descent.

We also practiced autorotations from a hover. All were totally powerless practice landings to the ground. Slightly less emphasis was placed on minor cockpit emergencies. I quickly became competent at autorotations. Helicopter pilots understand the adrenaline rush of not just surviving, but excelling at controlled crashes.

Autorotations were demanding and exacting. The descent profile was remotely similar to a portion of the Apollo moon landing. A specially rigged Bell H-47G was actually used in engineering studies prior to the first moon landing!

I commuted to class with warrant officer candidates Corky Franklin, Jack Grass, and Avon Mallette. All three had prior military service. We were all married students, permitted to live off post during the latter half of training at Fort Rucker. As I got in the car, there was the usual, good-natured banter. Avon joked, "Marshall, you gonna pass that damn check ride today, or you gonna be a grunt and pack a rifle?"

"Hell, I'll pass that check ride. I'm not about to go walking the jungles," I replied. Everyone had a good laugh.

It was Friday the thirteenth. As I filed into the briefing room, I looked on the blackboard and found my instructor pilot's name on line thirteen. The aircraft tail number had seven digits, ending with thirteen. To top it off, it was parked on pad thirteen! I thought to myself Oh man, this will be interesting.

Later that morning, after the weather briefing, I met Mr. Harry Baldwin, a former warrant officer who had retired as a major then become a civilian standardization instructor pilot in the Huey course. We completed the preflight and took off. We went through the standard autorotations and a detailed review of emergency procedures.

During the last trip around the traffic pattern, Mr. Baldwin simulated a failure of my primary electrical buss. I slowly lost my engine instruments. While I had my eyes out of the cockpit, Mr. Baldwin pulled two circuit breakers. The first disabled the flashing yellow caution lights and red warning light system. The second circuit breaker disabled my inverter, the source of electrical power for my critical engine instruments. To further complicate matters, he turned the inverter switch off.

As we continued around the pattern, I began calling out the prelanding check from memory. "Engine, transmission, instruments . . ." Then I noticed they were not green (normal). I was surprised to see them at 30 percent of the normal level since I'd had no caution or warning light indication.

After a few seconds of mentally reviewing the procedure, I checked a circuit breaker and found part of the problem. Obviously I had an electrical problem. First thing to check, all circuit breakers. Aha! Two disabled, I thought to myself. I looked back at the instruments, still no change. That was obviously only part of the problem. I recycled my essential and nonessential electrical buss circuit breakers. Damn, stumped! I kept visually checking for something else, all the time still flying in the traffic pattern, watching traffic, maintaining speed, heading, and altitude. As I looked up at the overhead console, I mentally reviewed all the steps; then I found it! The inverter, the source of electrical power for the instrumentation, was switched off.

I immediately recycled it, and the instrumentation instantly came back on.

Mr. Baldwin said, "That's enough for today." I'd passed! We landed and hovered back to the tie-down. In the debriefing, Mr. Baldwin explained in detail what he'd done. I had properly handled it, although slowly. He then explained other options and possible causes. I was overjoyed to remain in my class without being sent back or thrown out of flying altogether.

"Mr. Baldwin," I asked, "do you have any advice for a future W1 heading off to Vietnam?" Warrant Officer, Grade 1, would be my rank after flight school. In those days there were four grades of warrant officer; today there are five.

He looked at me, and without a smile said, "Be extremely careful. Don't volunteer for anything. Don't do anything you haven't planned. And most of all, I'll tell you what I told my son—don't get yourself killed over there." His son Larry was also in a warrant officer flight class.

"Thank you, sir," I said. We shook hands and I continued on with my class. With that sequence of events, I concluded thirteen was obviously not a sign of bad luck for me. It would be a day I'd remember clearly, ten months later.

In celebration of passing the check ride, which coincided with Valentine's Day, I bought my wife a very nice, short pink slip.

My final four weeks of training were devoted to gunnery systems. I was checked out in the various armament systems used in the UH1-B and Charlie-model Huey gunships. We finished our last four weeks of tactical training, and graduation soon arrived.

Warrant Officer Rotary Wing Aviator Class 70-5 graduated on April 7, 1970. In the jubilation of class graduation, none of us could have known that nearly one-third of our combined (with 70-3) graduation class of 130 men would be dead in the next twelve months. Apparently, there are some things the army does well. Statistics must be one of them; as a class, we'd been told one out of three would be killed in action and others would be claimed by accidents. Of course, each of us believed the other guy would become the casualty. The term decimation originated in the days of the Roman army, when it meant one out of ten people was chosen to be killed. WORWAC Class 70-5 was not much different from most army helicopter pilot classes. High casualties were anticipated. Those who volunteered for the Warrant Officer Candidate Program knew that well in advance. And, we had already volunteered for duty in Vietnam. That was part of the application for army helicopter training.

The year before, I'd entered three months of army basic training at the armpit of the universe, Fort Polk, Louisiana. Afterward, we entered flight school at Fort Wolters, Texas. We then trained for nine months, which included eighteen hours of daily harassment in preflight training. The days evolved to sixteen hours of classrooms and Link instrument trainers. We also logged 220 hours of student pilot stick time in TH-55, TH-13, and UH-1 helicopters.

Most of us believed we would live through the war. Our greatest fear was becoming a crispy critter, one who survived a crash and fire, minus nose, ears, fingers, and toes. The speaker at our last safety meeting prior to graduation at Fort Rucker, was a warrant officer who had undergone reconstructive surgery at Fort Sam Houston, Texas. He was a grim reminder of the risks and realities we faced.

However, having been drilled in the virtues of duty, honor, and country, we were highly motivated volunteers, eager to accept the physical and mental challenges. When I'd enlisted, I went through the routine batteries of qualifying exams given all enlistees. During basic training at Fort Polk, Louisiana, I was offered a slot in officer candidate school or the army preparatory school for West Point.

I wanted to get married and fly helicopters, so I refused the schools. Most importantly, I feared I'd miss the war if I opted for either school.

The warrant-officer rank, higher than enlisted and noncommissioned officers (sergeants) but below commissioned officers, was adopted by the army in the early 1960s for aviation specialists. It allowed a pilot specialty with requisite officers club privileges, without diluting the ranks of the managerial level commissioned officers. Warrants referred to commissioned officers as RLOs (real live officers). Their in-between status was just fine with the warrants, who simply wanted to fly. Nearly 80 percent of all army pilots were warrant officers.

During the final flight physical prior to graduation, I was put on a medical hold to evaluate borderline high blood pressure. While on my medical hold, I was assigned as the assistant executive officer of the airfield company at Fort Rucker. This was the company that housed the radar operators and air traffic controllers. They provided the staffing and training of tower personnel and air traffic control specialists.

Capt. David Anderson was the commanding officer. His executive officer was 1st Lt. Gary Moffatt. During the weeks after graduation, I would come to learn a lot about the inner workings of the army and dealing with the system or the "Green Machine" as it was frequently called, all of which was new to me since my family had no military background.

I enjoyed my time with Captain Anderson and Lieutenant Moffatt. Moffatt and I had gone scuba diving a couple of times in Pensacola and Destin. We often spent weekends together. On June 14, 1970, I was cleared for flight duties by the flight surgeon at Fort Rucker and was expecting orders to leave. The following Friday night, my wife and I were invited to dinner with the Andersons. We spent the evening watching slides and movies of his tour in Vietnam. The most interesting were his movies of his UH-1C gunships operating from a navy barge docked on the Mekong River, in the Delta, the southernmost region in South Vietnam. "Tom," Anderson said, "be sure to take lots of film. Always keep your camera on hand, and if you can, get a good movie camera. I've enjoyed my movies much more than the slides. But, sometimes you'll be too busy to take photographs." We enjoyed a good laugh.

A few days later, Captain Anderson called me into his office. In proper military fashion I reported. "Good morning, sir. You requested my presence?"

"Yes, Mr. Marshall. Have a seat. Your time with the Airfield Company is coming to a close. You've done an excellent job here. I'd like to recommend you apply for voluntary indefinite status as a warrant officer. I believe you could receive a transition into a Chinook or some other aircraft prior to going to Vietnam. Have you thought of this?"

"No, sir. I haven't," I replied. However, having gotten to know Captain Anderson during the past two months, I would trust his advice. "What do I need to do, sir?"

He said, "I'll have the paperwork started for you. You go ahead and sign it, I'll take care of the rest. We'll have it telexed to the Headquarters, Department of the Army, and see what we can do with the warrant officer branch there."

"Thank you, sir. I'll do it immediately."

The next day, I had the paperwork filled out and forwarded to the chief of the warrant officers' personnel branch, in the Department of the Army, Pentagon. Two days later, I received notice of my assignment to the OH-58A Kiowa transition class. The army officially called the OH-58A the Kiowa, but it was commonly called the Jet Ranger. It was viewed more as a luxury civilian aircraft rather than an army helicopter. It was not the massive twin-rotor Chinook I had envisioned but a tiny, four-seat, light observation helicopter. I was not impressed. I cautiously asked Captain Anderson if it was worth pledging a voluntary indefinite (lifer) status for.

Captain Anderson explained, "Tom, you've seen my movies and slides. Remember my slides near Cambodia with the slicks down. (We called Hueys slicks.) The way things happen in combat, you want to be anywhere but in a Huey's cockpit. When gunships get shot down, more

Hueys are lost. Even flying scouts is more survivable than a hot CA (combat assault) in Hueys."

I suddenly understood that when the sleek, fast Cobras were shot down, the much slower, bigger Huey was a much easier target, much more likely to be shot down. I'd never heard that explained in flight school. I requested the training slot.

## August 1970, Fort Rucker, Alabama

In the month of July, I completed the transition at Fort Rucker. The OH-58A was a dream to fly, but it had extremely sensitive controls for a new pilot. I had a very difficult time the first ten hours of student flight. I was beginning to wonder whether I'd master it at all. With only 220 hours in flight school, I was not an experienced helicopter pilot. I did, however, have experienced instructor pilots who were very patient. By the time I completed the twenty-five-hour course, I could at least take off, land safely, and perform autorotations. With the course successfully completed, I departed for two weeks' leave at home, Pensacola, Florida, on the way to South Vietnam.

On the evening of July 25, while home in Pensacola with my wife and parents, we watched television news. The correspondent was standing on a pad at Camp Evans in I Corps. The 101st Airborne had an emergency evacuation of Firebase Ripcord under way. In the background, you could see smoke from a mountaintop and a near continuous stream of Hueys going to and from. The crash of artillery fire sounded in the background. The 101st Airborne was obviously evacuating a firebase in danger of being overrun. I proudly and confidently thought to myself, Well, hang on, men. I'll be there soon.

I was eagerly awaiting my involvement, my chance to participate in history, having no earthly idea what changes that experience would entail. I believed that training and dedication would allow me to control both fear and fate. Acolyte warriors always believe that. Combat veterans, I would learn, know better. They are aware of the horrifying circumstances and actions that identify heroes and unfairly claim lives, even those not supposed to die!

On August 2, I was enjoying a final two-week leave prior to departing for Vietnam. As I began reading the *Army Times* and looking through past issues, I realized my flight class had many members who had been in country since the first of May. Word had already come that George Berry was killed on May 23, in country only three weeks. He was with the 158th Aviation Battalion of the 101st Airborne Division. He was killed while flying as a copilot at Firebase O'Reilly.

Dan Dewey died on June 5. He was hit by 12.7 mm machine-gun fire in an OH-6A observation helicopter.

Charles Richardson was also killed on June 5. Flying with Bravo Company, 2d of the 17th Cavalry, 101st Airborne. He had been killed by small-arms fire from AK-47 rifles.

Gene Mizer, a copilot in a UH-1C gunship, had been killed on July 15. His death was reported as an aircraft accident. They were flying low-level at high speed up a steep ravine, lost power, rolled over, and exploded. It sounded like they'd been hit by antiaircraft fire, but there was no verification. There were no close-up witnesses. With nothing left of the wreckage proving enemy fire, the army had a policy. Without witnesses or wreckage showing from antiaircraft fire, crashes would be chalked up as an accident rather than a combat loss.

On July 18, 1970, Mike Duckus was the left seat observer during an OH-6A flight orientation to a scout platoon. His aircraft took intense ground fire, crashed, and burned. He died of burns in Japan.

Also on July 18, Jim Dunnavant's gunship crashed west of Tam Ky. He was with the 176th Aviation Company. He was a helicopter air casualty by ground fire.

Ed Crouse died on July 20, 1970. He was shot while riding as a gunner observer on a Loach (OH-6A). He was simply training for aircraft commander of an OH-6 helicopter for low-level reconnaissance missions.

I hadn't even left the country yet and six flight-school classmates had been killed. With the knowledge of their loss, I had taken the first step of transformation, becoming a veteran. The war was taking on a personal dimension I had not anticipated. The sacrifice of classmates' lives meant the losses of friends; their deaths were not just statistics. I was slowly becoming aware of my own mortality and the lethal environment I'd volunteered for.

## Week of August 15, 1970, Camp Eagle, South Vietnam

WO Ken Mayberry had been selected to train as the Phoenix Company instrument instructor pilot. The 101st Airborne Division anticipated the need for instrument-proficient pilots with the pending fall monsoons, rain, and fog. In October and November, the weather would make for the worst possible flying conditions in a mountain environment. Mayberry traveled to Camp Eagle to complete instructor training. One afternoon off, he killed time reading a Stateside magazine at the division library.

He heard someone clear his throat and ask, "Excuse me, sir."

Mayberry looked up at a young PFC standing in front of him. "Yes."

"Sir, were you one of those pilots on Ripcord?"

"Yes."

The young PFC stuck out his hand and said, "Thanks,"

and walked away. For Mayberry, one word and a hand-shake justified his twelve-month tour of duty.

## Phoenix Company Headquarters, Camp Evans

Two new warrant officers were being assigned to the Phoenix Company at Camp Evans. WO1 Larry Baldwin and WO1 Pat McKeaney had just completed their in-country orientation and briefing at Camp Eagle. They sat in the company headquarters, being briefed about the company and receiving their orders. The captain asked them which platoon they wanted to be in. There was one slot open in 1st Platoon and another slot in 2d Platoon.

Baldwin looked at McKeaney and said, "I'll take 1st Platoon if it's okay with you."

McKeaney casually replied, "Okay."

A simple choice by one with the acquiescence of the other, left one man with six weeks to live. The other would become a member of the survivors' club.

On August 18, I boarded a National Airlines jet from Pensacola, Florida, to New Jersey. I out-processed with another warrant officer from Pensacola, Chris Rummel, a Cobra pilot. After one night in Atlantic City, we boarded a military charter flight for South Vietnam. On August 20, we landed in Anchorage, Alaska. It was a beautiful modern airport, in absolutely gorgeous, clear, cold weather.

The morning of August 22, we landed at Bien Hoa Air-field near Saigon. We had enjoyed a fairly comfortable but long flight across the Pacific with a short stop at Yokota, Japan. The doors opened and we stepped off the plane into the most oppressive heat and humidity I had ever experienced. Worse even than Pensacola on a sweltering July day. As our eyes became accustomed to the bright sunshine, we broke out into a sweat.

We rode an army school bus with chain-link fence over

the glass windows to protect against grenades being thrown into the interior. A sign at the reception center showed I was about 11,500 miles from home. I was thirteen hours ahead, in the next day, compared to Pensacola.

I had hoped to be immediately assigned to a unit and get shipped out right away, but I spent the next two days filling out paperwork, and briefing with the personnel officer. He told me that he expected me to be assigned to the 4th Infantry Division, which was getting newly arrived OH-58s. The reason I was assigned there was the pending inventory of Jet Rangers with few trained pilots.

That afternoon, I was sipping a beer in the officers club when sirens announced a rocket attack. It hit at Long Binh, ten miles away. I didn't even hear the explosions.

By Monday, August 24, I was tired of sitting on my can with nothing to do. Chris Rummel had left to fly Cobras in the Delta. I was supposed to leave for An Khe, but the air force C-130 that was to take me there had mechanical trouble. I was told I wouldn't get there before August 26. Typical army situation. Hurry up like hell to get there, then hurry up and wait, and wait, and wait.

The next day, August 25, Barry Godfrey, another classmate, died during a high-speed, low-level turn. His main rotor blades hit the ground at Bien Hoa Airfield, not far from where I was awaiting orders. He died during an orientation and demonstration flight. Army flying is a high-risk endeavor.

I killed time looking around the PX and gift shop, and ended up buying my brother Steve a carved wooden elephant for his birthday. It cost only four dollars but was an attractive piece. Eighteen years later, we'd see how they were made. It would be shown in *The Deer Hunter*, to the chagrin of my brother.

# 4

# Central Highlands

## An Khe

On August 28 at 4:30 A.M., I packed up my duffel bag and boarded a school bus for the air force flight line. We were dropped off beside a large, four-engine, turboprop transport, a C-130 Hercules. Our bags were secured in cargo netting on the rear ramp, and we assumed our seats in the web frames along the windowless fuselage. In a roar of turboprop engines, we departed for An Khe.

A little more than an hour later, the C-130 made a steep approach into a very small airfield at An Khe, which was just outside Camp Radcliffe. After a rapid descent from approximately ten thousand feet, where the air was cool and dry, we were again hit by the wave of heat and humidity. There was the smell of jet fuel, the noise of helicopter operations, and outgoing artillery fire. The noises were quickly overcome by the smell of burning feces, which were incinerated in a mixture of gasoline and diesel fuel. My senses were staggered as I looked up at nearby Hong Kong Mountain with a sixth-sense awareness, a distinct feeling of someone watching . . . someone who'd like to kill me.

An Khe was the central mountain plains headquarters area for II Corps and home of the 4th Infantry Division. The 4th was a standard army infantry division with helicopter airmobile assets assigned to give it mobility. It was not an airmobile unit like the 101st Airborne Division or

1st Air Cavalry Division; helicopter companies were assigned (attached) to it indefinitely, but were not organic parts of the 4th Infantry Division.

An Khe was situated on a broad mountain plain one thousand feet above sea level. It was midway between Qui Nhon on the coast of the South China Sea to the east and Pleiku at the Cambodian border to the west. I was assigned to the bachelor officer quarters at the replacement unit. I was then informed I'd have four days of indoctrination and acclimatization. The enlisted men had only been through basic training and advanced individual training that covered less than four months. As a warrant officer candidate, I had been through basic infantry training plus nine months of flight school and ground school. With the addition of four weeks of training in the OH-58 afterward, it had been a very long year. Four days of classes and acclimatization sounded like a waste of time. I was fresh from the States with a very positive attitude. I was determined to do my very best as a warrant officer and helicopter pilot. I was like a racehorse, chomping at the bit to get going, start flying, and win the war!

The army, however, had different plans. I had already been in country since August 22. I was told I was scheduled for four days of indoctrination and two days of intelligence briefings. Then I would serve as a communications officer in a bunker twenty-five feet belowground until my OH-58 arrived sometime in late September. So I'd have one month in-country time before I even started flying. I thought it was absurd I wasn't flying the next day.

On Saturday morning, August 29, I began my aviation briefing with the division aviation officer, Captain Hunter, at division headquarters. He was well organized and had the entire area of operations mapped with major areas of activity and incidents marked. He looked at me as I came in the door. "Mr. Marshall, a newbie to fly Jet Rangers."

"Yes, sir."

"I bet you're full of piss and vinegar, anxious to get

going. You want to go out and hop in one and start flying tomorrow, right?"

"Yes, sir. I'm ready."

"Well, you're going to find the army has different plans, and you'll be doing it the army way." He gave me volumes of information to read regarding the area operations, nature of the operations under way, and precautions to take in day-to-day operations. After the initial briefing, the realities of the Green Machine were sinking in. I was sent away with reading instructions and orders to return that afternoon.

Later that day, concluding the afternoon session, he asked, "You want to end this tour alive?"

"I fully intend to."

"Well, you'd better understand something," he continued. "You'll have to make decisions that may not be popular with those you're working for. The 4th Infantry Division is not airmobile. The men and officers of this division are not as well trained in helicopter operations and tactics as designated airmobile units. They will ask you to do things, thinking you can do *anything*. It is your responsibility to keep the aircraft safe and deliver its occupants safely. Remember these rules or you won't make it out of here alive.

"The first basic rule while flying with brigade or battalion is critical. You will not do any hovering reconnaissance or slow, low-level flying. The NVA are out there. They will not let you see them until they want to, and they will shoot you out of the sky. It may be months before you see the first live NVA soldier out there, or it may be the first day. Hovering single-ship, without cover, will guarantee your being shot down. The last Loach we had shot down was four months ago. The pilot was a new guy like you. He got low and slow, and they shot him out of the sky. They captured him and an artillery lieutenant, tied their hands, physically beat them near death, and then shot them each in the head. Single bullet executions. We recovered the aircraft and the bodies. Luckily for their families, they won't be listed missing in action. With incidents like this, it's pretty clear the NVA aren't interested in prisoners of war. If the pilot had obeyed the rules, it would not have happened.

"Secondly, never commence any activity without knowing your personal capability of accomplishing it safely. Your aggressive nature and sense of independence will be the two factors that will cause you the greatest risk and ultimate harm. Remember that."

I thought to myself, Yeah, yeah, let's get on with the program and fight the war.

"Last," he said, "obey the rules of engagement." Captain Hunter then began talking abut the My Lai incident, which had only been a year and a half earlier. The trial was still pending. I signed the rules of engagement. I was also given several pages of security forms to acknowledge security levels, security codes, and communication procedures.

On the following day, Tuesday, I got my orders. I was assigned to the Headquarters Company, 1st Brigade, 4th Infantry Division. I was designated a command-and-control pilot, carrying lieutenant colonels, majors, and captains around "at altitude." I was getting a brand-new Jet Ranger, which would be brought in from Saigon within two weeks. I was elated.

I bought a Yashica GT-35 electronic eye camera. Captain Anderson had impressed upon me the importance of a good camera, always loaded, for the combat tourist.

My ration card allowed three cases of beer, four bottles of wine, and three fifths of liquor per month. That sounded like a more than reasonable amount. I didn't think I could drink that much in a month if I had to. However, that, too, was about to change.

On the afternoon of August 30, 1970, I completed my intelligence briefing with Captain Hunter. I was one of four officers briefed. Captain Hunter concluded, "Remember the basic rules. You are not to do hovering reconnaissance. Don't get yourself or your passengers killed."

"Yes, sir!" I walked back to the BOQ, thinking to myself that the intelligence briefing was more aviation safety than area-of-operations history. I was thinking, Safety awareness is okay, but where's the war?

An hour later, the war revealed itself. I was sitting just outside the replacement hootch, writing a letter home. It was overcast and cool. I noticed a flight of Hueys in formation above the An Khe Pass, a mile or two to the southeast. I heard explosions. Then the artillery cranked up on Camp Radcliffe. They fired at the nearby mountaintop.

As I sat outside my hootch, I watched Cobra gunships begin diving and firing rockets in the direction of the mountaintop, which was less than two miles away. Four Huey helicopters made a formation approach in, and then there was a tremendous ball of smoke. A gray, metallic-looking fire, fueled by oil and jet fuel from a burning helicopter, rose quickly in a small mushroom. Three Hueys flew out, no longer in formation. It was obvious one had crashed or been shot down in the landing zone. Then there were additional Cobra gunships and UH-1C Charlie-model gunships actively circling the area, making continuous strafing dives. A major fight had just begun within sight of the camp perimeter.

An ambush had been unleashed on a convoy going between An Khe and the An Khe Pass. The military trucks were badly hit, and the military police escort vehicles had been disabled or destroyed. In an effort to rout the ambush, ready-reaction troops were inserted into the nearest clearing on the mountaintop to work their way down behind the ambushers and clear the area. However, the landing zone was a carefully planned trap filled with North Vietnamese spider holes. A brand-new warrant officer, riding with the Blackjacks on his first combat mission, had his leg ripped open by an AK-47 in the landing zone as they crashed, on fire.

North Vietnamese were hiding under thatch manhole-type covers. Once the aircraft hovered, they opened fire. In two minutes, sixteen GIs of the twenty-four who had been placed on the ground were wounded, and one helicopter had been shot down with the pilot severely wounded and copilot disabled. Three other aircraft limped home with major battle damage and wounded crew members. As I watched the battle unfold, I got the facts of the story from an officer just returning from headquarters. I began to understand that Vietnam could be a dangerous place. The final casualty count on that minor skirmish was six GIs dead, fourteen wounded, out of twenty-four. All of the wounded and the bodies were recovered by another ready-reaction force by the end of the day. I suddenly appreciated Captain Anderson's advice.

Having watched four Hueys go into a landing zone and three come out, I was thankful I wasn't a slick pilot. I then viewed flying slicks (troop-carrying Hueys) the same way Capt. David Anderson had. You had to be part of a larger team effort, and everything you did had to be coordinated with the people next to you. I wanted the latitude and self-determination of the single pilot reconnaissance or VIP bird. That kind of duty gave one a sense of personal control. It was obvious that a particular mental attitude and frame of reference made some men especially good at slick piloting, while others preferred more flexible, independent operations. After having witnessed the combat assault and aircraft fire, with the casualties including pilots, Captain Hunter's words suddenly became much more believable.

I received my call sign, Bird Seven, the seventh man to fly in the 1st Brigade's Hummingbirds. It was hard for the brigade to get aviation help, so they really appreciated the few pilots they had. I'd never felt so welcome among so many majors and captains as I did that day.

I wasn't scheduled for an aircraft until sometime after September 15. Until then, I'd serve in the brigade headquarters bunker as an aviation communications officer. Although word was the 4th Infantry Division would be moved to the coast by December, another rumor had started that the 4th Infantry Division wouldn't be shipped home until next June or July 1971. I hadn't even started flying and rumors were rampant, the war might be over. A truce and cease-fire might be announced, any day.

## Hummingbird Seven

On Sunday morning, September 6, 1970, I took my first helicopter ride in Vietnam. WO Jim Grant, one of the two Loach pilots, took me on a maintenance check flight in his OH-6A. I hopped in and asked him where we were in relation to the area of operations and what I could see while we climbed out. He took me up to about two thousand feet, did a couple of hammerhead stalls, low-level swoops, and then high-speed, low-level runs with cyclic (vertical) climbs to see if he could get me sick or nervous. I just relaxed and enjoyed the ride.

After the flight, Captain Jones, the brigade aviation officer, called me into the Mole Hole. "Mr. Marshall, you should be getting your OH-58 in a couple of weeks. In order to get you ready for it, we need to get you some AO (area of operations) flight time. We are going to assign you to Jack Jones, who is Colonel Fear's personal pilot. You'll be his newbie peter pilot for the next few days. They'll be working in the area of operations down east of Cheo Reo, northwest of Tuy Hoa. This should be an excellent way for you to get flight time, learn the area and our procedures."

"Great!" I said. Then I was given the time and place to

meet Jones the next morning. I mentally began preparing for my first day of flying in "the Nam."

Col. Tom Fear was the 1st Brigade commander, a career officer who'd gotten his start as a 2d lieutenant in Bastogne during the Battle of the Bulge in 1944. As 1st Brigade commander, he had the nicest, newest Huey in army inventory in the An Khe area. Colonel Fear also had a personal pilot selected for his skills, experience, and safety record. The Huey was equipped with a commander's communications console that permitted simultaneous contact with multiple ground units as well as other aircraft and the base of operations.

The next morning, I was up at 4:30 and at the Blackjacks' ready room. I met CW2 Jones,* who was obviously unhappy at having a newbie assigned to him. It meant he had to do all the work.

I assisted in the preflight inspection of the aircraft. We then strapped in, going through the start-up checklist procedures before flying a short distance to the 1st Brigade pad at the foot of Hong Kong Mountain. Our passengers came walking out and jumped aboard.

Colonel Fear welcomed me aboard once he was on. I then spent twelve hours in the cockpit, listening and observing intently. I had limited time to learn the major landmarks, areas of operations, and the areas of high risk, so it was very intense on-the-job training. It had been a lucky coincidence for me that the last major operation south of An Khe involved the area east of the Ia Drang Valley. The area was southeast of Pleiku, stretching eastward to an area northwest of Tuy Hoa. A small town there, named Phu Xuan, had a small landing strip that dated back to the days of the French. It served as the command post for operations.

---

*Warrant officers above W1 are all formally "chief warrant officers," hence "CW2" Jones.

From that point, a move was made westward into the southern foothills of the mountain range, which ran southward from An Khe to the lower plains. An artillery firebase overlooked a large expanse of plains. Several companies were dispersed throughout the area of operations. We overflew combat assaults that were placing the troops on the ground, and we monitored resupply operations under way. The colonel and Major Swinford, the battalion operations officer, were our day-long passengers. I listened carefully to as much radio traffic as I could and quickly became adept at simultaneously listening to two or three conversations on different channels.

The next several days were long ones. For six days, we left at 7:00 A.M., got back to the golf course by dark at 7:00 P.M., and were in our hootches by 9:00. Dinner was C rations in my room. It became obvious that getting up at 4:30 A.M. and sitting in the cockpit for twelve hours, typically logging seven to nine hours of flight time, would become quite tiring. And this was the best job a Huey crew could have!? After a few more days of flying, I began to get the feel of the Huey and was a little better "peter pilot."

In fact, I was so good, Jones let me use the radio once.

Takeoff times were 6:30 A.M. I flew over fourteen hours in two days. My name had become "Newbie."

On September 15, I received word my 58 was on its way. A cherry (new) aircraft, it would have approximately ten hours flight time when I received it. Jim Grant and Bruce Finney were teasing me about the 58 being underpowered and not as agile as their OH-6A Cayuse. The Cayuse was only called the Loach. We eventually got down to serious discussion comparing the operational capabilities in terms of speed, range, endurance, and load capacity.

I asked Grant and Finney if they had been shot down or

had lost their engines. Grant shook his head, no. Unknown to him, it was merely "not yet."

Finney assumed a very serious expression and then began to tell me of his autorotation after an engine failure. He was flying near Firebase Truman, northeast of An Khe, heading back one afternoon when the turbine engine just died. He made a steep autorotation onto a sandbar in the middle of the river, all the time calling out Mayday and giving his location. He explained that he'd kept his airspeed up, made a steep approach, ending with a slow deceleration, then a major decelerating flare just prior to a vertical touchdown with no forward sliding. He explained the technique and how it worked best with the Loach. It had been taught to him by an in-country instructor who had suffered the same problem. He landed vertically, with no damage to the aircraft.

Finney slowly and seriously shared his story. "Hell, I un-assed, waiting for a fire or an explosion. Nothing happened. Hell, it wasn't even smoking. I had my pistol in one hand and fire extinguisher in the other. Then I realized I was all alone, in the middle of a river sandbar. The middle of Indian country, and no friends nearby. I immediately tried to look as small as I could."

Within two minutes, a Huey flew in and picked him up. Another Huey circled until a maintenance crew and security force were brought in. It turned out that the cause was a minor engine problem, but it had caused a total engine failure. His Loach was sling-loaded by a Chinook back to An Khe. He was up and flying three days later with a new engine. A living example of the army's successful emergency training procedures.

On the seventeenth, my pay records caught up with me. I then realized I only had eleven more paydays in Vietnam. Unfortunately, they came thirty days apart. I also discovered that letters to and from my wife were about ten days behind actual conversations.

On the morning of September 18 was my last flight with Jack Jones and Colonel Fear in the 1st Brigade command-and-control Huey. We flew to Firebase Washington, where Colonel Fear met with two lieutenant colonels, one the passenger of WO Jim Grant.

I waved at Grant in his Loach as he departed, carrying the lieutenant colonel. He also had aboard a second lieutenant artillery observer, sitting on the floor of his passenger compartment. His feet were dangling outside. The lieutenant colonel had finished a short briefing with Colonel Fear southeast of An Khe. They took off in Grant's Loach and headed on to their daily routine while we headed south to Phu Xuan.

When we arrived at Phu Xuan, we got the tragic news that Grant had crashed and burned! He was critically injured but got off a distress call prior to impact. He'd been picked up and medevacked to the Camp Radcliffe army hospital. The lieutenant colonel was dead, as well as the artillery lieutenant, who'd been sitting on the floor in the back of the Loach. Everyone, including me, was shaken by the news. We'd just left them thirty minutes before. Now, two were dead. Simply gone.

I returned to base late that evening. Bruce Finney had already gone over to visit Grant in the hospital, and I went as soon as I got back. Grant was lying in the hospital ward bed, hooked up to an IV. With bandaged arms and hands, he looked like hell. Deeply sunken eyeballs and burns told the story of what he'd survived.

"Jim, what the hell happened?"

"I don't know. I felt a click in the back and then lost all power. The engine was running, but I lost all power. There wasn't anywhere to go but straight down."

I asked, "Wasn't there anything you could've done?"

"Man, I don't know. I didn't have any rotor pitch control, no collective when I hit bottom. I pulled pitch. Nothing happened—just pancaked right on top of the hill. I must've lost collective (control) or both (collective and engine). The colonel must have died on impact. The lieutenant (in the back) had his feet pinned beneath the fuselage. I tried to pull him out, but the fire—so intense, I couldn't do anything so—well."

He was badly shaken, having watched his passenger burn to death. The young lieutenant had been on his stomach, clawing the ground to crawl from the fire. He'd died screaming, consumed in the fiery wreckage. The magnesium alloys in helicopters incinerated wreckage and occupants alike. Fires usually left only a small piece of the tail boom and a pile of gray ash.

Grant had vertical compression of the spine. He'd also suffered very bad burns to his arms and face trying to save the lieutenant. He would probably never fly again.

The next day, Grant was transferred to a larger hospital, and I never saw or heard from him again. The next night, back at the hootch, Finney and I returned late and began drinking with other officers. One of the infantry captains asked Finney what "really happened," implying pilot error. Finney erupted in anger. "Damn it! Every time something happens, they want to blame the pilot first. Don't they realize this is fucking Vietnam?! Grant felt a metallic click, might have been a round hitting him from behind. No one knows! Everything's melted into one little puddle of molten sheet metal. The gooks are all over out there. A lot of times they shoot from behind, where you can't see and don't even know you're being shot at."

Well, I thought to myself, so much for aviation safety. If they're going to blame it on the pilots first, make sure you've got witnesses or proof if you get shot down. Obviously, it would be best if you had witnesses. Everyone suspected Grant had been shot down, but it was only speculation without bullet holes in sheet metal. The fire left no evidence.

Earlier that day, Finney had flown out and recovered

Grant's M-16, which had been melted into a molten pistol-like thing. A grotesque ornament, a reminder of death, it hung on the officers club wall. A Ranger captain, who was older than most, looked over at me and jokingly said, "Well, Mr. Marshall, you want to make this a career?" Without answering, I started laughing hysterically.

Laughter, lubricated with alcohol, eased the tension. It was a pattern of response to mortal stress, one I would refine and greatly intensify over the coming ten months.

Rumors abounded that the 4th Infantry Division would be long gone from Vietnam by December 1. Firebases and operations that had been anywhere from thirty-five to sixty miles away from An Khe were pulled back to just six to twelve miles of An Khe.

I was relieved to have made it into the war before it ended, and bewildered, wondering whether there really was a war going on.

## Sunday, September 20, 1970, Quang Tri, I Corps

First Lieutenant Al Finn, Phoenix 1st Platoon leader and aircraft commander, and WO1 Larry Baldwin were conducting another combat assault mission in a Phoenix Huey. With six Papa Company Rangers, long-range reconnaissance patrol (LRRP), in the cargo bay, they flew northwest of Dong Ha headed for the northernmost side of the DMZ, which separated North Vietnam from South.

The Huey entered the DMZ at an altitude of less than ten feet and a speed approaching one hundred knots. It was a demanding ground-level sprint across the barren mudscape of the DMZ to insert the LRRP killer team. The exit would also be as fast and as low as the Huey could fly. North Vietnamese Army bunkers with .51-caliber machine guns were dispersed throughout the area. Flying even at fifty feet above ground level invited death at the hands of NVA .51s. Suddenly the Huey smashed nose first into the ground, flipping tail over nose, into a flaming mass of war's debris. Four helicopter crew members and five soldiers died quickly. One Ranger was thrown from the aircraft and miraculously lived even though badly injured.

For the Phoenix, the afternoon of the twentieth was unlike most others. Word began passing on the radios, among friends. "Did you hear? Two-six went down, no survivors." The words shocked those who knew the crew. It would be a somber evening in the Phoenix company area.

That evening, back at the Phoenix Nest at Camp Evans, the word of their deaths was absorbed. Sp5. Larry Frazier had lost two good friends, Felts and Dotson, from the crew. Frazier remembered Lieutenant Finn had asked him to be the permanent crew chief for Finn's bird, but Frazier hadn't felt comfortable with the request and declined. He hadn't wanted to leave his friends in the Phoenix 2d Platoon. The event eerily reminded him of another day, when he had stood before a promotion board review a few weeks earlier. The crew chief who replaced Frazier so he could make the board that day had been badly wounded. It would take a while for him to assimilate the grief of his friends' deaths.

The pilots returned to base, finished their postflights, and headed for the shower. By eight o'clock they began to make their ways to the club. The pilots of the Phoenix went through the ancient warriors' ritual, mentally examining the action. Questioning why their friends died. What really happened. Were their deaths caused by ineptitude or carelessness? Was someone to blame? Each pilot dealt with such events in his own way. Some would think, I'm a better pilot than he was, or I'm luckier. Some would think, I'm more careful. Others would simply accept the losses in prayerful thanks; it was someone else. This was not a ritualistic search for meaning in their deaths, but a very personal search for individual assurance, a sustaining belief that "next time," it would again happen to someone else.

In the aftermath of the action, the truth would not be known. There was no specific evidence proving enemy fire caused the crash. To the pilots, it didn't matter how or why it happened. One of the dead was the son of retired Major Baldwin, who'd given me a standards check ride, the same Major Baldwin who'd told me, "I'll give you the same advice I gave my son—'Don't get yourself killed over there.' "

In the following month, October, after his son's funeral, the retired major journeyed from Dothan, Alabama, to the opposite side of the earth: the Phoenix Nest, Camp Evans, I Corps, South Vietnam. As a helicopter pilot and Vietnam veteran, he knew the questions to ask. The maintenance . . . weather . . . training . . . the mission.

What went wrong? Where? How? Why?

As a grieving father, he'd find no answer, no meaning, no one to blame. Only the timeless tragedy of a child lost in war. The pain had not changed since the beginnings of man.

Late that evening, a young specialist four at Graves Registration in Da Nang dutifully recorded the aircrew loss. UH-1H, number 67-17597, was lost in combat at military map grid Yankee-Uniform 112731. Those who understood the map system, knew it came to destruction nine miles due north of Camp Carroll.

Camp Carroll was the largest, northernmost position. It was named after a Marine captain tragically killed in action by friendly fire, a short round fired by a tank. The firebase was facing the most likely path of a North Vietnamese Army assault into South Vietnam. But that event was eighteen months in the future. No place on the face of the earth was as tragically misnamed as Defense Secretary Robert McNamara's demilitarized zone. It was a landscape of mythical Mars, the god of war, reddish-brown death.

The Phoenix pilots and crewmen had yet to be visited by Larry Baldwin's father. But the Phoenix understood, even shared his feelings; he was a grim reminder that death could claim anyone. The Phoenix would keep their distance from Baldwin's father, not wanting to become victims of his grief. To maintain survival instincts, the Nam attitude of "it don't mean nothing" allowed calloused composure.

WO Pat McKeaney would remember that September 20, for it was his birthday. He'd entered the Phoenix a few weeks earlier, with WO Larry Baldwin. McKeaney's birthday would never again pass without remembrance of Larry Baldwin.

## An Khe

On September 20, I finally flew my first solo-mission day in an OH-58, 9.5 hours. I was the command-and-control bird for two combat assaults, two platoon pickups, and all sorts of good fun things in between. Really had a ball!

I carried a major and a lieutenant colonel around, who supervised two company moves from the Phu Xuan into the mountain range above. I marked the first landing zone (LZ) with smoke grenades. My passengers decided I shouldn't do that on the second one. Rank had its privileges, and it was their choice to avoid unnecessary exposure to enemy fire. Not knowing better, I'd been eagerly anticipating enemy fire.

At the end of the day, I was released to return to An Khe, still a forty-minute flight away. The weather turned bad, with showers and fog covering the mountains and passes. Traffic control recommended I divert to Phu Cat

Air Base northwest of Qui Nhon, which I did, landing my new Jet Ranger in my normal eighty-knot traffic pattern behind two F-4 Phantoms going 140 knots. I got the VIP treatment and a ride to the air force snack bar. It was a heady experience for a young WO. Later that night, after the rain clouds cleared the pass at nine P.M., I flew back to An Khe. I also made my first night GCA (ground controlled radar approach) in country.

On September 22, the action suddenly became even more dangerous in the Cheo Reo and Phu Xuan area. I served as C & C for a battalion move. We marked the landing zone on top of a small ridgeline west of Phu Xuan, and ten ships made an insertion of troops. We found a large structure that looked like a thatched two-story barn. On a steep hillside with elephant grass all around and above it, the barn was very difficult to pick out. Once we made the adjustments, it was easily destroyed by artillery, but I had to correct the artillery observer in the backseat when he radioed, "Drop a hundred meters." "No, you need to add a hundred meters," I said. With the artillery adjusted, they had direct hits.

"Fire for effect!" the observer radioed. I found out later that we had one confirmed NVA kill from white phosphorous (WP) howitzer shells. The NVA soldier had been burned to death in his observation post, a tree. When I was told of my first confirmed kill, I personally thought it was no big deal. It was, however, a very big deal to the dead guy, who'd been immolated in white phosphorous.

Three days later, we were flying between the outpost and Phu Xuan when my passenger, an infantry lieutenant in the backseat, became very excited. He kept making the form of a triangle above his head and pointing down. I asked Rodriguez, my crew chief, "What's he want?" Rodriguez didn't understand his motions either, and I didn't have a headset for him. We had virtually no communication. I looked around and didn't see anything on the ground. We continued on and landed a couple of minutes later. As soon as he got out, he told me he had seen a column of forty North Vietnamese troops. I then learned the triangle-shaped signal above the head was an infantry symbol for the enemy.

It was a fun time to be flying. I was too new and uninitiated. I couldn't recognize the dangers obvious to the more experienced. I was, however, rapidly building valuable flight time and experience in the aircraft.

A few days later, an incident happened that would commence the learning curve we referred to as combat experience.

A unit made enemy contact and found a North Vietnamese Army base camp. As they assaulted the position, they overran a bunker complex. One previously wounded NVA was captured. The others escaped. In order to remove him to a prison hospital, they had to use a jungle penetrator from a UH-1 medevac ship. Per his standing orders, the medevac would not hover with the penetrator unless he had gunship cover. No gunships, no extractions.

There were no gunships available. At the recommendation of Colonel Fear, his pilot offered to simulate the noise of a Cobra by diving and making gun-run type passes. I offered to hover around him offering what little distraction I could.

The medevac pilot thought that sounded stupid enough to distract the enemy. A bird colonel's Huey, imitating the sound of a Cobra gunship's screaming dive noises. A newbie hovering around in a Jet Ranger, as an alternative target. All this for a wounded NVA, the enemy. The press would never have believed it and certainly wouldn't have reported it. Apparently NVA prisoners were few; Colonel Fear thought it worth the risk.

I circled the hovering medevac within thirty yards, on the treetops, at ten to twenty knots airspeed. As I slowly circled, I heard my first close shots, small-arms fire. They were our M-16s, not AK-47s. The infantry below us was reconning by fire, shooting up everything as they searched the camp.

The medevac hovered for less than two minutes, then quickly climbed away.

The next day, I had down for maintenance. I walked into the brigade officers' mess at lunch. Sitting in the small officers' section was Colonel Fear, alone. He motioned me to have a seat at his table. I was somewhat humbled, a lowly W1 having lunch with the brigade commander, a bird colonel. In a nervous effort to start small talk, I asked him where he was headed in the reassignment process. He explained to me that few were going home from the 4th Infantry Division. Only some enlisted men. All officers were being reassigned to other units in Vietnam. I asked his opinion of the pending standdown of the 4th Infantry Division. He became very stern. "It seems the president and his political advisers, in their wisdom, have determined the best way to win this war is through the Vietnamese people's armed forces (the basis for the Vietnamization process). It remains to be seen how effective it will be."

Changing the subject, he asked, "Was that you hovering yesterday down by Phu Xuan?"

"Yes, sir. I was just trying to provide cover so the medevac could come in."

"Well, Mr. Marshall, you've certainly been doing your job, and you're making quite an addition to the brigade."

"Thank you, sir." A compliment from a bird colonel! I felt pretty good about myself.

That evening, Bruce Finney came into my room, livid with rage. "Newbie, you stupid shit, what's this about you hovering down at Phu Xuan!" I looked up at him, surprised. I calmly explained what I'd done. I told him that I'd hover only when there were other aircraft in the area. Finney looked down at me, almost shouting, "If you keep pulling stupid stunts like that, you're not only gonna get yourself killed, but everyone with you." He stormed out of the room, in a torrent of expletives, interspersed with "Newbie!" Finney had months of experience and fully comprehended the risks. I still had a lot to learn.

After I thought about it, I slowly began to understand Finney's anger. I'd broken the first rule given to me by Captain Hunter. I'd been flying very long hours, accumulating time in my new OH-58. I was flying between five hours and nine hours per day, solo. I was eager to do the best possible job and loved flying as much as ever. Flying was as much a joy as I had ever dreamed it would be. The mountains were spectacularly beautiful. The sense of freedom, flying my helicopter on missions I controlled, had been overwhelming at times. I was, however, slowly beginning to realize I'd overstepped the bounds of common sense. Finney had chewed my ass for good reason.

On Saturday, September 27, 1970, another classmate was killed. Mike Bradley, with the 237th Medical Detachment, a medevac unit, died as a helicopter-combat casualty. He was a pilot in a hovering extraction, a jungle penetrator extraction just like the one I'd given hovering cover at Phu Xuan the day before.

Sunday was another typical day flying south near Phu Xuan and Cheo Reo. I spent most of my time carrying captains and lieutenants around between the battalion headquarters, overflying the platoons out of the field. The platoons on patrol, walking the jungle, would typically fire a pen flare to mark their location (which, obvious to me and everyone else, kept their location marked for the North Vietnamese also). Two platoons reported having trail followers and had unsuccessfully tried to ambush them.

During lunch, we flew over to Phu Xuan and landed at the former French airstrip. The airstrip runway was made of pierced steel planking (PSP). An OH-6A observation helicopter with the air cav unit was taking off. A skid hooked the PSP, and one of the landing skids was ripped off. It was quite funny to watch the pilot hover as sand-bags were set up for him to lean the damaged side of the aircraft on. He'd been sloppy in his takeoff, hooked the PSP with his skid, and damaged his aircraft. It was not only a dangerous accident, which nearly flipped the heli-copter upside down, but it embarrassed the hell out of him as all of the other pilots were watching, pointing, pho-tographing, and laughing. He'd rather have been shot down than endure that humiliation! One thing about army pilots, they loved watching someone else screw up. This event was no exception. Cameras blossomed in the cockpits. As I was walking back to my 58, I saw Avon Mallete, my flight-school, car-pool buddy, leaning into my cockpit. I shouted at him, "You can look, but don't touch."

He looked up. "Marshall, I'll be damned. I can't be-lieve you're flying this pretty little thing. But it's a piece of crap compared to my Loach."

I laughed. "You Loach pilots are all the same. But I'll keep my Ranger anyway." We got to talking about our wives and his new daughter, Tammy. He showed me a picture of her, and I asked him how it was going.

"Man, it is hot as hell over west of Pleiku and down southwest of there. We're kinda happy to be over here where it's a little easier to work. Everywhere we go, the dinks are there. And we've been losing people, too."

"Well, be careful, man," I said. We shook hands.

The days passed without names. Working straight through Saturday and Sunday left no sense of a week's time. We were too busy, and too tired, to notice. Flying my own Jet Ranger, feeling part of a larger American effort with no apparent enemy opposition, was feeding me a perspective of the war that simply wouldn't apply to areas north, I Corps. In country for nearly six weeks, I hadn't even taken ground fire yet.

## October 1, 1970, North Vietnam

The Ho Chi Minh trail was the general name for several supply routes, all leading from North Vietnam into various western border areas of South Vietnam. It began in the early 1950s as a simple jungle footpath connecting China, Vietnam, and Laos, bypassing French colonial outposts. By 1970, it was mostly invisible from the air, over twelve thousand miles of improved limestone roadways and paths dispersed among five major routes. The trail was a combat engineer's work of art, a testament to the people's persistence. It provided the men and materiel for all of the major battles that occurred in Vietnam. After the battles, it was a sanctuary approved by their enemy. The Congress of the United States of America forbade American ground forces to pursue the enemy into "neutral" Laos and Cambodia. President Johnson, his advisers, and Congress, gave life-sustaining sanctuary to the North Vietnamese Army.

In the initial Ia Drang battle in 1965, which was the commencement of American helicopter-borne (airborne) operations in Vietnam, the North Vietnamese attacked from the trail in Cambodia, just across the border. The same occurred in the 1967/1968 siege at Khe Sanh. The North Vietnamese Army troops besieging Khe Sanh attacked from Laos, a fact apparently lost on the media and, consequently, the American public. The battle for Hamburger Hill in 1969 again involved troops crossing a mountain trail from Laos into the A Shau Valley of South Vietnam.

Strategists on both sides knew that supply lines determined the war's outcome. A war simply could not be prosecuted without men, arms, and food. After the 1968 Tet offensive, bombing intensified in Laos and Cambodia, but by then it was too late; the trail was an impregnable highway, with underground service areas, field hospitals, and a fuel pipeline that stretched to the riverbanks of the Song Ba (*Apocalypse Now* country) near Loc Ninh, eighty miles north of Saigon.

On a single day in 1970, U.S. surveillance counted fifteen thousand trucks and jeeps on the trail. The air force, the army general staff, and intelligence officers did not reveal to lower-ranking officers or the press, the extent of development or the level of activity on the Ho Chi Minh trail. Americans would drop twice the total bomb tonnage used in World War II against the Ho Chi Minh trail, without stopping it.

General Vo Nguyen Giap carefully monitored the May 1970 Cambodian invasion, when American troops and South Vietnamese had crossed into the Cambodia base areas destroying huge caches of supplies, weapons, and munitions. In Cambodia, the North Vietnamese had evacuated the areas with delaying actions, snipers, and other tactics, but they attempted to avoid a major ground battle with American troops in Cambodia, knowing they would lose.

It was also clear to General Giap that the Americans would make an eventual move into Laos. Spies in Saigon, as well as Soviet intelligence, confirmed his suspicions. The trail was the key to all North Vietnamese Army resupply efforts throughout southern Vietnam, and it was the main artery of life support from North Vietnam to the North Vietnamese Army. The importance of this was not lost on the Americans and South Vietnamese.

The loss of supplies in Cambodia was not a permanent blow to the NVA, and the action resulted in a major propaganda coup for Giap. American antiwar demonstrators flooded the streets of Washington, D.C., San Francisco, New York, and other urban areas. American troops were still present in South Vietnam, but the American public's support of the war was a fraction of what the popular support had been in 1965. With the prior year's announcement of Vietnamization and withdrawal of American units, a political victory of sorts was at hand for North Vietnam. There was simply no reason for North Vietnam's leaders to negotiate anything. Time was on their side, as it had been with the French.

Early in October 1970, General Giap established total control over North Vietnamese Army divisions located in Laos, the DMZ, and the lower part of North Vietnam. He ordered the newly formed corps to prepare for an ARVN offensive along Route 9, the road leading from Khe Sanh to Tchepone. The crossroads at Tchepone was the center of North Vietnamese Army logistics activity in Laos. Beginning in October, the Communists prepared defensive positions and ambush sites in the area. Antiaircraft positions were prepared deep in the ground, many connected by tunnels, all perfectly camouflaged. They were impervious to all but a direct bomb hit.

Artillery positions were tunneled through the mountains overlooking Khe Sanh and the Laotian plains, just as had been done over Dong Khe and Dien Bien Phu in 1950 and 1954.

The NVA registered artillery on helicopter landing sites described in stolen plans and orders. Some critical supplies were shifted out of the area. The North Vietnamese Army made simultaneous preparations to repel an attack into the DMZ or the southern portion of North Vietnam. When the northeast monsoon ended in January 1971, the North Vietnamese were ready. Twenty antiaircraft battalions, manning a total of nearly two hundred pieces of antiaircraft artillery ranging from 23mm to 100mm in caliber, were placed in Laos between Tchepone, the DMZ, and Khe Sanh. Each emplacement had specific engagement rules and a limited area of sky to cover. Hundreds more 12.7mm heavy machine guns were also dispersed in the area.

General Giap commanded the Viet Minh troops that defeated the French expeditionary force at Dien Bien Phu in 1954; Giap commanded North Vietnamese forces at Ripcord. It would also be Giap who commanded the forces in Laos.

Many years later, we'd learn he wasn't clairvoyant, and not necessarily a military genius. The worldwide military intelligence network of the Soviets supported him. Among others, a U.S. Navy man, John Walker, had supplied the Soviets with crucial cipher keys and other data. The Soviets, Vietnamese, and their allies intercepted our messages and fed the data to the North Vietnamese Army units. Combined with the North Vietnamese Army spies planted in the highest levels of the Saigon regime, Giap was able to plan well ahead of the allies.

The placement of antiaircraft battalions between Tchepone and Khe Sanh was destined to elevate the intensity of the air combat operations. As later reported by the army, it created an antiaircraft "threat environment," second only to areas surrounding Hanoi and other important areas to the north. It proved to be the most dangerous helicopter environment of the Vietnam War. Pilots would simply call it hell.

In Laos, the North Vietnamese Army would stand and fight, something they had infrequently done in the past. Again, the cost in lives would be horrible for both sides.

American military leaders, and General Giap, were about to learn a lesson in airmobile warfare, emerging from the dutiful competence of army helicopter aircrews.

Giap knew when and where the army helicopters would come. He entrenched his antiaircraft forces and waited in ambush. He would learn that even twenty battalions of antiaircraft troops, two hundred pieces of antiaircraft weapons with highly experienced crews, could not stop the army helicopter crews.

## October 7, 1970, Washington, D.C.

In May 1970, an SR-71 Blackbird reconnaissance aircraft took highly detailed aerial photos that suggested POWs might be held at Son Tay, a prison in North Vietnam twenty-four miles northwest of Hanoi. It was believed that Son Tay might contain sixty-one American prisoners. On July 10, Gen. Donald Blackburn endorsed the concept of a Special Forces raid on Son Tay to attempt the freeing of any prisoners of war there. Col. Bull Simons, a distinguished Special Forces veteran, secretly gathered fifty-eight volunteers at Fort Bragg, North Carolina, to select a smaller number for "a classified mission." A complex plan, involving HH-53 Jolly Green Giant helicopters, one of which would serve as a gunship, would assault the guards' camp. An HH-3 Sea King helicopter would silently autorotate into the nearby POW camp with thirteen Special Forces troops to rescue the prisoners. After the Special Forces soldiers killed the guards and freed the POWs, the Jolly Green Giants would carry them to freedom. After countless practice sessions and drills, every step of the mission had been rehearsed. Every conceivable obstacle or possible glitch in the plan had been prepared for.

After the full dress rehearsal was successfully completed on October 7, the plan was submitted through channels to Henry Kissinger. After some delay, it would be presented to President Nixon and a small group of officials for final approval on November 18.


## Camp Radcliffe, An Khe

On October 8, President Nixon addressed the nation. The Armed Forces Vietnam radio network carried his speech, the formal announcement that the South Vietnamese government would be taking over major military operations. The Vietnamization process was then fully engaged. The withdrawal of American units in Vietnam would accelerate dramatically. President Nixon then announced that an offer had been extended to the North Vietnamese to "discuss a potential cease-fire."

In our hootch, the overall feeling was that we were

simply abandoning the war, quitting. Demoralizing words for those in country! Several of our captains were incensed. There were heated discussions and angry curses about our losses. The most sarcastic and biting comments were from a second-tour captain, a Ranger, commenting, "Looks like it's gonna end just like Korea." That meant, no victory, no satisfaction. We didn't know it would have a far more tragic ending, arising in part from the political distraction of an event yet to be called Watergate.

I couldn't help but think of all the losses and injuries, especially the loss of Jim Grant. It was obvious we could go in force anywhere we wanted. But it was equally clear, the North Vietnamese Army was everywhere, though varying in strength and weapons. The war would continue but, after the sacrifices and losses, the 4th Infantry Division colors were simply being packed up and returned to the World. The troops would be reassigned to other units in country.

While eliminating American units from Vietnam, we were carefully enhancing, with in-country transfers, the combat strengths of units remaining. Military strategists knew that the most difficult military maneuver was a strategic withdrawal (retreat). In fact, the 9th Infantry Division had already departed the Mekong River Delta, down south in IV Corps.

The following day, with time off for my bird's maintenance, I began unwinding. Rodriguez, my crew chief and door gunner, was working on the aircraft. Around lunch, he came back and told me that a Cobra had taken hits from antiaircraft air bursts. The Cobra was at the civilian tech-rep maintenance hangar. I thought, "Man, this sounds real interesting." We rode over to take a look at the Cobra, a new King Cobra with a 20mm Gatling gun in the nose turret. Up until that morning, the pilots thought they were hot stuff with the heaviest Gatling gun in army inventory.

The technical representative of Bell Helicopter was standing there, along with the representative of the gun manufacturer. Also there were the battalion safety officer and the Cobra pilot's platoon commander.

I listened as the Cobra pilot explained how they had pulled out at fifteen hundred feet and the air began to explode around them. The second Cobra broke off its pass, they both hit the deck and then *didi maue*d (Vietnamese for "hauled ass"). The Cobra pilot saw the anti-aircraft bursts and knew he'd taken hits. He landed at Cheo Reo, checked it out, then flew back to the golf course at An Khe.

I chuckled to myself. He'd been showing off his new weapon to the NVA. They apparently weren't too impressed, and one-upped his 20mm gun.

The holes in the Cobra looked like fragmentation hits from a mortar round.

The officers were standing around the nose of the Cobra, the battalion safety officer generally doing most of the talking. Then the safety officer said, "You guys screwed yourselves by flying too low. We tell you not to break out too low. I think you were just flying on the treetops, shot too close, and took your own fragments." The Cobra pilot, instantly infuriated, repressed his rage, and red-faced and just short of shaking, said, "The bastards have 37mm, probably radar guided. That's what did this." An argument ensued.

I walked away shaking my head. The Cobra pilot had the deeply serious look of one who'd nearly bought it. It was obvious that 37mm was in use in Cambodia and Laos. Stories about it were rampant. The fact that they might have it just inside the borders of South Vietnam should not surprise anyone. It disgusted me that the safety officer would first accuse the pilot who, in this instance, happened to be alive and well. I thought the safety officer was choosing to ignore the realities of flying in a combat theater; he simply chose to blame on the pilot something that did not fit his picture of the war. *Catch 22* was slowly evolving into a very meaningful theme to me. To me, the safety officer was displaying the arrogance of one ignorant about or uncaring of the risks that existed. I would later find the same attitude in the 101st Airborne Division.

The next day, we were told the 4th Division would be getting no more replacements. We suspected it could be the first step in a division withdrawal from Vietnam. It really looked as if the war had been declared over.

I'd been scheduled to carry our forward air controller (FAC) today as my gunner. Our air force FAC, a major, decided that one helicopter ride with me was enough for him. I'd taken him on a low-level run at ninety knots between the trees the night before. There were two tall trees on a hilltop just outside the sentry wires. The distance between them was less than the diameter of my rotor disc. I flew toward the trees at ninety knots, banking ninety degrees as I flew between them (to fit my rotor disc). My passenger was looking at the ground as we passed between the trees.

I personally thought it was an excellent display of the little helicopter's capabilities. I mistakenly thought my passenger was unimpressed, so I did a cyclic climb, zeroing out the airspeed. I asked him what he knew about helicopter stall speeds as we came to a hover at twenty-five hundred feet, him straining forward in his shoulder harness. I then held the nose steady and started backward at a hover, which gives some people a queasy feeling in the stomach, rather like falling off the bed in your sleep. He didn't appear nervous enough, so I asked him if he knew what settling with power was. Then he got nervous. I told him conditions weren't right to show that. He was obviously relieved—until I dropped my collective pitch, reducing power into a simulated autorotative free fall to the pad. That produces the sensation of one's stomach rising to one's mouth, as in a falling elevator. The little bird was much more fun than a sports car!

The air force major, however, decided the introductory flight was adequate.

On the morning of October 12, we took off at first light, just before sunrise. We flew just below a very low overcast that kept most birds down. I had Rodriguez in the front and two captains in the back. As we overflew a hill northeast of Firebase Washington, just under the clouds at two hundred feet above the hilltops, we chanced upon two North Vietnamese harvesting some type of food. It was an obviously well-cared-for field. I circled back, with Rodriguez firing as they ran for the trees. We missed them. I then noticed a lot of laundry drying on top of the bushes at the edge of the field. We raked the area with M-16 fire, called for artillery fire, and left. This occurred not far from where Grant had crashed. I was convinced he had been shot down; I saw two live, uniformed North Vietnamese Army regulars in their khakis and distinctive pith helmets. I finally had a visual image of the enemy. But I still hadn't been shot at . . . yet. That evening, my activities were reported to Colonel Fear in the brigade briefing. He asked if Mr. Marshall considered himself a gunship. I was then told to be careful and to avoid that type of activity.

The next day, northwest of Fire Support Base Washington, we found an entire base camp of hootches that appeared uninhabited. We overflew it several times, crisscrossing at different altitudes and high rates of speed, ranging from 105 knots at fifty feet on the first pass down to as low as 60 knots and ten feet on the last one. Our artillery observer called for permission to shell. A heavy bombardment destroyed it. No one could accuse me of hovering that time.

The following day, I spent all afternoon hovering up and down the Bong Son River, northeast of An Khe. Two GIs apparently drowned in it during a patrol. We had two Loaches, my Kiowa, and two Cobras searching the area until weather and low fuel made us leave. We did not find them.

The latrine, a large screen-enclosed room with three big pedestals where the toilet seats were mounted, was located adjacent to the row of officers' quarters. Underneath each was the lower third of a steel drum. The waste-barrel was taken out daily and the contents burned in a mixture of gasoline and diesel fuel. A man we thought of as an elderly Vietnamese, with chin-whiskers like Ho Chi Minh, had the job of changing out the oil drums.

I went in to use the facilities. A captain came in and took the pedestal next to me. A few seconds later, he screamed, "Aaaaah!" and, flailing his arms and legs, jumped off the pedestal with his pants around his ankles. "What the hell was that?" It turned out that "Father Ho" had come to change the oil drum below the captain's seat while the captain was sitting there. Father Ho had politely tapped the captain on his cheek, scaring the living shit out of him. The captain didn't know if a snake had bitten him or what! I had cramps for the rest of the day from laughing. Father Ho would later die in the perimeter wire, during a sapper attack in mid-November.

Lieutenant Phillips had the room next to mine. On his wall was every *Playboy* playmate that had appeared during his twelve-month tour. He was, by this time, very short, and was to leave within the next few days. A young Vietnamese hootch maid brought in his laundry and spit-polished boots. She looked at the wall full of pinups, then looked back at the lieutenant. "Hey, Ell Tee. You make beaucoup money?" Phillips looked at her and said, "Yes, officers are well paid." Then the young Vietnamese girl, all of fourteen or fifteen years of age, put her hands on her hips, started tapping her foot, and pointed to the wall. "If you make so much money, why come all you girlfriends have no clothes?" We all cracked up.

On October 20, I was down for maintenance. Rodriguez came by at lunch and picked me up from the Mole Hole. A Kiowa had been shot down just six miles outside of An Khe. The warrant officer pilot had been killed. The crew chief/door gunner had been seriously wounded. They'd found a column of thirty or forty NVA. The crew chief opened up on them as the pilot slowed to a hovering circle. Unfortunately he slowed before the gunships overhead could dive and fire. AKs riddled the aircraft, killing the pilot instantly, badly wounding the crew chief.

During the crash, the crew chief was thrown from the aircraft, which lodged in the trees forty feet above ground. He was restrained by his harness, dangling just below the cargo bay in midair, luckily still holding his M-60. The aircraft settled into the trees with the engine screaming, the rotor blades stopped. When the North Vietnamese came running up to take a look, the crew chief killed several of them with his M-60. Some returned fire, wounding him before running away because the gunships were overhead. A few minutes later, a security team recovered the crew chief and the body of the pilot. Within an hour, the wreckage of the Kiowa had been sling-loaded under a Chinook and brought back to the golf course.

I'd been in country two months. I'd done some stupid things yet had been generally careful. As I looked at the twisted, broken, bullet-riddled hull of the shattered Jet Ranger, minus its skids, tail boom, and rotor mast, I cynically wondered to myself if they would call this pilot error. My crew chief, Rodriguez, silently shook his head. It was a case of fubar (fucked up beyond all recognition).

Later that night, I was writing kind of big, had been drinking a little, four beers and an unknown number of rum and Cokes. Had a good little party for a guy leaving tomorrow. Lucky him.

## October 21, 1970

The standdown was bringing everything to a roaring halt. Things would really slow in early November, when the hootch maids and KP help would be let go. One hootch maid was a particular problem to a captain, who didn't like the way she polished his boots. He had a heated argument with her and canceled her permission to come on post, thinking that would be the end of the difficulty. But that night, the hootch maid got even. Our hootch was bracketed by mortar fire. One round landed within fifty yards to the west, other rounds landed anywhere from fifty to one hundred yards beyond. They had been carefully walked right across our hootch, narrowly missing.

All the base sirens were going but I slept right through the mortaring, which only lasted thirty seconds or so. I finally got up and went outside to check out the noise. Everyone was supposed to be in bunkers, but instead, they were outside taking pictures of each other in their underwear and steel pots. It was quite funny, typical army humor. Even so, the word was passed, don't fire any more hootch maids until the day we leave!

Orders came down from on high that we would turn in our aircraft on November 15. I would be transferred within a week of that date. Everyone was getting ready to move.

I was told a drive-shaft change between my engine and transmission might be necessary because it'd been throwing grease. It might have only a bearing problem, but there could have been something more serious. If not fixed, it could cause a short-shaft failure, meaning a forced landing or worse.

**November 2, 1970**

The standdown continued. Truman, the last firebase used by the 4th Infantry, was on the Ba River (Song Ba) about twelve miles to the northeast of An Khe. The day after the firebase was closed down, I was carrying Major Swinford and Colonel Fear to a corps briefing in Qui Nhon. It was the only time I carried them as passengers. The flight from An Khe was above pretty scenery, at thirty-five hundred feet altitude. With a little difficulty, I found the corps headquarters pad adjacent to a large antenna field. The landing pad was encircled by telephone poles sprouting miles of antennae.

I commenced the engine cooldown and a shutdown checklist, expecting Colonel Fear to spend one or two hours there at headquarters, but moments after I shut down, they were hurrying back to my aircraft. They requested that I take them directly to Firebase Truman.

We departed and climbed out northwest of Qui Nhon, heading for the Bao River valley. En route, Colonel Fear explained to me that an action had just occurred there and that he was determined to have a final personal visit to the field of battle, the last for the 4th Infantry Division in Vietnam.

I met up with Cobras and Charlie-model gunships, which circled above, covering us as I dropped the officers off at the firebase. It had been closed the day before but an ambush party had remained behind, hidden to see if the NVA would visit to scrounge for anything useful left behind. At first light, a column of twenty NVA made their way onto the firebase. The U.S. infantry, hidden in ambush, used claymores and killed sixteen North Vietnamese, wounding those that escaped.

At Truman I dropped off my passengers and climbed away. As I climbed out, the gunships called that I was taking machine-gun fire. I could not see it behind me, but

I immediately began a sharp turn and a maximum performance climb. A gunship pilot called out I was "still taking fire" as he rolled in. He called, "Coming hot," firing rockets and miniguns at the source of tracers. For an instant, I didn't want to believe them. I hadn't seen or heard anything! I accelerated in a very steep turning climb, quickly passing through six thousand feet to the relative safety of altitude.

A few minutes later, I was summoned down from seven thousand feet, where I thought I was invisible to the gun crews, to pick up Colonel Fear and Major Swinford. This time I made a steep, high-speed, diving approach. On short final, I used my pedals to kick the aircraft sideways, decelerating my rate of descent and speed from a 120-knot free fall to a hover. I quickly picked up my passengers and then flew out with gunship runs under way on two NVA machine guns. I began to realize how close death had been on the way home. I was slowly losing my bulletproof attitude, but the transition had taken two and a half months.

I was quietly surprised that Colonel Fear would let me fly him into that environment. I guess he just had to see the enemy who, for the most part, had eluded us. In that one ambush, more NVA were killed than during the previous month of hunting them around the firebase. It was the last field of battle for the 4th Infantry Division in Vietnam. From my perspective, it had to be a less than satisfying end to a brigade commander, who'd started as a second lieutenant, victorious at Bastogne, in World War II.

I had finally taken antiaircraft fire. I was disappointed that I hadn't seen the tracers. I was even miffed that I hadn't lost my cherry taking my first hit.

The following day, November 7, was the fifty-third anniversary of the Bolshevik Revolution. Old Charles had a party and included us in the celebration. We got twelve big mortar rounds (120mm) on the golf course. My 58 was wounded. Actually, I could still have flown it as there were only two fragmentation holes in the vertical stabilizer. It was sitting in the revetment, but since there were only ten aircraft on the field, all were bunched together to reduce the night guard requirement. That's when the North Vietnamese Army decided to show they were still around. Work crews patched the Jet Ranger up and I'd be flying the next day. Since we only had one unit left in the field from 1st Brigade, there wasn't much flying to do. Thus far, I'd accumulated 175 hours in my 58, over 500 hours total flight time, about 60 percent in-country time.

The fourteenth of November was really busy. Friday the thirteenth we received a rocket attack, five 122mm rockets. Nobody was hurt and no damage done, but they were loud (meaning close hits). We started countermeasures the next morning. I would be flying the rocket launch belt from six to seven A.M., eight to ten A.M. and six to seven-thirty P.M. until we left. The idea was to surveil the rocket-range area and try to prevent recurrences.

The counterrocket measures were the most fun flying to date. I was turned loose in my Kiowa, my crew chief/door gunner and an artillery lieutenant with a radio in the backseat. We were cleared to cruise low level, and that we did. I flew low-level S turns between the trees at ninety-five knots. With the doors off the Kiowa, wind whipped through the cockpit and the cargo bay. It was very exhilarating. I was free to do whatever I wanted, even though the rules of engagement precluded our firing first. The artillery officer could call batteries without approval other than the artillery officer at the base. If we could see the NVA, all we had to do was keep visual contact, and the artillery would take care of the rest.

At the end of the day, I asked my passenger if he wanted to cool off in the higher altitude, and the lieutenant agreed. I took the Jet Ranger up to 10,500 feet. It was the highest I'd ever flown in a helicopter, and it revealed a spectacularly beautiful sunset. We could see the Mang Yang Pass to the west, where thousands of Frenchmen killed by the Viet Minh were said to have been buried standing in place, facing the rising sun.

The An Khe Pass (Deo Mang Pass) and the South China Sea could be seen to the east. The exhilaration of flying, the elation of controlling my own aircraft was pure joy, amplified by the fifty-degree temperature at altitude. After a few minutes of circling, we began a slow spiraling descent back to the golf course, ending another day in the Nam.

I turned in my OH-58 at Qui Nhon on the sixteenth. I was through flying with the 4th Infantry Division. I also picked up my orders.

During my out-processing I received orders for a Bronze Star medal, for achievement and meritorious service against an armed, hostile enemy force. Most combatants got one, it was like "thanks for coming." I did get it kind of early, though. I already had enough time for five or six air medals. They were awarded on the basis of one for each twenty-five hours flying combat assault or fifty hours of general support.

On the seventeenth, I out-processed for the 101st Airborne Division in northern I Corps. I took a C-130 from An Khe Airport to Da Nang and another north to Hue. I then had 238 hours in 58s and 525 total pilot time. Pretty good bit of solo flying time for two months; 280 hours in the Nam.

*November 19, 1970.* WO Stan Struble was riding as a passenger in an OH-58A Kiowa just outside An Khe. He was killed in a hail of AK-47 fire. He had been a flight-class buddy. His dream was simply to serve his tour and return to Colorado and be a ski bum. At the time of his death, I was a passenger in an air force C-130 on my way to Da Nang, connecting to Hue/Phu Bai, home of the 101st Airborne Division (Airmobile).

# 5

# The Phoenix Tribulation

**November 20, 1970, Camp Eagle, I Corps**

I arrived at the 101st Airborne in Phu Bai, north of Da Nang, almost in Hue. I rode up with a guy who'd just finished a Loach transition. He assured me that I Corps wasn't much hotter than any of the other three corps tactical zones (CTZ). He did warn me that there were no REMFs (rear echelon motherfuckers) north of Da Nang.

I in-processed finance and personnel the following day. I was told that I could expect letters from home in about three weeks. It'd take ten days for my letter to get home, and another ten days for me to receive a reply.

The following day, I went through in-country orientation, again. It was boring, but shortened to one day for in-country officer transfers. I learned I was going to C Company (assault helicopter company), 158 Aviation Battalion, 101st Airborne. Lt. Col. E. P. Davis, commander of the 101st Aviation Group, had an office in a command-and-control bunker in Camp Eagle that was fully air-conditioned, well lighted, and looked like a Stateside office. He talked to all of the pilots, congratulated us (as if we really believed him!) on our assignments there, and gave us a big pep talk.

I asked him if there was any way I could be transferred to any unit with observation helicopters. He said emphatically, "No, the army needs you right where you're going. You are assigned to Charlie Company, 158th Aviation Battalion, an assault helicopter company." I became pissed with the Green Machine and decided that I didn't particularly care for the colonel either.

## Camp Evans, I Corps

On November 24, I moved into my new home, C Company, 158th Aviation Battalion, 101st Airborne Division, Airmobile, an assault helicopter company with call sign Phoenix. It was located at Camp Evans combat base, twenty miles north of Camp Eagle and forty miles south of North Vietnam. My first look at the Phoenix hootches was with dismay. The well-kept grounds of Headquarters Company, 4th Infantry Division, at An Khe were a paradise compared to what I saw at Camp Evans. It had been raining for no less than six solid weeks. Everything was red mud and green-black mildew. It reeked of urine, sulphur, and JP-4 (jet fuel). The constant sounds of helicopters taking off and landing were peaceful compared to the roar of the outgoing eight-inch artillery fire.

The Phoenix hootches were typical army barracks-type structures that had originally been built for the Marines by navy Seabees in 1967/68. They were simple wood-frame structures with corrugated steel roofing and corrugated steel shutters along the side of the building over screen window sections. Fifty-five-gallon oil drums filled with sand had been placed against the walls to provide protection against mortar and rocket shrapnel. At the entrance to my hootch, sandbags were collapsing.

The inside finish included a bar counter with a field phone and ground lines connected to headquarters. It had electricity and a refrigerator, plumbing, but no running water.

Gathered in the 2d Platoon hootch were warrant officers Butch Doan, David Wolfe, Ken Mayberry, Tommy Doody, David Rayburn, and myself. The hootch area was colorful. A large rebel flag overhung the table we used for eating. On the facing wall was a map of the United States, with colored pins designating the occupants' home towns. Our cots were placed on elevated wooden pedestals in separate mosquito-screened room areas. One wall was decorated with the 2d Platoon flag, Thunder Ducks, with the motto "Bottles and Throttles." Assorted ladies' undergarments from USO shows and R & R trips hung on the wall. David Rayburn had a body bag tacked up on the wall in his hootch, with his name boldly printed on it.

The night I got in, I unpacked my Nomex fire-retardant flight suits in the sleeping cubicle near the entry door. Don Mears was on R & R, so I temporarily took his space. A crew chief was leaving the next day, and Butch Doan and others were drunk, silly, and singing. I was the new guy and not a part of that particular celebration. I did, however, have new music, including a recent Chicago tape, which was quite an attraction to the others. Kris Hunt came in and introduced himself. He liked my music and asked me to turn it up. All in all, they were a rowdy group venting pressure from a series of long days, flying general support missions and combat assaults in northern I Corps.

Of the group, WO Tommy Doody was the quietest. He and Hunt were good buddies. We got to talking, and I asked them what had been going on in terms of enemy activity. One volunteered, "You can expect a 122mm rocket attack about once a week. Mortar attacks are less frequent, but they last a lot longer. If this hootch is ever hit, run like hell, because if this place goes up in flames, you want to be a long way from this little box." Then he pointed to a bench seat near the door. He lifted the seat up, revealing a complete arsenal of Special Forces weaponry, including "cherry-bomb" hand grenades, Swedish-K 9mm submachine guns, Thompson .45-caliber submachine guns, grease guns of World War II vintage, and weapons I did not recognize.

They got into a discussion of their assignments, and it

became evident that the CCN (Command and Control North, a Special Forces reconnaissance unit) mission was quite hairy. They mentioned having to carry extra personal weapons, including cherry-bomb hand grenades and extra personal side arm ammunition. One pilot even joked, "Across the fence, save the last bullet for yourself."

The sudden awareness of *extremely* high-risk missions swept over me. It became clear that these guys were playing the most deadly of games and enjoyed doing it. I had mistakenly believed that you had to volunteer for those kinds of missions. The Special Forces CCN missions were simply routine for the Phoenix. The real war was still on, and the Phoenix worked the vortex. The war was very much on, no holds barred. Oh hell! I thought to myself. I Corps was obviously the place for adrenaline junkies and warriors!

On November 25, I began settling into the routine with my new unit. At first, flying slicks in an assault helicopter company left me greatly disappointed, but I resigned myself to getting used to it. I thought I might even enjoy it once I became an aircraft commander in February. At least I was in a unit that had all the mission assets. Ken Mayberry, our platoon instructor pilot, said everywhere we went, we'd have assets—gunships and other slicks with us. If one went down, another went down to get them. I wasn't the only guy getting the shaft. There was a second-tour Loach pilot in the company with one thousand hours scout time. He was despondent.

I tried a MARS (military amateur radio station) call home but couldn't get through. It was really getting frustrating. In a letter home, I requested goodies, dried dinners, dried soups, and dried drinks. Told my wife that, due to our hours, I'd miss a lot of meals, and I'd be eating in the hootch most of the time. We had a poor mess hall, and it was over a quarter mile walk away, in the rain and inch-deep red mud.

The worst thing was, no hootch maids. We had to do

our own laundry and polish our own boots. Luckily, I had four sets of Nomex. I'd wash underwear and Nomex in a metal foot pan as I showered at night. Talk about a pain in the ass!

We did have a nice officers club, and it was very well used. It was the best at Camp Evans. We were twenty miles north of Hue and about thirty miles south of Quang Tri. I was told I'd soon be living at Quang Tri. There we'd fly in support of the 1st of the 5th Mechanized Division. The support duty would run from December 15 to January 15. It was really close to the DMZ and Laotian borders. I'd be flying all over, north and west of Evans, which included the lovely A Shau Valley. Told my wife she'd hear about us on the news quite a bit. A big Tet offensive was expected the coming year.

In our area of operations (AO) there were several famous firebases, Rakkassan, Ripcord, O'Reilley, and Mai Loc. Anything with the 3d Brigade, 101st Airborne Division, and I'd be in support of them. There were also big rumors of "drops" for everyone. The rumor went like this: because of Vietnamization and the American withdrawal, everyone with DEROS dates after April 1, 1971, would get a sixty-day drop. If that came through, I'd be home by June 20, 1971. That would be a dream come true. I reapplied for my R & R. That was my dream, meeting my love in Honolulu! I was assured it would be between March 15 and 25.

The following day, I spent my first day flying as copilot for Capt. David Nelson, the platoon leader. He'd been a first-tour warrant officer in Hueys, then he'd accepted a direct commission and became a real live officer as well as a Huey instructor pilot. It was an eye-opening time, a very long day. We spent most of the day sitting on the pad, the engine running at flight idle, waiting for a quick dash to carry a hot Thanksgiving meal to troops in the field, just over the first ridgeline of the mountains. Although the troops were only fifteen miles away, the mountain ridge at ten miles was impassable due to clouds and rain. We spent the entire morning on the pad with engines idling, then had to go refuel and come back and again sit at flight idle. Nelson was becoming furious that we were burning up engine time (decreasing the time before scheduled maintenance) and increasing maintenance problems. The platoon could have saved five to six hours turbine-engine time by just shutting down on the pad.

Nelson had a heated exchange with the battalion commander, complaining about keeping the aircraft running all day long, too much engine time being used up. The exchange became so bad, I thought he was going to get an Article 15 reprimand out of it. However, the lieutenant colonel in command of the situation demanded we keep running because there might only be a twenty-minute break in the weather. Finally, the call came, deliver the meals. A Loach had made it over a narrow mountain pass. We dashed across the fifteen hundred foot ridgeline between four thousand foot mountains, among the treetops and clouds, barely one hundred feet vertical clearance. We found the landing zone in a cloud-shrouded valley, a hover hole that was just big enough to get one Huey in straight down.

But the boys in the mountains got their hot lunches. As we hovered down to deliver the load, a lieutenant to the right front of our cockpit was trying to direct us to land. However, he could not be seen by Nelson; I sat there quietly as the guy on the ground, thinking I was flying, got more frustrated. The infantry lieutenant finally threw his helmet to the ground in disgust, but Nelson had it taken care of. We hovered, one skid touching a log, and the cargo was off-loaded. We hovered out and reversed our path through the mountain pass.

We'd eaten lunch in the aircraft with engines running. That night we cooked our own meal. It had been a short, but challenging day of flying. Going in and out of mountainside hover holes, just large enough to get one Huey in and out vertically, was demanding for the pilots and the aircraft. It required the maximum performance of the Huey and the highest degree of care by the pilots and crewmen. Nelson was highly experienced and understood more about what was going on than any of the first-tour people and many of our superior officers. It was obvious that the warrant officers looked up to him and respected his experience.

We finally had everything finished by 3:45 and made it back to the Phoenix Nest revetment area. By 4:30, I was in the hootch, and several others were drifting in, exchanging the usual banter at the end of a long day. Suddenly, the ground shook, there was a loud crash and a dust-raising *whompk!* Then another *whompk!* Two 122mm rockets hit within twenty-five yards of our hootch, impacting at the former surgical hospital, which had been shut down several weeks earlier. The impact of the rockets had been an incredible ground-shaking clap of thunder. They left three-foot-deep conical craters nearby.

We all dove for our individual cubicles, hitting the floor. Then two more rockets impacted slightly farther away. Then, just as quickly as it had begun, it ended. We found out later that two Redskin (D/158) Cobras, which had been in their revetment area, were left mangled pieces of metal by the attack. Although I had been subjected to rocket and mortar attacks at An Khe, the impact of 122mm rockets within twenty-five yards is one experience you never forget.

As the dust settled, a guy came running in. He had hit the ground outside and was laughing hysterically, saying, "You should have seen it. The first rocket hit as a Loach was on short final, with a dude carrying a briefcase standing on the skid. After the rocket hit, he yanked pitch, hauling ass straight up, with the guy just hanging on by one hand. And then the other rockets hit." I didn't know it but that was Capt. Bill Gordy and a security courier, a specialist five named Jackson. Jackson was building a reputation as being a "magnet ass," attracting all sorts of enemy fire anywhere he went. Even normally safe places like the center of Camp Evans and the Phoenix hootches!

I was scheduled for my instrument check ride a couple of days later. If I passed it, I'd be released for daily missions. I was still looking forward to flying. At least I'd be able to say I flew in the "real war zone." Most men there were proud of being in the 101st. The pilots agreed I'd enjoy working with the 1st of the 5th Mechanized Infantry out of Quang Tri, whose tanks and personnel carriers were dispersed around I Corps. I was also told I'd be working with very well trained ARVNs, ARVNs as good as many of the GIs. When they were that good, you didn't mind working with them.

I finished *The Honey Badger*, another good novel about love and sex, this one about seven hundred pages. Then I started James Michener's *Iberia*. It appeared that the rumors of drops in tour length were based on opinions that the army would have to do something drastic to keep up with the forecast withdrawal figures. Obviously the war was over in some areas, but not with the Phoenix in I Corps.

On the twenty-seventh, I slept late and stayed in the hootch waiting on the MARS line. Washed the rest of my dirty clothes and got them dried, which was an accomplishment because of all the rain. We actually had warm sunshine for two hours, a real event. In a letter home, I requested a small extension cord and two light sockets with switches. We used the lights to keep clothes dry in our closets; everything was wet all the time during monsoon rains.

I was shocked to see even former CH-54 Skycrane pilots flying UH-1s. The accumulation of officers in all units was due to the deactivation of many big army units.

I was really pissed with the Green Machine. I'd gone voluntary indefinite (lifer) to fly a specific aircraft, the OH-58. I had three months in-country time and a great deal of experience in the Central Highlands flying the Jet Ranger. I wanted back in a Ranger. The thought of flying the Huey on ash-and-trash missions was repulsive. After the An Khe Pass fiasco, the thought of flying combat assaults was simply scary.

I had enjoyed every day of flying the Jet Ranger, and getting back to the routine of normal supply missions and combat assaults was not what I wanted. Even though the battalion commander had told me I could not transfer, I went to the commanding officer and requested in writing a transfer to the air cavalry or any unit that had Jet Rangers. I stated the reason for transfer was I'd been trained in them and had three months in-country time. I'd much rather be a scout looking for the enemy than a target sitting in a Huey.

When I told the guys in my hootch I was requesting a transfer out, after having been there only five days, I immediately became an outsider and would stay one. They were a close-knit bunch who had worked together, fought together, and covered each other's asses numerous times. Suddenly they had a newbie who didn't want to be there. They told me of several other pilots with similar in-country experience and qualifications. All had been denied transfers. The joke was, the only way out of the Phoenix was DEROS or die.

In very quick order, I'd concluded Camp Evans was the armpit of the universe. The living quarters were next to Stone Age. The missions given the company were the worst in I Corps. We were one of three northernmost assault companies, where combat action was frequent.

I began to reflect on my discussions with infantry officers and other pilots in the 4th Infantry. We had joked about how the war was over and units were withdrawing. I remembered listening to President Nixon's speech about the Vietnamization process, even talk of a possible cease-fire. With all that under way, and the 4th Infantry and the 9th Infantry already gone, it was obvious that politicians had reversed the direction of the war since I'd enlisted. The recision of the Tonkin Gulf Resolution the summer before, had started a process that the army was snow-balling, an accelerated effort to remove American units from Vietnam. The primary exception being the 101st Airborne Division, where I was.

I mentally reviewed my experiences to date. I'd made some mistakes in judgment but without injury to myself or my passengers. Although I was a newbie in the 101st Airborne, I had a full three months of in-country experience that, I thought, gave me the ability to recognize risk and exposure and to develop the intuitive awareness of danger.

I was then fully immersed in the maelstrom of a war we obviously weren't going to win. The game of war I'd enjoyed so much at An Khe had dramatically changed. It became a game we had to play, but only death could be the winner. The Phoenix pilots lived by example. You'd feel the strain but show nothing. Most importantly, you'd do your job well; other lives depended on you.

I thought back to the words of David Anderson and others: "Truly believe you'll do your duty and come home safely, and it will happen." Those sentiments were echoed in other conversations with Jimmy Thornburgh, a Green Beret with five years in Vietnam, later a warrant officer, Cobra pilot, and flight-school classmate.

No one wanted the distinction of being the last man killed in Vietnam. I did know that I wanted to have a greater sense of control over my fate. Flying a single-pilot aircraft on single-ship missions, I could at least do what was in my personal interest, should the circumstance dictate.

I'd begun to realize that the kick-ass attitude that I, and most others, brought in country quickly went by the wayside after arrival at the 101st Airborne. These guys were still fighting a serious war. I knew that in the Central Highlands and farther south there was an obvious attempt to avoid major contact by both sides. In fact, some units to the south had orders not to engage the enemy during the drawdown. I believed those restrictions were a direct result of the My Lai tragedy. The attitude down there was, we don't bother them; they don't bother us.

At Camp Evans, the North Vietnamese were just outside the perimeter with mortars and made an event of weekly shelling with 122mm rockets and mortars. What a difference from the Central Highlands. But, for the time being, there was no choice but to continue on with the missions at hand.

I'd finally found the real war!

The following day, I had my first check ride in the Phoenix with WO1 Ken Mayberry, an experienced pilot and really nice guy from Nebraska. He was getting short and was the unit standards instructor pilot. We flew north to Quang Tri where I flew ground-controlled instrument approaches and automatic direction finders (ADF). I had a very good instrument practice session in a brand-new H-model Huey. Mayberry told me a lot about the Phoenix Company and the missions we flew, acknowledging calmly that missions were frequently under enemy fire, but noting that we had the best assets (gunships and forward air controllers) with us at all times. That was the difference between the 101st Airborne Division and other units. Mayberry was an accomplished pilot with combat experiences many army pilots would only read of. My training flight was strictly professional, no anecdotes, no war stories or BS.

He had me put the Huey through its paces, practicing emergency procedures and actual instrument flight. We flew an ADF approach into Quang Tri and a GCA into Camp Evans. I only had sixty-five hours of Huey time after flight school. I'd had no experience with heavy loads or troop insertions in country. I would learn that although I could fly a good check ride, I'd had no useful practical experience in a Huey to prepare me for I Corps.

I began flying regular missions on November 29. I didn't like the idea of being peter pilot again, but I had no choice. A peter pilot was the copilot. His goal was to become an aircraft commander (AC). Peter pilot came from the aircraft logbook code for copilot (PP). However, in army pilots' humor, it referred to the body part the copilot was permitted to control during flight. I'd just start the grind as a copilot and patiently wait until things changed.

The next day, I was told I'd spend the night in the hangar as I would be the copilot for one of the ready-reaction-force birds. The experienced pilots derisively called these missions the ready rat fuck. We'd be on fifteen-minute standby all night long, sleep on a cot, fully dressed with boots on, ready for instant takeoff. Sleep was not exactly peaceful due to the 175mm cannon fire as needed, twenty-four hours a day.

The rain made life miserable. Leaks everywhere in my room were so bad that someone before me had drilled drain holes in the floor to let the water out. Actually, it wasn't as bad as it sounds, it was worse. Everything stayed damp and musty.

Oh! An Khe! It was a bit of heaven. I didn't have a bed in the Phoenix, just a cot. It was reasonably comfortable with a sleeping bag. Of course, as tired as I was at night, a plywood sheet would have been comfortable.

On the thirty-first, I had a 4:30 wake-up call, the usual for copilots. I preflighted the Huey in the dark and the rain. Inch-thick red mud, greasy with tarlike permaprime everywhere. The one thing I hated more than anything was climbing up on the tail stinger so I could check the tail rotor gear box oil level and the pitch-change links attached to the tail rotor, but I didn't dare not do it. We typically would have everything ready to go for the pilot. I then met WO Darryl Keith, who was my pilot for the day. He was a slender "kid" (about the same age as me) with reddish-blond hair and extensive I Corps experience.

We took off from the Phoenix Nest (i.e., the revetment area) and flew down to Camp Eagle to pick up some engineer officers we were to carry down to Da Nang. We circled over Camp Eagle, and it was fogged in. There was, however, a hole, which Keith referred to as a hover hole, over the engineer pad where our passengers were. I held on as he made a dizzying descent, flying visually through IFR (instrument flight rules) fog. I had been introduced to Darryl Keith's IFR techniques. With months of experience, he was finely tuned, but it was scary as hell for a copilot who could fly instruments pretty well.

We picked up our passengers and departed for the engineer pad on the river in Da Nang. We had a beautiful flight over the Hai Van Pass. Then we descended to fifty feet, down on the beach. We passed an air base, then a Vietnamese residential district, which everyone called Shit Beach because the residents walked out in the mornings to bathe and use the bathroom. There were no sewers in that section of Da Nang. It was quite funny the first flight over, seeing all the people out there doing their daily business, waving at us, passing fifty feet above them at eighty knots.

That evening, I went across the road to visit a flight-school buddy. Rick Lukens, a Redskin Cobra pilot and maintenance officer, was drinking Scotch. I had not been a Scotch drinker, but after the second one, I became one. He had really nice living quarters finished out of rocket boxes and their foam insulation. We got to talking about classmates. He'd been an avid reader of the *Army Times*. Having had former service experience, Lukens was keeping up to date on all the facts. He had come in country after me, having spent six months training in the army maintenance command prior to coming to Vietnam.

"Did you hear about Struble?" Rick asked.

"Yeah, I heard it talking to a couple of other guys from An Khe. Seems the day that I left, he was riding as a passenger, screwing around, and the North Vietnamese decided to come out and play. I believe they killed the pilot and Struble, riding as copilot, along with the door gunner in the back." Struble had been a flight-school buddy. He didn't even have to be on that flight. He was bored. He'd talked to his friends of the desire to put his time in the army and then go back to Colorado to be a ski bum. No longer.

Although Lukens had been in country less than two months, he had seen a lot of action flying gunships and knew where all the hot spots were. The Redskins were considered among the best. They had the daily experience to prove it.

## December 1970

On December 1, 1970, WO1 Stephen C. Sellett, a classmate in WORWAC 70-5, died as a helicopter air casualty while serving as pilot.

I was back to flying again, wet and cold all day. I discovered I needed a set of long underwear. Yes, even in Vietnam. Just then temperatures were in the low sixties, with 100 percent humidity and rain. That's not really cold until you get tired and wet. The crew chief and door gunner had it much worse in their wells, moving through the air constantly at one hundred miles per hour, windblown and soaked.

Everything inside and outside the hootch smelled musty and was damp. There was just no way to get dry. Most of us expected little action until February or March, when the rain stopped.

I spent the following day flying with Mike Cataldo, who had just returned from Stateside leave. We had a troop insertion in the foothills, just east of the mountain ridgeline, west of Camp Evans in the foothills north of Fire Support Base Barbara. Cataldo was a wiry guy with a good sense of humor. He truly enjoyed flying the Huey. He was another experienced Phoenix pilot, about as good as you could get in flying proficiency.

The combat assault involved an insertion of troops. We had six troops on board to drop off, and then were to return to the pad for another six. As we approached from two miles out, Cataldo asked if there were gunships on station; there were none. It was supposed to be a cold insertion, in a free-fire zone. The crew chief asked if he could "go hot" on final, firing machine guns. Without thinking, Cataldo said yes. Then he said, "Well, newbie, here's your chance to fly a CA. You take the lead ship in." Cataldo sat with his left foot propped on the door, smoking a cigarette and enjoying the view.

Newbie Warrant Officer 1 Marshall was given the controls, completing the approach, touching skids down in the small landing zone. But the nose of the aircraft yawed abruptly three feet to the right the instant troops were getting off. Simultaneously both crew chiefs opened up their M-60s. Our yellow tracers were ricocheting back, passing within feet of our windshield! If Cataldo had not been restrained by his seat belt and shoulder harness, he would have jumped from the aircraft. "What the hell?" he shouted in the intercom. I had not applied adequate left pedal to compensate for the increase in torque and engine power that would be felt as our passengers departed and the guns opened up. The crew chief cracked up laughing. "Well, sir, it looks like Peter Pilot broke one guy's leg, he's lying on the ground laughing and crying, he's obviously goin' home." Because I slightly undercontrolled the yaw of the Huey at touchdown, the skid broke the leg of an infantryman below the knee when the aircraft yawed to the right. His foot had been planted in the mud, and he now had the fabled "million-dollar" injury. Cataldo had momentarily forgotten he'd given permission to the door gunners to open up since we were the first ship in. Later that evening, he told me how he had taken heavy fire not long before on CCN in Laos when the aircraft yawed with golden tracers bouncing around us from our own machine guns, déjà vu.

I had once again let the impact of flying the much more sensitive controls of the Jet Ranger undercontrol the movement of the much larger and less agile Huey. I still had a lot to learn about flying a Huey, but my poor performance was aggravated by the fact that I didn't really *want* to fly it.

As the afternoon dragged on, we completed a supply drop near Eagle Beach and proceeded south over the marshlands and salt flats. I was having a decent afternoon flying despite the morning's fiasco, but I hadn't been keeping my left hand on the collective, as Cataldo had repeatedly insisted. Flying an OH-58 solo frequently required the pilot's hand to be off the collective while changing radio frequencies and writing grease-pencil notes on the overhead greenhouse window. In a Huey, however, the person flying was expected to maintain both hands and both feet on the controls, at all times.

I was happily cruising along at twenty-five hundred feet, with my hand off the collective when Cataldo cut the throttle on the Huey. The correct response, very frequently practiced in training, was to immediately lower the collective (rotor pitch control) while entering a forced land-ing (autorotation).

I was stunned to immobility, shocked by Mike's having done something only an instructor pilot would do!

I looked at the main rotor RPM gauge unwinding. Mike asked, "What you gonna do?"

I slowly responded, "Lower the collective," as I pushed it down.

"Better do it," he calmly said as the main rotor RPM approached the red line, which indicated catastrophe.

With the collective down, I mentally recovered from my surprise. Cataldo had already begun recovering the engine RPM and said, "I got it," as he took over the flight controls.

"You might want to be faster next time," he said.

I'd screwed up terribly; I'd reverted to a complacent newbie, enjoying it too much. It was my most profoundly humiliating embarrassment as a copilot. That day would be remembered as one long, unforgettable flying lesson. Stay on the controls, alert at all times. Sounded simple, but anything less could get you and from three to nine others killed.

That night, I returned to the hootch with a case of Lurps (compact freeze-dried rations) courtesy of the crew chief. We didn't have time to eat during the day, so we fixed our own at night. Had some really good chicken stew. Usually had a cup of hot chocolate for breakfast. I carried a rock-hard C-ration candy bar (a "John Wayne") with me just in case I needed some quick energy.

The following day, Cataldo and I were flying typical ash-and-trash missions (general resupply) while the crew chief kept saying something was wrong. He didn't know what was making him feel bad, but he was *very* unhappy and reminded us frequently. At first, I thought he was just bitching, but he was serious. Our last three trips were with very heavy loads, ammunition resupply to Firebase Holcomb, which was situated on a three hundred foot high pinnacle, with vertical drops to the valley foothills. A heavily loaded Huey could mean catastrophe if the engine failed on approach. We successfully completed the resupply and returned to Camp Evans. At the end of the day, Cataldo remarked that despite the crew chief's bitching, everything had gone pretty well. We had the aircraft fueled at Camp Evans POL before returning to the Phoenix Nest.

As Cataldo lifted the Huey from the fuel point, the short drive shaft between the turbine engine and the transmission broke, and the aircraft yawed violently to the left with the jet engine screaming. In a powerless crash, we landed on the skids in a ditch, dirt walls on both sides rising to our eye levels. I looked up and kept watching the main rotor blades to see if they'd come crashing through the cockpit and kill us both.

Cataldo had had a total power loss while headed diagonally over a ten-foot-deep gully. He'd centered the aircraft with the length of the ravine and safely crash-landed. He'd also kept the rotor disk centered at an angle to avoid hitting the ground (within three feet of the blades). Astonishing me, he'd simultaneously rolled down the throttle, preventing a catastrophic engine overspeed! It was an autorotation successfully completed during a critical phase of flight, by reflex, at the end of a very long day.

It took only a violent two seconds to yaw left and fall to the ground; the absolute horror came afterward. For an eternal minute, I watched the main rotor blades slowing and flapping, just inches above the ground, outside our ditch. If they slapped the ground, imbalance and inertia could have sent them slicing through the cockpit and me.

Cataldo kept them stable. He had shouted for me to cut the fuel but I didn't understand him in that loud and violent two seconds. He then shut the fuel off himself. In elation, as the blades stopped, he reached over, grabbing my shoulder. "Are you okay?" In shock, I mumbled, "Yeah."

The crew chief said again, "Man, there it is." A few minutes later, we were able to get out, shaken, amazed, and thankful. A small crowd of equally impressed onlookers gathered, including our commanding officer, Major Lord.

Cataldo's skill and reflexes saved our lives from a major aircraft accident. He had kept us from either going upside down or having the blades slap the ground. The practice autorotation he'd surprised me with the day before had displayed his confidence in flying. The autorotation just completed was testimony to his skill.

The CO and maintenance people came running over and inspected the aircraft. With the replacement of a bearing, it was immediately flyable. It took half an hour for the mechanics. I was given the choice of flying the aircraft back to the hangar or taking the truck. I rode the truck.

To end the day, I'd been given perimeter line duty officer, on the bunker line, all damn night long!

That night, December 2, by chance, I ran into Rick Lukens again.

Lukens and I walked the perimeter, showing our presence as duty officers. I asked him if there had been any activity on the bunker line. He replied, "Well, the activity we've had has not been North Vietnamese. I'm told a couple of months ago, one of our Redskin pilots was the line duty officer. They called him Baby San. He was trying to get some sleep (you're permitted to nap, but not to sleep all night). People kept calling in, telling him there was somebody in the wire. He would go out and look, didn't see anybody, and went back to bed. The fourth time they came in and woke him up and told him there really was somebody in the wire. Baby San hopped in his jeep and drove to their position. On the way over, the guards requested permission to fire. Baby San gave the order.

"Well, they opened up and killed the guy. It happened to be a GI coming back from a drug run to the local village. He was high on heroin. An M-60 put a tiny hole squarely in his forehead, expelling his brains out the back. It put Baby San into a real depression. He felt responsible for killing a GI. He grounded himself and declared himself a conscientious objector. He refused to fly any missions in Cobras so they shipped him out to a unit down south. The 163d Aviation Company."

The drug problem was serious enough that guys were going through the wire at night to buy heroin and bring it back. We also heard of a lot of hashish and marijuana, but the heroin powder, smack, was the real serious stuff.

But Baby San's tragedy was not yet played out.

### December 4, 1970, Mac-V Compound, Quang Tri, I Corps

Quang Tri, forty miles north of Camp Eagle and Hue, was the last major town in South Vietnam below the DMZ. The Special Forces compound was operated by the Military Assistance Command, Vietnam, Studies and Observation Group (MACV-SOG). It was located on the western side of the airfield, an assortment of wood-framed, barracks-type buildings, no different than the single-story tropical barracks seen in World War II and the Korean War. The compound was next to a small asphalt landing pad, which could hold a platoon of ten helicopters. As a newly assigned warrant officer, I was one of several pilots getting the initial security and intelligence briefing prior to my first Command and Control North (CCN) mission.

The CCN Special Forces compound was subtly different from the rest of the Quang Tri airfield and combat base. It was a carefully secured compound, inside the western perimeter. To soldiers, the helicopter pad was referred to as FOB (forward operations base); to pilots and crewmen it was the "flight over border" pad. Depending upon your mission and need to know, acronyms sometimes had very different meanings.

The buildings were clustered around the helicopter pad. However, we quickly observed the special features of construction. The buildings were elevated above the ground, and shutters covered the normally screened upper half of the walls. Security was very tight. The small compound had its own fenced security perimeter inside the much larger Quang Tri airfield security perimeter.

The new pilots and veterans filed into the briefing room, taking seats on benches arranged in a Spartan classroom setting. The briefing was commenced by Captain Correll, a painfully serious-looking Green Beret. The captain began, "Everything we do here is classified top secret. No one, and I mean *no one*, is permitted to discuss any activities here with anyone not involved in the mission. You are not permitted to take photographs. And you are not allowed to discuss the missions in letters home." A young warrant officer, forewarned by my Stateside duty with Capt. David Anderson, I instantly decided to keep my camera handy. I thought that I'd finally have an opportunity to take some interesting photos.

As part of the first mission, we were shown a wall-size map covering I Corps, Laos, and the lower part of North Vietnam. The map showed all confirmed North Vietnamese Army antiaircraft positions. There were pins of green, blue, and red, which we knew indicated the size of the NVA weapons.

The map was heavily speckled with multicolored pins. There were occasional clusters, obviously dense concentrations of very heavy antiaircraft artillery. The Special Forces officer asked if we knew what the minimum-sized weapon was on the map. Having three months in country and sitting on the front row, I spoke out, ".51 cal." He smiled and shook his head, "No, Mr. Marshall, these are all larger than 12.7 millimeter." That meant that the weapon positions marked were twenty-three millimeter and larger. The pilots in the group took a collective deep breath as a strong chill swept down my spine, radiating to my extremities.

That meant that if they could see us, they could shoot us down, regardless of our altitude. Within South Vietnam, we generally considered ourselves safe from small-arms fire at twenty-five hundred feet above ground level. The rules of the game had just changed, decidedly in the enemy's favor. We were going to operate eighty-knot Hueys at World War I airspeeds, in a radar-guided anti-aircraft environment dangerous for five hundred–knot "fast movers" (jets).

The briefing continued with a Special Forces sergeant describing the Special Forces teams fielded by CCN, their assignments, and personnel. The sergeant briefly commented that the NVA in these recon areas were "not known to take prisoners of war" among the Green Berets, their Laotian and Vietnamese teammates, or the aircrews supporting them. This bit of information seriously jolted us. Then it got worse. We were told there would only be one attempt at extraction if we "went down." The euphemism for being "shot the hell out of the sky" then became very personal. After that one effort, we'd be "on our own." Simply put, it was just too easy for the North Vietnamese Army to set up an ambush on second rescue attempt.

CCN was not going to be the fun and games I'd thought at the beginning of the briefing. I saw others sitting near me grimace at the same sudden awareness. We'd been committed as players in a very special contest. No POWs, simply life or death. The gravity of the situation overpowered a highly professional presentation. Following the advice of other veteran Phoenix pilots, I was carrying cherry-bomb hand grenades in both of my lower leg pockets. If I had a choice, it would be fight, escape, and evade.

The briefer continued with an even more disturbing pronouncement. If we were "lost," we'd be listed as "killed in action—body not recovered" since we were not legally operating in either North Vietnam or Laos. The euphemism for killed in action was not lost on those present.

We were then given the security clearance papers acknowledging the top secret nature of our work. We were also given the rules of engagement to sign, defining when our crews would be cleared to fire their weapons. We signed the rules of engagement as a formality. We knew that once we crossed the imaginary fence into Laos or the DMZ heading north, anyone we saw would be enemy.

When the briefing was finished, Captain Correll told our platoon leader to stand by, ready to launch our Hueys on short notice. He reported that an unnamed recon team with two Americans and six Montagnard scouts was in contact with the enemy after having been discovered by North Vietnamese patrols. We weren't given the team's name or location. I reflexively thought we'd be going into Laos. We'd have an air force forward air controller direct us in. They were in enemy contact, another euphemism, for close infantry combat. Unknown to us, the team members were running for their lives through the mountain hillsides of North Vietnam. A deadly game of cat and mouse was being played on the cat's turf. It was a game where the winner lived. Each time the North Vietnamese Army closed in, the covert team would ambush the lead element then escape and evade to another ambush site. They did this to extract a high price in enemy casualties for pursuing them and to slow down the enemy's pursuit. The team hoped to slow pursuit enough that it could break contact long enough for helicopters to extract it.

The Special Forces soldiers were the best of America's forces, volunteering for incredibly dangerous missions. But the CCN missions were totally dependent on helicopters to get them in, out, and safely home. They knew the risks of helicopter extractions. To demand a hot extraction might result in a helicopter being shot down, right on top of them. The team leader knew that if contact could not be broken, his last resort was a string extraction (i.e., lifting the team out on a long rope; see the cover photo) under fire. The men of the Special Forces team also understood they were on a 70/30 mission in North Vietnam; 70 percent routinely didn't come back during the course of a year. It was the most dangerous mission behind enemy lines. To the pilots, Laos and North Vietnam were Conrad's *Heart of Darkness*. One discovered the sum of all personal fears, the very real risk of dying in a foreign land for a cause America was quitting.

In the briefing, we were told to expect a hot pickup zone. The Griffins, Cobra gunships from 4/77 Artillery, would provide close air support. An OV-10, a small, twin-engine turboprop FAC (forward air controller, call sign Covey) would be high overhead to call jets and prop-driven Skyraiders if needed. Jolly Green Giants, armored search-and-rescue helicopters from Thailand, were also on standby in case we needed them to extract *us*. Another chill down my spine.

We quietly filed out of the briefing room and down the steps to the helicopter pad. We checked our aircraft once more. We then sat around the aircraft, discussing anything but the mission.

Twenty minutes later, Capt. David Nelson, our platoon leader, came running out of the briefing room. "Start 'em!" Within seconds, the main rotor blades had been untied by the crew chiefs and the blades displaced abeam. Copilots then began the starting sequence. The pinging of ignitor plugs was a call to action as the gas turbine engines spooled up, driving the rotor system. Two minutes later, we departed, a flight of four Hueys, climbing to an altitude of forty-five hundred feet. We flew at the base of purple-gray overcast, headed northwest from Quang Tri toward the border areas. Northwest of Camp Carroll, north of the Rockpile, we turned north. Only then did we realize our destination was North Vietnam! We continued north-

northwest over the DMZ, well east of Laos, in the lower part of North Vietnam. As we climbed out for the forty-minute flight to the pickup zone, we checked in with Covey (the FAC) to brief us on his last contact with the unit. The air force OV-10 Bronco would monitor our progress and call air strikes if necessary. We were to look for purple smoke on short final.

Captain Nelson was my aircraft commander. We were Chalk One, the lead aircraft. The phrase "Chalk One, Chalk Two," emerged from the use of chalk boards depicting the flight formation and crew assignments. The lead or number one aircraft was Chalk One. I was Nelson's copilot on my first CCN mission. I'd flown only six days with the Phoenix prior to the mission. Three months of flying a little Jet Ranger in the Central Highlands around An Khe was no preparation for North Vietnam! Nelson did all the flying, continually updating the others while en route. He ordered the plan of action. Two birds would pick up the eight men in a hot pickup zone. It would be a hovering, string (rope) extraction. Near the border area we assumed radio silence except for digital-scrambled FM radio. Without the same type of radio and the day's settings, the enemy could not listen to us.

In the cargo bay of our Huey, a Special Forces sergeant was flying belly man, along with our door gunner and crew chief. A string extraction required our coming to a hover a few feet above the trees and dropping 120-foot-long ropes to the four passengers, who would clip on to them with special rings sewn into the load-bearing-equipment (LBE) harness each wore. Then we'd fly them to safety as they dangled below while we climbed vertically out to five thousand feet.

From that moment on, we were a small assault helicopter team of four lift aircraft and four gunships, literally riding to the rescue like the cavalry of old. We were all aware of an unspoken commitment: Americans were in trouble on the ground, and we were their only way out; it was time to get them out or die trying. A vicious skirmish was under way, a Studies and Observation Group team was hopelessly outnumbered by North Vietnamese, equally willing to die in pursuit of the Americans. At that moment, we were living an absolute commitment to duty, honor, and country; we weren't proclaiming those virtues, we were committing them.

We had flown north-northwest from the Rock Pile, a conical mountain below the demilitarized zone. We proceeded north under a purple-gray cloud ceiling at six thousand feet; the mountains to our west rose to over fifty-five hundred feet elevation. Gusty winds buffeted us over unnamed mountains and ridges.

Several miles from the pickup zone, the four helicopters dispersed into one-minute intervals; the pilots behind us slowed to increase the distance between each Huey. We'd have one minute to find our passengers under attack, hover over them, and drop the strings. After they clipped on, we would climb vertically away, to safety.

Minutes later, we turned onto the final approach. Nelson called the sergeant on the ground and told him we were two miles out. His only response was, "Hurry." Nelson asked, "Is it hot?" The sergeant's response was not a military "affirmative," but a simple "Yes." Even in the second it took to key the mike for the single word, we heard the firefight raging.

We began the descent, leaving the purplish-gray glare of overcast clouds, into the reddish-brown haze of smoke and combat. The Griffins were diving their gunships in a continuous cycle of fire support. When one finished firing and began to climb away, another dived and fired!

As we descended to the pickup zone, clearly in sight, an indescribable sinking feeling wrenched my gut. The Huey was shuddering in deceleration. The whopping sound of our rotor blades heralded our approach to the mountain ridges. With adrenaline pumping, we focused on the mission: find the team, hover over it, drop the strings, get the men out safely. The business at hand, training, and respective duties took over. Fear was set aside during the final approach.

The Griffins were still shooting up the area as we approached the pickup zone. They were told to bring their firing closer. The team was obviously close to being overrun. We were committed to the final approach. We were their only hope! It was time to act, no decisions, only trained reflexes, monitoring the radios, engine instruments, mountain winds, and enemy fire. Control movements, piloting decisions, were completed before conscious thought.

On short final, still one-quarter mile from the pickup zone (PZ), Nelson said, "Get on the controls (with me), very lightly." Another chill down my spine. This was it! Combat! The real thing. Just in case he was hit, I was to be ready to take over the controls. As we came to a hover, the crew chief shouted, "About ten yards forward, sir, about five yards to the right." I felt the controls moving furiously, but Nelson had the bird at a perfect hover just below a mountain ridgeline without much in the way of visual aids. His piloting was complicated by gusty mountain winds. I kept my fingertips dancing lightly on the controls.

The Green Beret sergeant in our cargo bay looked over the side and said, "We're clear to drop, sir."

Nelson said, "Drop 'em."

The four 120-foot ropes went over the side. I looked over the side of my armor plate, and I could see we were taking fire. We'd hovered into the chaos of close combat, yellow tracers streaming beneath us, wisps of white smoke from NVA rocket-propelled grenades (RPGs), and concussion of Griffin 2.75-inch rockets going off all around us. I quickly looked back inside the cockpit, watched Nelson, and did not look down again. Instead, I focused on the landmarks of the ridgeline in front of us. I moved my focus in the trained manner, one second on the ridge-line in front, one second on engine instruments, one second on flight instruments, repeating the scan over and over. I also scrunched down into my seat to become as small as I could, behind my chest chicken-plate armor and the armored sliding door to my right. My simple existence depended upon successful mission execution, and the best of luck!

I glanced at Nelson, who was holding the Huey at a precise hover, ignoring the sounds of rockets and grenades. He was mentally focused, shutting down distractions in his mind. Fear would not disrupt the job at hand.

The crew chief called, "They're all hooked up, sir."

Then Nelson said, "Okay, coming up."

"Clear up left," shouted the crew chief, followed by "Clear up right" from the gunner.

Nelson then called over the radio, "Chalk One, coming out."

Chalk Two, on short final called, "Is it hot?"

"Affirmative," Nelson responded. With four passengers attached to the strings by McGuire rigs, we went straight up five hundred feet, with a slight forward movement once the men on strings were clear of the trees. We climbed up to the bottom of the clouds, near forty-five hundred feet, then proceeded southeast away from danger. Our time at a hover had been something less than thirty seconds. It had seemed like an hour.

The same action was repeated by the second Phoenix Huey. Both extractions were safely completed in less than two minutes. The two other circling Phoenix birds were backup ("recovery" birds) in case we'd been shot down. We turned southward toward South Vietnam, unwilling to relax, knowing we were still over North Vietnam.

A couple of minutes away from the pickup zone, Nelson said, "You got it, keep it steady, very steady." As I took the controls, he shook his gloved hands, and began clenching and unclenching his fists. He'd executed the extraction perfectly!

About twelve miles northwest of Quang Tri, north of the firebase Camp Carroll, was a large river valley. There we descended to a large sandbar and hovered down with the men still on the ropes. They were numbed beyond movement. The McGuire rig straps, as pilots referred to them, cut off blood circulation to their legs. Added discomfort came from being carried at forty-five hundred feet, dangling from ropes in forty degree temperatures while flying eighty miles per hour. They simply couldn't move. Our crewmen carried them into the cargo bay. We then flew them back to Quang Tri, FOB pad. After dropping them off, we headed home for the night at Camp Evans.

When finally back on the ground safely, in the revetment area at the Phoenix Nest, Nelson said, "You shut it down. I've got paperwork to do." He then left to write his after-action report, and I began the engine cooldown and shutdown checklist. It was obvious everyone had been under incredible tension.

I was impressed with the performance of Captain Nelson. He could do anything in my book! It couldn't get any more exciting! Any mission he would fly, I'd happily fill the right seat. I didn't think it could possibly get any worse. However, I would eventually be proven wrong. The first impression of him I'd had just a few days earlier simply didn't fit the impression I had after what we'd just endured. At the Phoenix, I first saw him hopscotching from one dry rock to the next, not to dirty his spit-shined Corcoran boots in the monsoon mud. I remember thinking to myself, this guy would be better suited for the navy! I'd seen many navy officers in Pensacola, immaculate, spit polished. We army pilots, however, were a different breed. We lived a different life in Spartan quarters near the front lines.

This was I Corps, the end of our front line. We'd just

completed an unimaginably risky mission in North Damn Vietnam!

In awe of Nelson, the crew chief, gunner, and Green Beret, I silently tried to assimilate the experience. During the extraction, waves of adrenaline had created in me a level of awareness so high that it transcended anything I had ever known in competitive sports. It had been interspersed with what I can only describe as time expansion, when a second seems like a minute, and a minute like an hour. That wonderful exhilaration and incredible sense of accomplishment after the mission was experienced by most. It took a while to calm down. We had been incredibly lucky. None of the aircraft had taken hits. All of the Special Forces team had been safely extracted while under heavy enemy ground assault.

That evening, as the emotions ebbed after our return, the reality of high-risk hovering extractions and exposure to enemy fire in North Vietnam settled in. This was a game you could play successfully only for a while; eventually, the odds would claim you. I began paying closer attention to the veteran pilots who were serving as first pilots, aircraft commanders with several months of CCN time. The phrase "combat experience" suddenly had an entirely new meaning to me, even though I had been in country over three months. Although my three months of introduction to combat in the Central Highlands had been deadly at times, all those events had been nothing more than a docile training mission compared to CCN.

After three and a half months in country, I'd finally found the real war. I'd landed right on the spear's tip!

I wrote in a letter home that rocket attacks on Camp Evans had stopped. The last had been Thanksgiving Day. Recently it had only been mortars, which, compared to rockets, weren't so bad. Spent about four hours with Rick Lukens. Sat around drinking Scotch and talking of classmates. He told me Aileo, a flight-school classmate, was also in Phu Bai. Bruce Baer DEROSed with wounds but was expected to be okay in a few months. We thought it kind of ironic that the guy who bitched the most in flight school got the worst injuries.

The next day, I flew CCN with WO John Michaelson. Flying again into the triborder area of North Vietnam scared the hell out of me! Michaelson was a first-tour warrant officer with a few months more experience than I had. It turned out to be another day of successful hot extractions from a mountain ridge, this time one we could actually put skids on. I took photos of the action. At the end of the day I bumped the cyclic, which made a strange creaking noise. Michaelson shouted at me, "Don't ever do that. You'll cause a hard-over (in the hydraulics)." His crew chief and door gunner glared at me as if I were the most stupid of all newbies. Maybe I was. There had been widely reported accounts of Hueys suffering hydraulic hard-overs, the aircraft inverting and crashing. It was an unknown, an uncontrollable risk, in the back of all experienced Huey pilots' minds.

Michaelson was a very intense, tightly focused pilot. He'd just received a Distinguished Flying Cross for rescuing a Marine aircrew twenty miles into Laos. Answering an emergency call from a forward air controller, Michaelson had flown his Huey twenty miles into Northern Laos, at treetop level, to rescue the crew without a gunship escort. Michaelson had accomplished it safely, in the most dangerous combat environment. He described the extraction to me as "interesting." They had taken sporadic machine-gun fire and rocket-propelled grenade fire going in and coming out. For his efforts, he was threatened with a reprimand by army superiors if he tried it again. In typical warrant-officer style, he did it again three weeks later. Unfortunately, on that occasion the crew could not be rescued, and luckily, Michaelson did not get shot down trying—or a court-martial.

I was not happy flying CCN with someone I didn't

know. I intuitively trusted Captain Nelson after my flights with him, and I eventually learned Michaelson was another excellent pilot, one totally aware of risks. He could think ahead of what was happening—he could tell me how I was screwing up before I did it.

He was very tough on his copilots, but he had the experience and safety record to justify his way. It simply worked, and I had much more to learn.

I was flight-line officer of the day on December 6, which amounted to having the day off. Got up at 5:30, reported to operations, then went to breakfast at 6:00. Back to bed and slept till lunch at 11:30. It was the proper way to spend a Sunday in Vietnam. We still didn't have running water or lights. The civilian contractors didn't work on Sunday.

While I was lying around the hootch, another Phoenix pilot had a long day of ash-and-trash missions. He was given pilot-in-command responsibilities, with a copilot of much less experience. The pilot was awaiting aircraft commander orders. In a mountaintop resupply at the middle of the day, after he had completed several runs, he handed the controls over to his copilot. The copilot came in underpowered and undercontrolled, and the pilot was just fatigued enough not to react in time. The result was a blade strike on the ground, inverting the aircraft and killing a GI on the ground. The Huey was totally destroyed. The Phoenix's safety record had also been destroyed.

The pilot had the tragic accident around 1:00. By 4:00, he had been checked out by the flight surgeon. His personal belongings had been collected from the quarters by another officer. There was no discussion of mitigating circumstances or any possibility of his continuing to fly with the Phoenix Company or the 101st Airborne Division. He'd been instantly grounded, removed from duty, and sent to a holding station with menial tasks to keep him bored until he DEROSed. He had been responsible for letting his copilot screw up. Michaelson's attitude finally made sense to me.

When word filtered through the Phoenix, it was obvious that pilots were disgusted with the treatment of the pilot. The pilots felt that the battalion commander, Lieutenant Colonel Gerard, had a genuine lack of understanding of their capabilities and responsibilities. The pilots were flying 130 hours per month. We had fourteen-hour days, nighttime standby, and additional ground duties and missions. All in the worst mountain flying conditions for helicopters.

If an accident messed up an aircraft, Lieutenant Colonel Gerard immediately grounded the AC (aircraft commander) and revoked his aircraft commander orders. If a copilot was involved in one, he was told he'd never be an AC with Gerard around. I'd come to Nam with a good attitude, and that really hadn't changed, but commanders like Gerard appeared stupid and were a demoralizing influence. It only made me more certain I'd be leaving the army. They expected you to fly heavy loads, in the mountains, with adverse weather, over enemy-controlled areas. A high percentage of the aircraft were showing wear and tear from constant use and make-do field maintenance. In those conditions, it only took a little bad luck, and I mean *luck* in its strictest sense, to have a catastrophic mishap. Absolutely no pilot error was required to have an accident.

Only years later could I begin to appreciate what Lieutenant Colonel Gerard had to deal with. One hundred forty or so young warrant-officer pilots, in the worst flying environment, working the worst area of operations. Safety had to be the paramount concern.

Having survived a powerless crash during takeoff with Cataldo, I realized how lucky we'd been. No damage or injuries. No having to face Lieutenant Colonel Gerard.

I thought that sometime around February or March 1971, I'd start looking for a good ground job, at least one that had less flying. I thought again about getting a transfer to fly 58s, but it began to appear that slicks might be a little safer. Having some combat time with the Phoenix, I just couldn't see myself flying a 58 in I Corps the way I did in the Central Highlands.

By this time, everyone in Nam, I Corps especially, was praying for an adjusted DEROS date. A few officers who had DEROS dates up to January 20 got thirty-day drops so they could be home for Christmas. That was a pretty decent move by someone in the Department of the Army.

On Pearl Harbor Day I finally received mail from home. It took eleven days for a reply to a previous letter. Found out I was being moved to the 1st Flight Platoon, flying with a different bunch of guys. That meant I wouldn't be flying out of Quang Tri over the holidays. After CCN, many Phoenix pilots considered support of the mechanized infantry the most challenging and rewarding mission.

I spent the day flying MACV support with Captain Nelson. We did a sling-load fuel-blivet resupply of Outpost Hickory, which was located on a mountain just south of the DMZ, overlooking Khe Sanh. Thirty-five knot mountaintop winds made the mission tricky, but Nelson handled it without difficulty. I provided excellent ballast in the right seat.

Only 246 days to DEROS, and the big 97 days for Hawaii.

The next day at CCN, we were without a serious mission. When we had free time, it was the routine to provide food for the Montagnard tribesmen who worked as team members with the Green Berets. They enjoyed fresh venison, so we were charged with the duty of bringing in a deer. The hills were home to numerous mule deer, which were very large and would feed the Montagnards for a few days.

This kind of mission was viewed as fun by a lot of pilots, who took along Swedish-K submachine guns, Thompsons, M3 grease guns, and other automatic weapons and personal side arms for CCN missions. Those who wanted to shoot, piled into the back of a Huey. Nelson was flying as the pilot. In the back were Ralph Moreira, Darryl Keith, Tommy Doody, another pilot, a crew chief, and a door gunner. I brought my camera and hopped aboard.

We flew low-level down the Da Krong River valley, southeast of Khe Sanh. There were two aircraft, one flying high and us, going low at about forty knots along the river. Once a deer was spooked, Captain Nelson maneuvered us into position and the most god-awful cacophony of automatic weapon sounds erupted. The deer stumbled and died quickly with multiple wounds. Nelson landed the helicopter a few yards away.

We all hopped out in the elephant grass. I had my camera and ran over to get a shot of the deer and the guys picking it up, struggling, to load it. It was heavy as hell, weighing well over 250 pounds. WO Ralph Moreira shouted at me, "Marshall, get your ass over here. Help load this damn thing, and let's get outta here." I took my photograph and then hopped in the back of the Huey with the twitching deer and the pilots.

The door gunners were intently scanning the landscape, looking for evidence of enemy activity. While climbing back to Quang Tri, the crew chief asked Moreira if he had noticed the bunker complex opposite the river. We all just shook our heads, knowing there were North Vietnamese Army bunkers everywhere.

Back at the CCN pad in Quang Tri, I took more photographs of WO Tommy Doody and crew members standing next to the deer. Doody had two very short months, and a day, to live.

I thought to myself that if we'd been shot down, the platoon pilots would have been wiped out. The photograph would become an indelible metaphor in my memory, capsulizing my time with the Phoenix. Of those in the photograph, one would survive the next three months.

As a consequence of the recent accident, the CO called a safety briefing for the next evening.

The 101st's safety record had degenerated to a series of accidents and incidents. Until the past few days, they had been without injury to the crews or passengers. Prior to the CO's meeting, discussions included a review of a series of accidents that plagued the 101st Aviation Group. South of Da Nang, a Huey had been reported as having a hydraulic failure and a subsequent hard-over. It was suspected that the cyclic control had jammed under hydraulic pressure during a right climbing turn, inverting and destroying the aircraft, along with the crew of four.

An instructor pilot in another 158th Aviation Battalion company had recently given the toughest Huey check ride ever. The instructor gave the guy a simulated hydraulic failure. A minute later, the instructor pilot reached down without watching his hand, and accidently turned the fuel flow off! They smacked onto the runway, spreading the skids, but walked away. The instructor pilot had flown his last check ride in the army. It was a near tragic accident, totally humiliating him.

The passenger fatality with the Phoenix bird had been the grievous end of good luck.

The Phoenix pilots were assembled in their well-used officers club for the company meeting. A few minutes after the meeting began, Captain Graves came running into the club. He was ashen faced, obviously scared as hell. He urgently motioned the CO and two other officers out of the meeting. Graves had discovered a man lying dead on the floor of his hootch, in a pool of blood. As word of the death filtered into the officers club, the meeting was summarily adjourned. It was a very eerie close to the night. With so many people facing death on a daily basis, to have one guy, with a relatively secure ground job, kill himself, seemed so senseless. Everyone was in a state of shock.

All the pilots had been facing deadly situations on a daily basis. Everyone present knew flying Hueys in I Corps monsoons and mountains was treacherous. Just to avoid a fatal accident, regardless of an enemy presence, required the peak performance of all crew members, as a team. For those who shared and nurtured each others' survival instinct, to have one man choose to take his own life was beyond comprehension. It left us stunned . . . even angry at him.

One day later, we were on CCN again. It was another hot pickup zone. The Green Berets were well north of the DMZ, in the southern part of North Vietnam, just east of Laos. We were the fourth Huey in line, Chalk Four. We were the last to pick up our passengers, who were under constant fire. The Griffins' Cobras were very effective, keeping the NVAs' heads down with aerial rocket fire during our approach. As we came in on final, I took photographs as Darryl Keith flew. With all my recent experience, I'd gotten overconfident once more. I was taking photos instead of following through on the controls, the way Nelson had taught me. Then a Green Beret came on the radio in the midst of the firefight. He told us to "Ignore bodies in landing zone. Not friendlies. Repeat, not friendlies!" I quickly put the camera aside and resumed my duties. We picked them up with Griffin Cobras firing rockets with flechettes in close to our helicopters. The Griffins' rocket impacts were so close that Dave Nelson, flying Chalk One (lead) took a flechette round (a metal dart) through his tail boom. Once safely back at Quang Tri, everyone wanted to check out Nelson's damage. We teased him, joking about it.

A few days later, on December 11, I moved into my new hootch at the end of the row of buildings, next door to the latrine and shower. A couple of guys teased me about being nearer the target, the Redskin ready pad, just thirty yards to the south. It had just gotten dark, and things were settling down at the end of another long day. I was sitting on my cot in my PT shorts writing a letter home. Then came an unmistakable *whompk*. I thought, not now! I'd already been closely mortared at An Khe a couple of times so I knew what was coming. Then came another one, and it was getting louder (meaning closer). Then came another one, even louder. Obviously mortars being walked my way. By then, I was in my flip-flops, on the run!

I sprinted out the door toward the large bunker. It was near the middle of the Phoenix row of hootches.

*Ka Whompk!*

The explosions continued louder . . . coming closer.

*KA WHOMPK!*

Ten yards to the bunker steps and safety.

*KA BAAM!*

Everyone was running to the bunker.

*KA BAAAM!*

All diving for the only stairway into the bunker. Another explosion, even louder and closer, shook the ground. It must have hit very close by. I flew feetfirst down the bunker opening.

As I went airborne down the bunker stairwell, my foot landed squarely and firmly in the back of a captain, who was just a little bit slower and shouldn't have been in my way. At the bottom of the stairs on the muddy bunker floor, I landed on him, one foot in his lower back. I collapsed with a knee in his shoulder blade, my rubber thongs flopping around my ankles. Out of breath from the sprint, I couldn't even laugh. The captain, however, was eating mud and had major-league bruises. Others piled on top of him as I rolled away. Then, as suddenly as it had started, the mortar fire stopped. I quietly made my way back out of the pitch-black bunker. Then the laughter began. We'd experienced the simple terror of incoming mortar fire.

The little bastards had missed again! I was later told Captain Hunt, our XO, was the man who ate the last few steps. He was having a rough tour.

The Redskin ready pad had been hit by mortars, one Cobra damaged on the pad, but there were no injuries to the crew, who had attempted to start it under mortar fire.

## December 12, 1970

Had a very long day with Darryl Keith. We were once again flying CCN. With a Special Forces sergeant assisting our crewmen, we were guided to our drop point in Laos by an air force FAC. We then flew a mapped flight path, dropping electronic sensors designed to report movement of vehicles and people along the Ho Chi Minh trail. We actually flew six hours flight time, but were on the flight line from 5:30 A.M. to 6:30 P.M. That night, I lost my wedding band in the shower. I'd been missing meals and losing weight to the point that my ring size changed. Weight loss was just a part of Vietnam experience. Practically the only exciting things I could write home about were taking a hot shower and marking off the calendar, each day another day shorter in the Nam. Mail call was the happiest hour of each day, even when you didn't get mail. The CCN missions were as hairy as they got. But, under security regulations, not the thing to write home about.

With the successful completion of each mission into North Vietnam or Laos, there evolved a combat veteran's wisdom in risk assessment. The awareness of danger became a repetitive analysis of pucker factor levels. High pucker factors result in hemorrhoids. Normal flying stress, on the pucker factor scale of one to ten is about a three. However, the pucker factor over Laos, the DMZ, and up North was a continuous maximum of ten.

The new OH-58A I had had at An Khe was a cherry. The Phoenix Hueys included replacement birds transferred in with weak engines. Some were D models converted to early H models with weak engines. The converted D models had nose-mounted pitot tubes providing air pressure for instruments, while the newer H models were distinguished by roof-mounted pitot tubes. There were a couple of newer H models, which had experimental self-sealing fuel cells. The cells were designed to reduce fire hazards in a crash.

Typical of all helicopter field units, the Phoenix maintenance was as good as possible, considering the field expediencies and difficulties.

Flying had become a long, tiring, risky job, not the pure joy I'd known in An Khe. Anytime we went west or north from Quang Tri, emotional stress maxed out. Even though we hadn't taken antiaircraft hits and only minimal small-arms hits, the awareness that it was the NVAs' choice, if and when, wore us down by day's end.

Nobody would have been disappointed if the war were suddenly over. Everyone, especially married men, tempered their desires to one singular objective, that of getting home safely. But a tragically large number would not make it home alive. Worse, some would never have their remains returned. I clung to the thought that, overall, the tour would have a pretty good effect upon me. It definitely was a profound life experience. With the politicians abandoning Vietnam, I felt lucky to have made it into the war for the experience. But my dilemma was a very personal one: to live the experiences but not to be sacrificed in a lost cause.

We spent the night of the twelfth in Da Nang, the officers' quarters at the Special Forces compound, CCN pad. Got to fly to the Marble Mountain Marine base to refuel. Army pilots in fixed-skid Hueys got a chuckle reporting to Marble Mountain tower "Skids down and locked." It was a required report for Marine aircraft turning to final approach. The most enjoyable thing about flying CCN was the availability of nights in Da Nang at their headquarters. A night there was like a mini R & R. It was an unbelievable luxury just to be able to sleep in a concrete-block, Stateside building with air-conditioning. There were beds with mattresses, tiled showers with unlimited hot water, and flush toilets. We got a real good night's sleep on a bed with a mattress instead of a cot with a sleeping bag. The last time had been in October at Phu Cat Air Base after my hydraulic failure. To top it off, I even got letters from home.

I spent the evening talking with Cataldo and Keith regarding other jobs in the company. Dave Wolfe had suggested that I consider taking over his parts supply job in maintenance. He said it was a pretty good job that gave minimal flying time but enough to keep you happy and current.

We'd been on CCN since the first of December. Although some of the missions involved resupply to Special Forces Outpost Hickory, near the old Khe Sanh airfield, and Firebase Fuller at the DMZ, we had been making routine missions in Laos: dropping sensors, inserting and extracting troops. We also completed one large mission extracting South Vietnamese troops from the southern part of North Vietnam, north of the DMZ. Politically and officially, we weren't doing those things.

Although the CCN missions had been "fun" (scary as hell), they were incredibly risky. We'd been extremely lucky, but at the end of each day, we experienced an increasing level of fatigue combined with the exhilaration of having completed another day without injury. We wondered how long the good luck would last.

*December 14, 1970.* Dustoff was the call sign of the Huey medical evacuation helicopter. They flew twenty-four hours a day in whatever weather. If there was any possible way to respond to a call and pull out a wounded GI, it would be done. Answering that call, WO Paul Brass and WO Randy Freeman of the 326th Medical Battalion

101st Airborne Division attempted a night pickup. Contact was lost. The next morning, a search party was sent out, and the helicopter was found destroyed on the side of a mountain. More classmates of WORWAC 70-3/70-5.

On the fourteenth, I flew six hours carrying troops from point A to B and vice versa. I decided to put in a formal written request for transfer. I thought I'd ask for a unit at Quang Tri or Dong Ha that had OH-58s. I'd be happier in them, even flying scout missions. I wrote home that I wasn't real unhappy or despondent, just dissatisfied flying Hueys and tired of the routine. With nearly two weeks of CCN missions, and being extended on them another month, I couldn't imagine our good luck continuing to hold. Although OH-58s might be more dangerous, at least it would have been my call when a bad decision was made. My new room had a closet that was a hotbox. It had a 150-watt light bulb that kept things dry. For the first time in four weeks, I had dry socks and underwear. I also had a reading light on my desk in my cubicle.

Word had come that warrant officers not on voluntary indefinite status were released from active duty one month after return from Vietnam. As it stood, wherever I was stationed Stateside, I faced at least an eighteen-month stabilized tour. That way, I could finish a lot of college.

They were really working us. That night, I'd have CDO (company duty officer) and another job afterward instead of the day off.

On the fifteenth, I put in a formal letter requesting transfer. I requested an air cavalry unit at Quang Tri or the 1st of the 5th Mechanized Division. I hoped to fly a Jet Ranger again. Although I felt it probably wouldn't be granted, I couldn't live with myself unless I'd at least tried to get out of Charlie Company. If not for my experience flying the OH-58 in the 4th Infantry Division, I might have enjoyed the Phoenix duties. I kept thinking of Captain David Anderson's comments regarding the Green

Machine and how to perform your duties and use the system while looking out for number one. Anderson had explained to me in very clear terms that I was simply safer flying anything but a Huey in an assault helicopter company. Based upon Anderson's advice, I had gone voluntary indefinite (lifer) to get the OH-58 transition. Captain Hunt, the Phoenix Company executive officer, was pissed at me. He needed warrant officers in a company that was overloaded in RLOs (real live, commissioned, officers). He personally assured me the request would be denied.

My time with the 4th Infantry Division, watching the withdrawal of a complete division covering central II Corps, had given me a perspective on the war that none of the Phoenix officers seemed to have. As far as they knew, the war was still on indefinitely. I had, in fact, seen the United States Army pulling out, and it continued, even though we weren't witnessing it.

In three weeks with the Phoenix, I'd witnessed more hot combat action than I could have imagined in three months over the Central Highlands. I'd participated in hot extractions from pickup zones, actually seen ground fire directed at me, and experienced antiaircraft fire, including flak, over Laos. It was more than I had even heard about during three months at An Khe with the 4th Infantry Division. The enemy threat didn't end when you entered safe airspace. At night in the hootch area, we'd been mortared and subjected to 122mm rockets; the Phoenix were unluckily positioned close to the Redskin Cobra revetment area, the perennial target of those attacks. The Redskins and Griffins kept the dinks pissed off. The Griffins were an aerial rocket artillery unit that also flew Cobras.

From my perspective, the war had been declared over by the president's Vietnamization plan announced in October. In December, total war continued for a select group of unfortunates committed as crews of the Phoenix, Lancers, Ghostriders, Redskins, and Griffins. The companies at Camp Evans. We couldn't win, we couldn't quit, but we'd continue to play the game, against the ultimate opponent.

The NVA were only part of the problem. Fatigue from long days, nighttime standby, and extra duties were a problem. Maintenance was good, but not without its problems and shortages. The weather was definitely dangerous. Operating Hueys in a high-altitude mountain environment, visually, was remarkably difficult. Added to the equation were fog and aircraft carrying loads heavier than they were designed for. The risk of a fatal catastrophe was constant. The NVA was the enemy, but the ultimate opponent was, quite simply, death, whether by accident or enemy action.

There appeared to be nothing going on with the North Vietnamese Army within South Vietnam. They evidently were preparing for Tet or something later. Still, the grunts were the only ones who got into contact and suffered casualties. During the past two weeks, there were more deaths from suicide or drug overdoses than enemy fire.

Even though I didn't like flying the Huey and didn't particularly like the missions, I had experienced real combat missions in the real war zone. I hadn't even been shot at in my first ten weeks at An Khe. Mayberry had been truthful. The Phoenix had the best support available. Cobra gunships and air force forward air controllers in OV-10 Broncos were always on hand for our CCN missions. I finally understood why. We were flying in an unrestricted war zone, with lots and lots of NVA.

I sensed my time with the Phoenix, Charlie Company, would be memorable. I also realized the routine of CCN missions was glazing over the initial shock encountered in the first mission. It began to seem easy, but I knew better.

The following day, I flew eight hours west of Quang Tri, carrying an Australian major. It was real interesting, a heavily accented day. Flew within a few hundred yards of the DMZ so we could get some good pictures. Had another day of clear blue skies with a sixty-degree temperature. Saw a Widowmaker, an army OV-1 Mohawk, entering North Vietnam on the beach at fifty feet altitude and about 250 knots airspeed. Glad it wasn't me.

*Pleiku.* On December 19, WO Avon Mallette was completing another day of visual reconnaissance, hovering, searching for the enemy, dropping CS, tear gas, and fragmentation grenades into bunkers. As he hovered past a concealed bunker position, a lone NVA soldier sat up with an RPG (rocket-propelled grenade launcher) and, from behind, hit him in the engine compartment and fuel cell. The aircraft exploded and crashed to the ground. His body and that of his crew chief were recovered by the command-and-control helicopter crew. My flight-school, car-pool buddy was another loss to WORWAC Class 70-3/70-5. He never got to hold his daughter Tammy.

## December 23, 1970, The White House, Washington, D.C.

President Richard Nixon approved the proposed Laos operation in principle, subject to final review at a later date. The president's decision was, in part, based upon the advice of Gen. Alexander Haig, who'd met with Gen. Creighton Abrams, commander in Vietnam. Abrams proposed a major multidivision offensive. The ARVN would move into Laos against the Ho Chi Minh trail. The operation concept was approved.

From the strategic viewpoint of Nixon and Kissinger, the Laotian invasion made sense. In a broader perspective, the United States had already begun a "strategic withdrawal" (i.e., retreat), from Vietnam in 1969. The best way to carry out any strategic withdrawal was by switching occasionally to the tactical offensive. Firebase Ripcord had been one of those offensive moves, Laos would be the last. The Laotian invasion was intended to buy a big chunk of time to permit the accelerated withdrawal of units from the combat arena. It would also put Vietnamization to the test.

The plan to strike at North Vietnamese Army base areas in Laos was risky. It involved United States troops along the DMZ clearing Highway 9 from Quang Tri to the Laotian border. In the second phase, there would be a three-pronged ARVN assault from South Vietnam, along Highway 9, to Tchepone, Laos. Additional ARVN units would attack northward from Highway 9 by heliborne assault and ground movement to A Luoi. Simultaneously, infantry elements would advance on a parallel axis south of Highway 9, protecting the flank of the central column. The goal was to capture Tchepone and raze the 604/611 Base Area of the North Vietnamese army. According to planners, that would take approximately ninety days. U.S. support would be in the form of helicopters, air strikes, and artillery fire from South Vietnam. The Laotian incursion would be accompanied by a minor ARVN operation into Cambodia. However, the Cooper-Church Amendment, passed in 1970, after the Cambodian invasion, forbade American ground troops from entering Laos or Cambodia. That prevented critical U.S. advisers, forward observers, and air controllers from accompanying ARVN ground units. The orders were issued to commence preparations for the assault at the end of the rainy season in early February.

## December 23, 1970, Camp Evans

For me, it had been heavy flying the past couple of days. More Command and Control North, and that continued to be real interesting. I'd been eating at Quang Tri MACV pad. Only one meal a day, and I didn't get hungry.

The place rivaled a Stateside cafeteria. Special Forces got the worst missions and the best chow.

Flying with Keith throughout I Corps was an eye-opener. Everywhere we went, there were helicopters. The broad landscape of Quang Tri Province was a panorama of continuous military action. Artillery strikes, jet strikes, and gunships, something going on all the time. OH-58s and Loaches were flying with Cobras and command-and-control birds above. I began to understand that flying an OH-58 in a single-ship capacity would not be safe in I Corps. In fact, flying anything single ship was not safe in I Corps if you were west of the mountain ridgeline. There were numerous instances of single ships taking fire, but multiple-ship formations not being fired on. The single ship passing over was too tempting to shoot at from behind. The pilot couldn't see it or hear it.

The scenery was beautiful in the big mountains. It had been raining for so long that all the mountain streams were running crystal clear. Wispy waterfalls fell throughout the ranges. We had had only three days' sunshine in the previous three weeks.

Had a really good Christmas Eve and Day. Was so drunk Christmas Eve, I couldn't sleep even though I went to bed at 11:00. Got up at 5:00 A.M., preflighting, and flying by 9:00 A.M. I wasn't intending to get drunk but everyone, and I mean everyone, was. I didn't have to pull bunker guard, luckily, so I had a good night. Every flare we had in inventory went up. We had continuous illumination with green, red, and white flares from 8:00 P.M. to 12:00 A.M. To top it all off, the airfield tower, one hundred yards from my hootch, played Christmas carols all night.

It was comforting to realize that I was well into my fifth month with only two months until Hawaii. Flew two hours today. Bob Hope was entertaining the troops in Phu Bai, and all available aircraft were up just to keep the dinks' heads down. Finished flying early enough to get my clothes off the line just as it began to rain. That was a real Christmas gift.

The mess hall outdid itself on Christmas Day. Ate all the ham and shrimp I could hold, plus raisin pie. Some of the guys got to fly up to Quang Tri and ate at MACV. They had wine and champagne at each table in Quang Tri. Heard there were some interesting flight maneuvers on the way back. That night I listened to Bob Hope on the radio, Armed Forces Radio, Vietnam. His jokes were as good as ever. I got cramps from laughing.

Only 221 days to go, 73 days to Rest and Relaxation with my wife in Hawaii.

The next evening, I was assigned to fly with Cataldo on the regional flare ship, ready to support wherever necessary. We slept in the afternoon and then, after dark, went to the hangar to stand by. I preflighted the Huey, which was loaded with illumination flares in metal canisters. The rigging of the canisters was checked carefully. There had been one widely known instance of a flare igniting in the cabin of the Huey, which melted prior to hitting the ground, killing all aboard. Flares were to be used over any fire support base under attack. We were prepared to illuminate the perimeter of Camp Evans or any other nearby areas that might come under attack.

Just before midnight, we got a call to go up. There had been enemy contact west of the perimeter at a night defensive position. The only problem was, there was fog and a one hundred foot overcast ceiling, strictly IFR (instrument flight rules) conditions. We cranked up and took off with GCA (ground controlled radar approach) vectors to the location. But the contact had already ended, and the flares were not needed. Cataldo handed the aircraft over to me and said, "Okay, Newbie, make a GCA." Taking the controls, I called the ground-control-approach handler, who directed us to the initial point of entry for a GCA.

The GCA required radar vectors to a final approach

initial point of entry at an altitude of eighteen hundred feet.
The initial point was approximately nine miles from the
runway. According to the instrument approach plate, if you
hit the initial point of entry with a 380-foot-per-minute
descent, you'd break out at the runway numbers. I was
nervous, but full of personal confidence that I could make
the approach. I had recently completed two with Ken
Mayberry in my initial check ride at Quang Tri. I was psy-
ched up to do my best.

The GCA controller called out, "Initial point, begin
descent." I steadied the aircraft as I slowly began a descent of slightly less than four hundred feet per minute.
Throughout the descent, I was able to maintain a correct
magnetic compass heading. Because there was virtually
no wind or turbulence in the fog, I had no crosswind
correction to make. During the descent, GCA called,
"On course, on glide path." Cataldo sat up, lit a cigarette,
looked around, checking everything, and then resumed
his normal slouching posture with a foot on the cabin
vent, smoking a cigarette. I was glued to the instruments
and continued trying to make everything as close as possible. We were literally "in the soup" in a blacked-out
night.

The GCA controller continued repeating, "On course,
slightly below glide path." I slowed the rate of descent
and continued on. The GCA controller called out, "Two
miles to touchdown. On course. On glide path." And then
he began talking continuously, giving "On course. On
glide path." We broke out of the fog at about eighty feet
above the runway. I thought I had done an absolutely perfect ground-controlled radar approach. It was a surreal
accomplishment in my mind; I'd been mentally in the
zone. I had experienced the sensation of being one with
the aircraft, executing control movements perfectly, before I consciously thought of them. Cataldo looked over,
flipped his cigarette out the window, said, "Not bad," and
hovered us back to the Phoenix Nest. I thought to myself,

"Not many people could do it that well." Cataldo was simultaneously thinking, "How many guys can be that lucky?" I felt I'd done it so well that the event had been a "religious experience," virtually no corrections from the ground during the last three miles. The sense of being one, connected with the aircraft and the clouds, is an exhilaration that only pilots can share.

Flew on the twenty-sixth all night long so I had the twenty-seventh off. Slept nearly all day. Had an upset stomach for the first time. Guess I ate too much rich food and goodies from home. Read the best book today, *Love Story,* by Erich Segal. The Phoenix pilots intentionally gave it to the new guys to see if they cried while reading it. Told my wife not to read it on the way to Hawaii. I also had to reexplain my location in letters home. We were about eighty miles north of Da Nang between Hue and Quang Tri at Camp Evans. No, it couldn't be worse. As for the flying, I explained, we did everything, all over northern I Corps from the DMZ to the Laotian border to the A Shau Valley. I didn't tell her of our flights over the fence (west into Laos) and up north into lower North Vietnam.

# 6

# Khe Sanh Revelation

On December 28, 1970, I was again Keith's copilot on CCN at Quang Tri. We were the lunch bird and flew all of the Phoenix pilots from the Special Forces compound to the MACV Compound at Quang Tri, the location of that excellent mess hall.

We had used about twenty minutes of fuel in cranking up, flying the pilots over, and shutting down for lunch. Afterward, we were cranked up again and flew everyone back. When we returned to the CCN pad, we were given an emergency call to pick up Green Berets and Montagnards in Laos. NVA had encircled them, and they were in danger of being overrun but hadn't yet been discovered by the enemy.

The four Phoenix Hueys immediately launched to recover the team. We departed west from Quang Tri, climbing to altitude. On the trip out to extract the Special Forces team in Laos, Keith and I had an inverter failure at six thousand feet, just southeast of the abandoned Khe Sanh combat base. There was no yellow caution light for the inverter and no red warning light for the transmission. The nature of the electrical failure initially indicated a critical loss in transmission oil pressure. The bad part was, we were under communication silence on the radios. We were the last of four aircraft in trail (one behind the other) formation.

After switching to the spare (backup) inverter, there was no change in the instruments. The transmission oil pressure continued downward. Once Keith saw the transmission oil pressure at zero psi, he initiated an immediate precautionary landing. Then, as we touched down, we lost the radios and engine instruments. Mistakenly thinking we were losing the transmission, we had completed an immediate forced landing at the abandoned Khe Sanh air strip. Keith got out with the PRC-10 survival (emergency) radio and tried to make contact with the other members of the flight. Since we were Chalk Four, or the fourth aircraft in a line of four, no one had seen us depart formation. The PRC-10 had a dead battery.

I sat in the cockpit, absorbing a long glance at the bombed-out moonscape, the infamous Khe Sanh combat base. I was sitting a few feet from the ramp where C-130s were destroyed by rocket and mortar fire in March 1968. I'd watched it on the evening news while at Florida State University. With that history in mind, I found myself sitting in the middle of it, in a Huey!

I quickly reviewed the emergency procedures, resetting the electrical buss switches, then circuit breakers, and found out we had no spare inverter. I reset the circuit breakers and recycled the main inverter, which instantly got the electrical system back on line, then rolled the throttle up. Keith heard the turbine engine rev and ran back on board. I was taking off as he strapped in, wanting to get the hell out of there! He asked what I'd found, and I explained the dead spare inverter. I was lucky the main inverter came back on-line after being recycled. We quickly accelerated, climbing until we caught up with the flight, back into the Chalk-Four position.

Nobody had even missed us. But we had used much more fuel at that point. I then realized it was the precise electrical problem I'd gotten my pink slip for in flight school, and the reason for my standards check ride with Mr. Baldwin. Mr. Baldwin's advice to me reverberated in my mind! "Don't get yourself killed over there."

A few minutes later we caught up with the flight after

they'd begun the extraction. We were deep into Laos, at the fuel limit of our Hueys. The pickup zone was southeast of Tchepone, heart of the Ho Chi Minh trail, and close to a place destined to be named LZ Liz.

We made the approach to pick up the last four team members on the ground. It was south of QL9, a major dirt road crossing Laos. Bloody Tchepone, as the air force called it, was a major crossroads of the Ho Chi Minh trail. Our crew chief dropped a rope ladder to pick up the Special Forces team from a fifteen-to-twenty-foot hover. The pickup zone was in the middle of a ghostly gray forest. Dead trees. Fifteen-foot stumps. Their tops blown off years ago. We couldn't hover lower than fifteen or twenty feet. We must have hovered there less than five minutes, but it seemed like hours. The team members were nearly paralyzed, cold and weak from exposure, lying motionless for days near NVA paths. They were suffering from exposure, soaking wet. The crew chief was mad they couldn't climb any faster, shouting, "Hurry!"

As they neared the helicopter bay, they were pulled in by the crew chief and the Green Beret on board. The first Green Beret sat up, made a triangular shape above his head. I knew he was signing that the NVA were closing in. He pointed in their direction and then collapsed into a fetal position, exhausted, shivering on the cargo-bay floor. I told Keith of the warning: "He pointed NVA coming at our seven o'clock."

"Hurry them up!" Keith ordered. As soon as the last two were dragged aboard, we began rapidly climbing. We heard the sounds of nearby antiaircraft artillery shooting at the departing Phoenix birds. *Us!* Nearing fuel starvation, the Redskins had long since departed. The last Phoenix bird out, we quickly passed through three thousand feet. Then the crew chief called on the intercom, "Sir," which instantly terrified Keith and me. They were rowdy, independent enlisted men who generally didn't treat warrant officers with proper military courtesies. He repeated,

"Sir." Another metallic shock through our bodies. "They're still shooting at us." Keith responded, "Bullshit" in disbelief. It was quiet except for the muffled *whompk* of anti-aircraft explosions. Flak. Close enough to clearly hear it above our Huey's noise!

Reflexively, Keith and I glanced at each other, simultaneously thinking, Oh shit! He pulled in more power and slowed the aircraft back. We assumed an even steeper rate of climb to seven thousand feet into the cumulus clouds. The Huey clawed us skyward, redlining engine temperature and torque. All aboard became silent. The crew chief was right. The slow intermittent *whompk* of 57mm flak could still be heard over the normally loud noises of the Huey. We were then jolted by our twenty-minute fuel-low warning illuminating. The flak was a problem we couldn't control. The caution light instantly got our attention. It was a yellow caution light that flashed brightly. It simply meant the engine would die—from fuel exhaustion—in twenty short minutes! I set the movable bezel on my Zodiac diver's watch. We picked up speed and headed directly to Mai Loc. The outpost, which had a refuel point, was soon in sight from our altitude, but we didn't think we'd make it. Keith and I began discussing options, i.e., where to complete an autorotation, considering the aircraft load. An autorotation (a powerless landing) didn't worry us, but the thought of being stranded in Laos absolutely terrified us!

The other three aircraft were not in trouble, since they had not been used as lunch birds and had not landed at Khe Sanh. They still had a twenty-minute reserve. We approached Mai Loc from seventy-five hundred feet in a dive with an angle and speed suitable for autorotation. We landed to a hover directly at the refuel point twenty-two minutes after the caution light illuminated. My hemorrhoids were apopping.

As the crew chief and door gunner began refueling, Keith radioed lead, informing him what had transpired. I collapsed deeply into my seat, beyond exhaustion, thinking, Thank you God, we made it. After refueling, I remarked to Keith, "Next time we're the lunch bird, we will stop and refuel on the way back." "Fuckin' A," he replied. Army helicopter combat operations were an intimate entwining of prayers . . . and expletives.

The day had been an emotionally exhausting, near catastrophic mission. That night, back in the safety of our hootch, Keith and I drank ourselves silly. We had folding aluminum beach chairs on the porch. Elated at having made it back safely, we got to the usual talk as the alcohol took effect.

"Who were the last guys to get killed in this unit?" I asked.

"Lt. Al Finn and a warrant officer, Larry Baldwin," Keith said.

An electric jolt coursed my nervous system, bolting me upward from my seat! "Was Baldwin's dad an instructor pilot at Rucker?"

Keith said, "Yeah, he was so upset about his son's death, he even came over and visited the company. He wanted to fly up and see where they went down. He wanted to understand what had happened. He was distraught.

"Finn was not a very popular lieutenant," Keith said. "Some warrants didn't think he was a very good pilot. Oh, he could fly; some thought he just wasn't natural at it. Baldwin was pretty good for a peter pilot. They were heading north of the DMZ past Charlie Two to insert a Ranger killer team. Nobody saw it up close, so it was written off as an accident. Yet it's the damn DMZ, where .51-cals are everywhere. A Cobra pilot thought Finn took a .51-cal round in his windshield just before they hit the ground . . . at one hundred knots. Everyone was killed instantly."

"You mean they called it a damn accident in the fucking DMZ!"

"Yeah. What do you think?" Keith said.

I was stunned. It was just what happened to Jim Grant in the 4th Infantry Division. Without certain proof of a bird's being shot down, the destruction was blamed on pilot error or mechanical failure. It was also similar to the King Cobra pilot who took flak southwest of Cheo Reo and the safety officer who'd refused to believe it!

In Finn's instance, there was simply no more dangerous place to be flying a helicopter. Finn lost his life, leading by example, flying as aircraft commander on an incredibly risky mission. Like all RLOs, Finn had been subjected to the usual bravado of younger warrant officers. They believed you had to be a warrant to be a real helicopter pilot. Capt. Dave Nelson was the exception among the Phoenix. But he'd served his first tour as a warrant.

Mr. Baldwin's words reverberated in my mind! His son had been flying missions on the DMZ with the Phoenix. I was flying CCN missions with the Phoenix, north of the DMZ. The inverter failure that we had just experienced was the very reason I'd gotten my pink slip in flight school. It was why I met Mr. Baldwin.

The identity of malfunction, mission, and unit was obvious and undeniable. I perceived a choice. It clearly became either fatalistic acceptance, or attempting a change of fate through a transfer out of the unit. I thought to myself, I'm dead. Simply dead!

I related to Keith how I happened to meet Larry Baldwin's father.

Keith was stunned by the story. I was unnerved.

At that point, I knew I was leaving Charlie Company, one way or the other. I would go down to headquarters the next day and reapply for a transfer to a unit I knew had OH-6 (LOH) helicopters in Camp Eagle and needed pilots. I would quietly do my job and duties. However, as Captain Anderson had pointed out, there were ways to move within the Green Machine. If it took an endless series of petitions for transfer, so be it.

I knew my commanding officer would again deny the request, saying I was too valuable to the unit and would be an aircraft commander soon. I would tell him I simply didn't want to fly UH-1s and wanted to get into Loaches or Jet Rangers, where I'd been trained. Haunted by the story of Finn and Baldwin, compounded by my personal experience with Baldwin's dad, I truly believed that if I stayed in the Phoenix, I'd not survive my tour of duty.

I was depressed as hell. I'd discovered fear of one's impending mortality.

Keith went to bed.

I stayed on the back porch, drinking Jim Beam from the bottle.

I awoke the following morning around four A.M., sitting in the aluminum beach chair, puking my guts into my lap. I showered off in icy-cold water, returned to my cubicle, put on fresh clothes, and went out to preflight the aircraft. No longer an acolyte warrior, I was absolutely confirmed, an army puke.

We saddled up, just another day flying CCN with Keith. I woke him on the way into Laos. I got to sleep some coming back. A day of quiet pickups and, luckily, no ground fire. Why they shot everything at us the day before and not the next day, I'd never understand. We had become numbed by the routine, and our incredible good luck. Nothing eventful, just unbelievably lucky. But in the back of my mind flickered constant reminders of WO Larry Baldwin.

That night, I went over to Rick Luken's Redskin hootch and had a couple of Scotches. He was emotionally down, and I was simply exhausted. Then he flipped me the *Army Times* and said, "Have you seen this week's edition?"

I said, "No."

He said, "Well, Avon got it in Pleiku last week." I was hammered with another shock wave of emotion. I had known Avon very well. Avon had been my car-pool buddy, and our wives were good friends. I remembered meeting him at Phu Xuan in September, seeing a picture of his daughter, Tammy. Avon never got to see her. We proceeded to drink until sorrow was drowned.

## December 30, 1970

I had been broke the past few weeks, which kept me out of the officers club bar. Totally penniless until I borrowed twenty dollars from a friend. I wrote home I wasn't working too hard. Still eating lunch at MACV compound in Quang Tri every day and flying CCN. It took one whole bottle of Kaopectate to get over stomach troubles. I couldn't say whether the stomach problem was nerves or bad water. Both miseries were common among the Phoenix. That evening, I was assigned to fly Nighthawk. We would circle the bunker line four hours each night. All-night duty, but we'd get the next day off.

That night, I went to preflight the Nighthawk Huey. It was loaded with a large searchlight and a minigun on mount for the crew chief. Most of the crew chiefs thought this was the greatest fun around. With seventy-two hundred rounds per minute fired through the barrels of an electrically powered Gatling gun, it looked like a golden hose. The searchlight, however, offered the pilots a problem. The bright light destroyed night vision when flying in fog or clouds.

Of course, it was just another foggy night in I Corps, an overcast of fog at about one hundred feet above ground level. A call came to send up the Nighthawk. Mortar fire was suspected from an area south of Camp Evans. As we cranked up and took off, Keith told me to keep monitoring the flight instruments and be prepared to take over for instrument flight, if necessary. I remembered Keith's IFR descent through a cloud bank into Camp Eagle weeks earlier on my first flight with him. I knew it was going to be an interesting night.

Because of the fog and overcast, we could make out no light for visual ground reference. The broad plain between the mountain range to the west and the coastline covered less than ten miles. The mountain foothills began approximately three miles to the west of Camp Evans. Even at a helicopter's cruising speed of eighty knots, you could end up crashing into the fifty-three-hundred-foot-high mountain ridge in less than two minutes thirty seconds. After sunset, the mountain ridge simply vanished into the blackness of night. We could not see the ridge and needed to stay in the low flatlands of the coastal plain. We called GCA to monitor our progress and give us warnings of altitude and terrain clearance. We then headed south along a free-fire zone, south of Camp Evans. Keith was flying, and we would range between fifty and eighty feet above the ground, twenty feet below the ragged overcast ceiling. We were doing sixty to eighty knots, and from time to time, a flock of birds would surface in front of us and blind us with a cloud of white flashing by. I don't know how many we killed with our rotor blades.

Then we were requested to use the searchlight in a specific area to the southwest of Camp Evans. It was much closer to the ridgeline. I was getting nervous: eighty knots airspeed; a pitch-black night; a hundred-foot, ragged overcast ceiling just a few feet above us. I started calling out angles of attitude (pitch of the nose, up or down) and degrees of bank (left or right turn). We had forward landing lights and searchlights on as well as the huge xenon searchlight out the side of our ship. Because we had the landing lights and searchlights on, neither of us had pilot's night vision, the normal sensitivity of the eyes at night was negated by the bright white light. I asked Keith if he was losing visual reference.

Keith said, "No. I'm okay. You just stay ready to take over, but keep watching and calling out."

I was calling out such unusual attitude and bank angles as "Pitch down thirty (degrees), pitch up forty (degrees), left turn twenty-five (degrees), right turn forty (degrees)."

Keith was laughing his ass off. He had a very good sense of where he was and what he was doing in pitch-black night. I was totally uncomfortable flying visual conditions in the blacked-out night on searchlights, him ignoring the flight instruments.

I remained ready to take over the controls on instruments if he said to. After several tense but uneventful minutes, we returned safely. I made a silent prayer that I would never have to fly Nighthawk with him again.

The next morning, meeting with other pilots, someone asked him how I'd done on Nighthawk. Keith said, "It was a little hairy. Marshall was about to load his pants. He kept calling out all these crazy pitch and bank numbers, but they didn't make much sense." I just shook my head in disbelief. I knew what we had done was incredibly risky, only three or four seconds from fatal catastrophe, but Keith took it all in stride. To him it was part of the daily work.

The newest rumor from Rumor Control was a twenty-one-day drop coming for all officers, which might be increased as summer neared. This came from Phu Bai, so there was supposed to be some truth in it.

I continued flying, mostly with Keith, on missions alternating between ash-and-trash around the area of operations and CCN. We flew several engineering missions down to Da Nang. I became reaccustomed to the Huey and finally began to enjoy flying it.

I wrote letters home stating I was glad I had at least tried to get out of the unit and was resigned to accept whatever fate held at that point, with a clear conscience. I would find out later that really shook up my wife. In my own way, I'd faced the beast, fear, and accepted whatever fate would deal me. Emerging from the personal

understanding that death would not be my choice allowed
me a sense of relief from that acceptance.

I pulled from my wallet "A Guide for the New Year." I
had saved it from my hometown church bulletin, the East
Hill Baptist Church, the prior New Year, knowing I was
on my way to Vietnam:

### A Guide for the New Year

Live each day to the fullest. Get the most from each
hour, each day, and each age of your life. Then you
can look forward with confidence, and back without
regrets.

Be yourself—but be your best self. Dare to be different
and to follow your own star.

And don't be afraid to be happy. Enjoy what is beautiful. Love with all your heart and soul. Believe that
those you love, love you.

Forget what you have done for your friends, and remember what they have done for you. Disregard what
the world owes you, and concentrate on what you owe
the world.

When you are faced with a decision, make that decision as wisely as possible—then forget it. The moment
of absolute certainty never arrives.

And above all, remember that God helps those who
help themselves. Act as if everything depended upon
you, and pray as if everything depended upon God.

—S. H. Payer

Amen.

I had New Year's Eve day and night off.

Got all my washing done. Even got to lay around and read some. About 8:00, I went over to the officers club to see what was going on. The New Year's Eve party was under way.

The Redskin pilots were joining the Phoenix pilots in the New Year's Eve celebration. The Redskins were second to none in drinking and hell-raising. One notable Redskin party ended in a pistol-shooting contest among drunks. Ever mindful of aviation and firearm safety, the participants agreed to simple ground rules. Each man would be given one bullet at a time. The contest ended when one round exited the officers club wall, where the target hung, and killed their electric generator and lights.

As I walked into the Phoenix club on New Year's Eve, I saw "Little Shit," the Redskins' company dog, a very small Vietnamese mixed breed. It was walking on the Phoenix bar. The dog was drunk and wobbly, lapping out of any glass sitting on the bar. The music was loud, the voices louder, everything was cloaked in smoke. The stories were incessant, all beginning with "This is no bullshit!" Whoops, hollers, and catcalls sounded as the storytellers continued.

By 9:30, it got worse. Two Redskins were in a contest to see who could eat his *glass* faster. I was getting drunk, but these guys were eating their drinking glasses. One actually finished eating his glass with a bloody smile, to the cheers of onlookers. I thought to myself, time to leave. I had a nightcap and left for my hootch.

## January 1, 1971

During the first week of January, orders came down from division headquarters directing two pilots be transferred from the Phoenix to the 163d Aviation Company, call sign Roadrunners, which flew out of Camp Eagle, the division headquarters. Since I had twice requested a transfer, my name came up. I also had all the qualifications. The Phoenix executive officer approached me outside the hootch. When he asked me if I wanted a slot if it came open, I didn't even hesitate. I instantly replied, "Yes."

Without a word, he spun and hurried on to headquarters. I was left feeling as if I'd quit the varsity high school football team in the midst of the season. I was both relieved and sickened.

Later, word circulated among the Phoenix. I was envied by some, disliked by others. According to most rumors, the 163d was a rear echelon outfit. Flying the OH-6 was very similar to the OH-58. I looked forward to it, praying that fate might let me go.

*January 3, 1971*

> In my sleep,
> death visited,
> not coming to claim,
> but to remind,
> standing in my doorway,
> cloaked in fog and darkness.
> He turned and walked away,
> not me,
> not this time!
> not this war!

I awoke startled. For a moment, I could not discern the void between nightmare and reality.

Later that morning, I very cautiously asked another pilot if he'd had any eerie dreams. He laughed and said, "It was probably the fireguard making his rounds."

I wasn't convinced.

\*   \*   \*

On January 5, Keith and I were flying ash-and-trash resupply missions in the vicinity of firebases Barbara and Sally. Toward the end of the day, we had completed our last drop-off and were headed back to Camp Evans. We were just a mile or two east of the mountain ridgeline, which always had areas of hostile activity. Suddenly, the red fire-warning light flashed on. Keith immediately elected to put the aircraft down on a small, one-lane dirt road in the middle of Indian country. He gave me the controls to set up the approach, then began Mayday calls. We made it on short final to the trail. Keith made the final touchdown and shut the aircraft down. My pitiful little .38 pistol drawn, I jumped out with the crew chief and gunner. Keith stayed on the radio trying to talk to maintenance personnel back at Camp Evans. Within a couple of minutes, I was situated away from the tail of the aircraft, with a fire extinguisher in one hand and my pistol drawn in the other. The crew chief and gunner had opened the engine cowlings looking for fire. There was none.

I suddenly realized I was in the same posture Bruce Finney had been in in the riverbed at An Khe. We were out in the middle of Indian country, and I began to make myself look as small as possible. A few minutes later, a Huey circled and radioed that we were clear of any approaching enemy. About fifteen minutes later, a maintenance bird arrived from Camp Evans with a crew chief on board who had experience with the firelight warning system. It was immobilized. The aircraft was cranked up and inspected for fire damage. There was none, so we hopped back in and flew it home. It had been an unsettling experience. In an army helicopter, a red warning light means "land now," not in one or two minutes but *now*. We were relieved that it had only been a warning-light malfunction.

I was still trying to get transferred to any unit with OH-6s or 58s. I'd found an open slot in a VIP unit at Hue but my commanding officer decided I was too valuable to release. So that ended it. In a way, I was relieved that there was no chance of transfer. I could finally accept the Phoenix as home.

That evening, I found out a friend had been killed Stateside, in a car wreck. Bruce Horton, at Fort Bragg. Really shook me to hear that. He had been a crew chief for one tour in Vietnam, then entered the warrant officer program. Having survived a tour in a slick only to die in a car accident! Heard it from Richard King in A Company (A/158 Ghostriders). They shared our mess hall. He also told me that Pete D'Agostino, from Pensacola, was in B Company (B/158, Lancers).

I began to realize how Vietnam had changed my taste. I'd eat bologna and cheese on a hamburger bun, plain, and it tasted good. It was the only sandwich we could get. Usually available about three days a week if they were brought up from Phu Bai. Any time we got near a PX at Hue or Quang Tri, we stocked up. I'd eat one meal a day when possible, then have a Coke and some type of canned food in the evening. There wasn't time for anything else.

It was surprisingly cold. Stayed in the low sixties most of the day, middle fifties at night. Lots of people were using heaters and electric blankets. I wore long underwear all day and night.

I was still dreaming of R & R. Only two short months. Everyone coming back from Stateside leave said it was really bad. They said coming back from the United States was even worse than coming over the first time. But people coming back from Hawaii said it wasn't really too bad to come back.

## January 6, 1971

I had to explain in a letter to my wife that there were no Vietnamese women at Camp Evans. No hootch maids or anything. She had complained about the photograph of my Phoenix hootch with assorted ladies undergarments hung on the wall.

In the letter I'd just received, she told me that a guy had been trying to get to know her between classes at the University of West Florida. She was finishing her senior year. She told him I was a Cobra pilot, to encourage him to leave her alone. I was pissed! What I was doing was more dangerous than a Cobra pilot!

Then her letter continued with the most shocking news. David Anderson, commander of the airfield company at Fort Rucker, had been killed in an aircraft accident. On an instrument flight mission, he had apparently flown a Huey into a mountain in Kentucky. The very man who'd encouraged me to go voluntary indefinite and get the OH-58 transition, and initiated me in the ways of the Green Machine, was dead.

January 9, another CCN mission. Again, it was going to be a hot extraction. An SOG team in Laos was in the middle of North Vietnamese activity as they'd landed in an NVA bivouac area. They were totally encircled and had been on the ground longer than normal, six days lying motionless, totally encircled by a North Vietnamese unit whose men were moving and sleeping only a few feet from the concealed Green Berets. In an effort to draw attention away from the helicopter extraction of the team members, a series of explosive simulators was going to be dropped nearby. They would simulate firefights with other teams.

Prior to the string extraction, Keith and I were designated as one of the two birds to drop off the simulators. The only problem was, the area where we were going to drop the simulators was next to a known 37mm antiaircraft position on QL9, the two-lane road that ran from Quang Tri to Tchepone, Laos. Well, that was unsettling news. A little while later, we were instructed to drop the simulators westbound and then to make a left turn away from the highway. An air force jet bombed the 37mm, and it was "believed" to be destroyed. However, we knew that there were active antiaircraft artillery and heavy machine guns all along QL9. We were cautioned not to cross the road to the north.

Keith was selected to be the lead for the simulator drop. During our descent into the area, I could see the bombed-out 37mm position, and photographed it. I was permitted to fly the Huey in, coming to a low hover over a field of grass and reeds, just south of the highway. As we came to a hover, the Green Beret in the back of our helicopter threw out the simulator and yelled "Go!" We immediately made a high-speed climb with every ounce of power available.

We then initiated a steep, left-hand turn, trying to get above twenty-five hundred feet altitude as quickly as possible, while heading south from the road.

The second aircraft dropping a simulator was piloted by WO Rick Scrugham. He came in and dropped his simulator off. During his turn and climb, he became distracted by ground fire and continued his turn all the way around to cross *north* of QL9. As he crossed the highway, the sky lit up with green and gold tracers. Keith had me flying while he lit a cigarette. He said, "Did you see that?" "Yeah," I laughed. Keith said, "Well, watch this." Knowing what was about to happen, we both cracked up laughing.

We were safely climbing through three thousand feet, yukking it up. Keith was giving a Howard Cosell sports-like commentary of the event. Scrugham was back down on the treetops, making a U-turn a mile north of the road. He had to cross the road again, knowing that everyone in the world was going to be shooting at him, so he kept it low and hauled ass due south, right across the road. Again, the sky lit up, green and gold tracers arcing above him, but they missed. He continued climbing out, heading south. Even the platoon leader ragged him on the radio.

The Special Forces team was successfully extracted without wounds to the men or damage to the aircraft. We had witnessed a minor mistake, which could have become a fatal one. Rick Scrugham was experienced, and successfully worked it out safely. The phrase "watch this" meant "get your camera and be glad it's not you!" The phrase was a lasting joke among the Phoenix, and many other army pilots. It was going to be another very drunk night in the club, but this time in Da Nang at the Special Forces compound.

On January 14, Paul Stewart returned from Stateside leave. He had finished eleven months of a one-year tour with the Phoenix Company, call sign Phoenix Two-two. He was regarded by the Phoenix pilots as one of the most capable and skilled aircraft commanders in Vietnam. He was the standardization instructor pilot for 1st Platoon.

Stewart was Mr. Cool under fire. He had experienced everything that occurred in 1970, including numerous unnamed extractions in hot landing zones, along with the evacuation of firebases Ripcord, O'Reilley, and countless CCN missions. He could make the Huey do things less skilled pilots dreamed of.

Most importantly, if you went down, he'd come get you, no matter what.

I'd been on CCN since the first of December and was damned happy to have survived unscathed. Stewart had reupped for another six months and taken a thirty-day Stateside leave. The extension was canceled during his leave; the 101st Airborne had reached 150 percent of officer strength. Warrant officers who weren't voluntary indefinite, like me, were being released by the army after DEROS. Stewart had returned to work off his thirty-day leave, ending February 14, 1971. I couldn't believe he wanted another six months with the Phoenix!

Captain Hunt, the company executive officer, asked Stewart, the senior warrant officer in 1st Platoon, to talk with me to see if I would rescind my request for transfer. Stewart came into my hootch space and said, "Marshall, let's have a talk." I said, "Okay, let's go out back." It was a nice, clear, sunshiny day, which we were not used to. Behind the back porch of our hootch, I sat down on sandbags.

Stewart propped a foot on the sandbags, hands clasped, resting on a leg. He began expounding the virtues of flying a slick. The joys of successfully completing missions. The difficulty of accomplishing those jobs safely. He reminded me how important we were to the grunts. He talked of the importance of the missions, not to mention the excitement of CAs and of CCN in Laos and up north. He asked why I wasn't satisfied flying slicks with the Phoenix.

I looked up. "Hey, I went voluntary indefinite to fly 58s. I've got three months in-country time in 58s. I pledged myself voluntary indefinite and I feel like that's a contract with the army. The army owes me staying in 58s the rest of this tour. I enjoyed single-ship missions. I like flying reconnaissance, artillery spotting. I simply don't like having my ass sitting there (in the right seat of a Huey) like a pigeon in a shooting gallery."

Stewart shook his head. With one leg propped on the sandbags and his hands clasped together, he looked at me and slowly said, "I don't understand why you don't appreciate what we do. The grunts can't get along without us. Flying slicks is one of the most important things happening. It's the most enjoyable thing I've ever done in my life. I love it. Hell, I'll probably die driving a slick."

Stewart's bravado was wasted on me. I was young, disillusioned, and apprehensive. I looked at Stewart and thought to myself, This conversation is over.

"Well," I replied, "I don't share your feelings. I want

out, into any company with Loaches or 58s. I want my transfer request remaining in effect until I'm transferred out."

Stewart said, "Well, you take care of number one, but I think you're gonna miss a lot."

With that, we parted. No handshakes, no pats on the back.

There was a simple, but absolute, disagreement. I didn't tell him the CCN story with Keith or my knowledge of Finn and Baldwin. I withheld it, afraid to expose the magnitude of my fear. It was my personal revelation. I didn't expect others to understand it. Stewart would be dead in less than four weeks, driving a slick into Laos. He would have gone home only six days later, had he survived.

Later, I had twinges of guilt until I reverted to the thoughts of Mr. Baldwin and his son. But I mentally compartmented it. Whatever burden I had to carry mentally, I was leaving the company if the opportunity arose.

January 15 was a beautiful day, "field grade" weather. No clouds, limitless visibility, flew five thousand feet above Camp Evans. You could see the DMZ to the north, North Vietnam, and Laos. The mountains were beautiful. The bad news was that 1st Platoon got the old shaft from 101st Aviation Group headquarters again. We were supposed to have the next thirty days at Quang Tri with a much easier mission, supporting the 1st Battalion of the 5th Mechanized Infantry Division. What we got was an extension on Command and Control North. The Special Forces for another fifteen days. Screwed again! That made it six weeks for the 1st Platoon; seven weeks for me personally, since I started with 2d Platoon. I guess since we hadn't taken hits or losses, we could stand it till something happened. The way the commanders kept us on CCN, we must have been pretty good at it. I knew we were appreciated by the guys we picked up in Laos and North Vietnam. We'd only been doing extractions, not insertions, and extractions were definitely the more risky of the two.

I would understand years later; the Phoenix were being groomed to lead the Laotian invasion. In extracting Special Forces teams along the Ho Chi Minh trail, they were being familiarized with the future landing zones in Laos.

In less than thirty days, I would be over the hump and would have only twenty days until R & R. It was really funny how you'd start thinking like that. At times, it really got involved, counting down the days of one eternal year.

Got a new guy in company January 15, a West Pointer no less. Capt. Don Davis was a nice guy for an RLO (real live officer). In my opinion, he was getting the Green Weenie as bad as the rest of us.

I didn't know he'd actually requested the 101st Airborne!

### January 18, 1971, The White House, Washington, D.C.

President Richard Nixon finally approved the operation details for LAM SON 719. It required the reopening of the Khe Sanh firebase and airfield, along with American aviation support of an ARVN invasion into Laos. The Laotian invasion was reportedly an event of American parentage. Gen. Creighton Abrams had proposed the operation to Henry Kissinger, who approved it and passed it through the Joint Chiefs of Staff and the secretary of defense, who also approved it. They then passed it through the president, who ordered it carried out. After the operation concluded, everybody except Abrams would deny responsibility for the concept and the results of the operation. The greatest test, ever, of army-airmobile operational capacity and endurance was about to commence. The helicopter air crews would write a new chapter in military history.

On January 20, a dream came true, and a prayer was answered. I was transferred to the 163d Aviation Company at Camp Eagle, a VIP unit and about the best job in Vietnam or the 101st Airborne Division. I was told to move the next day. I'd be flying a slick (UH-1H, Huey) there for a month or two and then transitioning to an OH-6 (Loach). It would be much more enjoyable, easier, and the safest possible job. There were some really jealous guys in the Phoenix. A lot of people wanted a job there. I started packing and gave away a bunch of stuff, including khakis, to Rick Scrugham. I asked him to hold my mail for me. I had two duffel bags, a refrigerator, fan, laundry bag, and bedroll to move.

I admired and respected the aircraft commanders I'd flown with in Phoenix. They accepted their duty, in the most dangerous active area of operations in Vietnam. The Phoenix pilots performed their jobs with an intensely competitive attitude; you had to be at your best to overcome the mission risks of northern I Corps. The mountain pads, sling missions, fog, instrument conditions, overworked aircraft and maintenance personnel created a dangerous environment. Yet crews remained ready to answer an emergency call anytime, supporting the 101st Airborne Division and Special Forces anywhere. Even so, for the first time in two months, I was a very happy man. I was renewed in my faith, confident that I would be alive at the end of my tour.

## January 20, 1971, Stateside

Letter from Angie Franklin in Anderson, South Carolina, to my wife, Pat Marshall, in Pensacola, Florida:

January 20, 1971

Dear Pat:

Only a short letter to tell you the sad news if you don't
already know. Avon was killed 19th of December and
buried 29th December. I found out last Saturday when
I read it in the *Army Times*. I talked with Faye last night
but I don't know any of the details. Faye is taking it
pretty good. He never even got to see Tammy. I'll tell
you more when I find out. Faye may come up and
spend a few days with me next month. We had a wonderful R and R. Corky looked great of course and was
overwhelmed with Scott. We only have 113 days in this
terribly lonely year left. I guess you are trying to stay
busy in school. Scott really keeps me happy. He weighs
15 pounds now and is 25 inches tall and has one tooth.
Faye said Tammy had eight teeth and she is only two
days older than Scott. Hawaii was beautiful and you
thoroughly enjoy it. I'm watching *Hawaii Five-O* now
and I enjoy seeing some of the sights I saw in person
last month. Send Tommy my regards and write soon.

Angie

## January 21, 1971

In the maintenance bird, CW2 Dave Wolfe flew me
down to Camp Eagle and my new unit. I had just received
my box of goods from An Khe the week before. I personally pushed the box on a dolly from my hootch to the
aircraft at Camp Evans. At Camp Eagle, in the land of
REMFs, I had an enlisted man carry the box to my new
hootch area. I was temporarily asigned a room that had a
nice bed and a mattress with springs. No more sleeping
bag! The guy who lived there was on R & R in Taiwan.

There was an adjacent large room with several bunks where several warrant officers stayed. They were quite rowdy, drinking heavily and singing country songs when I arrived.

From then on, my address would be the 163d Aviation Company, General Support Air Mobile, 101st Airborne Division, APO, San Francisco, CA 96383. I was told I'd be doing nothing but flying VIPs—no combat assaults, resupplies, or anything else. Our Hueys carried colonels and generals. When I got an OH-6A, I'd have to carry majors. For all practical purposes, I thought, the war was over for me. I'd be flying very high in a new aircraft.

However, the entire war was about to start all over, and I would be very much a part of it!

# 7

# Woodstock One-Three

*Bear Cat.* The Cambodian border with Vietnam was monitored by the CCN equivalent of CCS, Combat Command South. The 1st Special Forces were rappelling into a drop zone, attempting to recover a downed Loach crew. WO William Seaborn was piloting the UH-1. It took heavy ground fire, flipped upside down, crashed, and burned. Another casualty for WORWAC, Class 70-3/70-5.

Camp Eagle, the headquarters of the 101st Airborne Division, Airmobile, was located south of Hue. I'd just transferred into the 163d Aviation Company in the 101st Aviation Group.

The OH-6A Cayuse (called "Loach" after the acronym for light observation helicopter, LOH) was a small, four-seat observation helicopter, the safest in the army inventory. On the evening of January 24, 1971, the commanding officer called the pilots to the officers club for a company meeting. Orders had come down to change the radio call sign Roadrunner to a new name.

The 163d was considered a company of rear echelon motherfuckers by combatants. It served VIPs and provided courier service to the headquarters of the 101st Airborne Division and other commands attached to it. By virtue of the missions and rank of their passengers, it was a privilege to be given a slot in the company. As the new guy, I quietly sat in the officers club listening to the banter and BSing going on among pilots. All were combat vet-

erans. Most had served honorably in other assault helicopter companies prior to joining the 163d.

I was just beginning to meet the other Loach pilots.
WO Jim Saunders was short. The son of an admiral, with
experience in Hueys, he'd been shot down on Firebase
Ripcord and shot up around O'Reilley. Baby San was by
then a conscientious objector who'd flown Cobras at Camp
Evans. He had been transferred south after giving the
bunker line guards permission to open fire, killing a GI
high on heroin who was trying to sneak back into the
perimeter. The bunker guards mistakenly assumed he was
an NVA or VC attempting to penetrate the wire.

Capt. Bill Gordy, the standards instructor pilot in the
company, was the top Loach pilot, having the most hours
in it. He was a second-tour pilot, having been a warrant
officer during his first tour. From Pottstown, Pennsyl-
vania, and Amish, he had a distinctly conservative, but
friendly, attitude about him. He was not a heavy drinker
like everyone else. However, he hadn't gotten to know me
yet, and his second tour of duty hadn't turned "hot."

The others included warrant officers who'd been with
the Kingsmen and other units. With the tragic exception
of Baby San, most people were shipped to the 163d Aviation Company as a reward for having served well in other
companies. It was as good a job and living conditions as
you'd find in I Corps. My record of service in the 4th
Infantry, coupled with the fact I'd gone voluntary indefinite, got me the job. Two months with the Phoenix assured
my intimate familiarization with the area of operations.

WO Stephan Cobb was also flying Loaches. He had
been a copilot in a Kingsmen bird involved in a midair
collision. On my first flight with Keith, when we had
joined up in formation with another Phoenix bird, a lieutenant colonel had objected to the formation flying. Keith
cussed and then backed off into a loose trail formation.
He then told me about the Kingsmen midair. In my eyes,
Cobb was a well-known survivor of a near fatal crash.

Cobb had been the copilot of the lead bird in a Kingsmen formation of two Hueys that meshed rotor blades. He flew the aircraft to the ground at high speed with no pitch control. In an effort to maintain the integrity of the cabin in the crash, he kept a high forward rate of speed and slid into a rice paddy. Without the benefit of collective or pitch force to reduce the impact, he, in a sense, glided it on, and it slid to a muddy stop. His quick thinking had saved their lives, but the colonels on board both aircraft, though uninjured, were entirely pissed. That became the end of formation flying in the 101st Aviation Group and, consequently, with the 158th Aviation Battalion, unless it was a troop move (a tactical need). Cobb was a white-headed kid from California. He had been employed at Edwards Air Force Base as a civilian technical rep repairing aircraft before he received his draft notice. Facing the draft, he decided it was better to go ahead and volunteer to fly army helicopters than to walk the jungles as a draftee.

I met the warrant officer I was replacing, Bruce Bender, from New Jersey. His Roadrunner call sign was One-three, 13. That was to be my call sign since I was his turtle, i.e., the man replacing him in the aviation lineup.

Bender warned me to be careful in the Rock Pile area, where we frequently carried couriers to outposts along the DMZ. Two rounds from an AK had left holes in the windshield that would serve as daily reminders for me.

Bender had the distinction of being the only pilot I had known in Vietnam who had been hijacked. An infantryman who was high on drugs jumped into his Loach at a firebase on the east side of the A Shau Valley. He put a pistol to Bender's head and said, "Take me to Saigon." Bender lifted off and took the guy flying. Bender got to talking with him and eventually convinced him to hand over the pistol without hurting him, even though the commanding officer of the man kept radioing Bender to take his own pistol and shoot the GI. As they were running out of fuel, Bender radioed to have psychiatrists and MPs waiting. While they refueled the aircraft, the guy was subdued without injury. He just wanted to go home.

Obviously, it was not only a crazy environment; there really were crazies out there besides the young warrant officers.

Earlier that night, we'd watched the movie *Woodstock*, seeing the bands, group love-ins and other festivities at the 1969 Woodstock festival. Watching Woodstock under starry skies of the Nam, after six months of being a nun (none) didn't help our attitudes about the Green Machine or Vietnamization. It looked to us as if the war had simply been declared over, not won or lost. Orders had come down that the Roadrunner call sign would be changed as part of the normal communication procedures, and several captains got into the discussion of proposed call signs. A number of call signs were offered and booed or cursed down. Baby San came up with the idea of using that little yellow bird from the *Peanuts* cartoon strip. "What's the name?"

For a minute, no one could think of the bird's name. Then everyone started cracking up, laughing and cursing, when all of a sudden, someone blurted, "Woodstock!" Woodstock was a perfect double entendre, well suited to our declining attitudes about the war. The company commander approved it, thinking of the little yellow bird. It was an appropriate call sign for helicopters carrying around rear echelon motherfuckers, as well as the 101st Airborne Division brass. The pilots embraced the new call sign, fantasizing about the orgies we'd just seen in the movie of the 1969 Woodstock festival.

Meanwhile, the withdrawal of units down south was accelerating. It looked as if the war really was ending, quickly. There hadn't been any significant military action in I Corps since Ripcord the previous summer. There was only combat when it was initiated by American or ARVN patrols; the NVA were lying low or had retreated back into Laos.

Our new call sign became a way of complying with the Green Machine while expressing our personal dissatisfaction with the general trend of things. From that day forward, I was Woodstock One-three. To me, Woodstock One-three was a perfectly acceptable call sign and number. I believed thirteen a lucky number for me. I found it in a bubblegum wrapper one day when I was six years old, and the fortune in my gum wrapper said thirteen was my lucky number. Since it coincidentally matched the August 13 wedding date of my parents, that was totally acceptable to me. Then I remembered the series of thirteens on the day of my check ride, one year earlier, with Mr. Baldwin. The same familiar chill hit, but it was awareness, not fear.

I'd been haunted by Larry Baldwin's loss with the Phoenix, so Woodstock One-three was an absolutely joyous appointment.

With the matter of the call sign resolved, the drinking continued along with the war stories. The conversation revolved around pullouts of American units, early outs for warrant officers not making the army a career, and the possibility of twelve-month tours of duty being shortened to accelerate the withdrawal of troops. It was a festive, jubilant atmosphere. The consensus was the damn war was over and life was great in a REMF unit.

However, Gen. Creighton Abrams and President Nixon had different plans. They would issue orders starting the whole damned war over. It would resume with the reopening of the infamous Khe Sanh combat base. From Khe Sanh, helicopters would fly deep into the heart of the Ho Chi Minh trail, Tchepone, Laos. The air force called it Bloody Tchepone because of its jet bomber losses there. What was bloody for five-hundred-mile-per-hour air force jets, would be worse, much worse, for Hueys operating at less than one hundred miles per hour. Army pilots, veterans of the Laotian invasion, would simply call it a nut wringer.

Within fourteen days, the 101st Airborne, supported by helicopter companies from down south of Da Nang, would move eight thousand South Vietnamese (ARVN) troops into Laos and support them for forty-five days.

Six hundred fifty-nine helicopters would be assigned to the operation.

Four hundred forty-four helicopters would be shot down. Losses would be heavy. Seventy-two pilots and crewmen would be killed or missing; 193 would be seriously wounded. American casualties, including ground forces, would total 1,402. 215 would be killed in action in forty-five days.

Of thirty in the room with me, most would take anti-aircraft fire during the next forty-five days. Many would take hits to their aircraft.

One pilot would be shot down and evacuated to the States with compression of the spine and burn injuries. Another pilot would narrowly miss losing his life, avoiding a midair collision but totaling his helicopter.

Two pilots would be shot down in Laos, amazingly without injury to crew or passengers. I would take rocket-propelled grenade fragmentation and AK-47 hits to my OH-6A.

Compared to the men of assault helicopter companies, we were to become the truly fortunate sons.

### January 25, 1971, Phoenix Nest, Camp Evans

Don Davis, a captain newly assigned to Charlie Company, spent the day flying ash-and-trash missions with WO Dean Grau. Because Grau was not yet an aircraft commander, but a first pilot, Davis had his first experience of flying in the left seat of the Huey. By the end of the day, Davis was assigned to fly as copilot on the Nighthawk aircraft with WO Don Mears, who was also flying as a right-seat first pilot. It was Davis's sixth day of flying missions with the Phoenix. He had never met Mears before the Nighthawk mission. The weather had been marginal all day. Even helicopters could be grounded by the winter monsoon of northern I Corps.

Late that afternoon, after a long day flying with Grau, Davis was preflighting the Nighthawk gunship. Capt. Dave Nelson came running up to Davis and asked if he could borrow Davis's chicken-plate chest armor. Nelson's was in another aircraft that had departed, and he had been called to take four aircraft up to Quang Tri where CCN had declared an emergency. Davis told Nelson he was flying Nighthawk that night. Nelson responded, "You don't need a chicken plate for Nighthawk. I definitely need it for CCN." Davis was new to the Phoenix, but he trusted Nelson, a highly respected platoon leader. So Davis loaned Nelson his chicken-plate vest.

Late that evening, about 11:30 P.M., a sniper team reported movement around them. The Nighthawk was called. Davis rode in the left seat; this was his first experience night-flying from the Huey's left seat. They departed with Warrant Officer Mears piloting. As they climbed out of Camp Evans, the weather became extremely poor. They headed toward the first ridgeline beyond Fire Support Base Jack. Mears, flying the aircraft, was between three and four hundred feet above ground level. He started going in and out of low-lying scud and banks of fog. Mears developed a condition known as vertigo, where the inner ear deceives the mind and provides incorrect balance and sensitivity information. When this happens, the senses contradict what the eyes report to the brain from the aircraft instrumentation, and the feel of the aircraft in the seat of the pants is wrong. Mears feared he was entering a catastrophic climb or roll and immediately told Davis, "Get on, take over on instruments!" Davis took the controls and descended them back out of the scud to marginal visual conditions.

After a few moments, Mears said he was okay and took

the controls back. Within another few seconds, he was back into a solid bank of fog. Again, he had Davis take the controls back to get them back to VFR (visual flight rules).

As they approached the mountain ridgeline, the cycle of in-and-out of the clouds continued. When Davis took the controls the fourth time, he found himself rising in a very fast updraft, as if the helicopter were being sucked into the sky.

They were climbing at close to fifteen hundred feet per minute. Davis reduced collective to flat pitch, no power, but the Huey continued to climb, obviously in mountain turbulence. They eventually leveled off between three thousand and three thousand five hundred feet. Mears then called Evans's ground-control-approach radar operators, who had been monitoring their progress. Mears asked them for an immediate ground-controlled radar approach back to Evans. Mears told Davis to continue flying; Mears was still screwed up by vertigo. The GCA controller instructed Davis to make right turns to get away from the mountains. Controlling the aircraft in a coordinated right turn for the first time was difficult from the left seat, and Davis sensed something was wrong with the controls. He suspected that something might have broken or overstressed during the turbulence that drew them up two thousand feet.

His task was complicated by the fatigue of having flown all day without sleep prior to the 11:30 P.M. Nighthawk mission. The difficulty was further intensified by the fact that the small attitude indicator for copilots in the left seat was not the full-size flight instrument in the right pilot seat, which Davis was accustomed to.

The elements of a tragic helicopter accident synergized, precipitating a crash. Davis was flying the Huey's left seat for the first day in two years of aviation experience. Unfamiliar seating, mountain turbulence, soupy fog, and his pilot in vertigo all entwined to make for a desperate situation! Davis continued flying instruments from the left seat. Eventually, GCA started giving him left turns and things were working well until they hit turbulence so severe that Davis lost control, and they descended from three thousand four hundred feet to two thousand six hundred feet.

Mears recovered from his vertigo and attempted to get control of the aircraft but to no avail, so he told Davis to take it back. Davis assumed the controls again, but by then, he'd also entered vertigo.

In an incredible few seconds, the nose of the Huey fell, inverted, from the clouds only four hundred feet above the ground. Mears glimpsed the lights of Camp Evans and saw they were upside down. With visual reference points to aid him, he resumed the controls, trying to correct the steep bank just prior to impact in a rice paddy.

They rolled sideways, throwing the rotor blades, engine, and transmission from the aircraft. The aircraft rolled at least once and possibly three times. The combination of actions between the pilot and copilot had narrowly avoided the ultimate catastrophe of death. It was an experience that neither one could believe and neither would ever forget.

For nearly ten minutes after the crash, Mears tried with the crew chief and gunner to free Davis, who was trapped in his seat. Davis was compressed down by the collapsed roof of the Huey. He could only take about a quarter of a normal breath in that position. At that point, Davis realized Dave Nelson had actually saved his life, because if Davis had been wearing the chicken plate, it would have crushed his larynx and probably killed him. Mears would find out later that he had serious spinal compression and would be hospitalized for it.

It was a horrible incident of night flying, complicated by fatigue, unfamiliar pilot seating, mountain turbulence, and pea-soup fog. All in all, it was an experience the crew would have preferred not to have participated in.

Shocked, Davis was slowly assimilating what he'd survived. He'd been in country less than three weeks. His Nighthawk mission had nearly ended as I had feared mine would when I'd flown it with Keith the previous month. They were damn lucky to be alive! The gunner, PFC John Robertson, was also thankful to have survived. But he'd be dead with CW2 Paul Stewart in eleven short days.

## January 25, 1971, Camp Eagle

Unknown to us, Operation LAM SON 719 had commenced. It was the largest airborne invasion since 1944, against an equally well prepared foe but one with superior intelligence. The first phase of the operation was an American operation known as DEWEY CANYON II, which was designed to make QL9, the single-lane dirt road, usable for military traffic from Quang Tri to Laos.

In the predawn darkness on January 30, the 1st Brigade, 5th Mechanized Infantry Division, from Quang Tri, moved an armored cavalry and engineer task force on the road to Khe Sanh. Simultaneously, the operation to lift equipment, materials, and the men necessary was beginning. I was a last-minute substitute copilot in the command-and-control aircraft (Huey) coordinating the CH-54 Skycranes and CH-47 Chinooks that were carrying men and materials to the reactivated Firebase Vandegrift south of the Rock Pile, midway between Khe Sanh and Quang Tri. A major combat assault was under way. Although we suspected one, we did not know that an invasion of Laos was imminent.

At first light, simultaneous combat assaults were conducted by combat engineers on the abandoned Khe Sanh airfield and a critical river crossing named Bridge 34. Two engineer platoons with two dozers, four three-quarter ton trucks, and a radio jeep were lifted by helicopter to Bridge 34.

Huey crews combat assaulting security troops onto

Khe Sanh were pleasantly surprised to find a Welcome to Khe Sanh sign awaiting them. It was from the Phoenix, C Company, 158th Aviation Battalion, 101st Airborne Division. WO John Michaelson and his crew had placed it there the night before.

Ninety-seven medium- and heavy-helicopter sorties were flown by army and Marine helicopters from Mai Loc to road positions along Quang Tri valley and the Khe Sanh plateau. From the moment engineers landed at Khe Sanh, around-the-clock work continued to construct a thirty-two-hundred-foot C-130 cargo strip.

I enjoyed flying as copilot in the command-and-control Huey carrying the air mission commander of the heavy-lift helicopter battalion as our passenger. The Chinooks and Skycranes were carrying bridge pieces from Mai Loc to bridge points along the QL9 Highway from Vandegrift to Khe Sanh.

It was an amazing feat to have an armed convoy heading westward, having bridges placed in front of them by Chinooks and Skycranes, barely slowing the mechanized infantry march westward to the Khe Sanh plateau.

My aircraft commander was a Hawaiian Airlines jet pilot who'd been drafted and was nearing the end of his tour. Unlike crew attitudes on a typical Phoenix mission, he was relaxed, even happy. He had me do most of the flying, which was essentially circling at two thousand five hundred feet while the colonels and majors in the back observed the progress of the bridge installations on QL9. It was a very interesting day to observe the operation and know the magnitude of what was going on. It was exciting to be a part of a very large military move.

# 8

# LAM SON

## February 3, 1971

It felt like they'd started the whole damn war over
again. I got twenty hours in a Huey over three days. The
R & R dates came down, and mine was to start March 19.
I was scheduled to arrive at Honolulu between 2:00 and
4:30 P.M.

I spent the day as copilot in a slick while we ferried
General Phu around. He went to college in the United
States and had virtually no accent. We flew him to Dong
Ha and Quang Tri. There were more aircraft up there than
I'd ever seen at one place. Quang Tri was said to be the
busiest airport in the hemisphere.

## February 4, 1971

Combat engineers had worked nonstop since January 31,
when they combat assaulted into Khe Sanh. In spite of
rain, fog, mud, and fifty-five-degree nights, they cleared
the bunkers and minefields left by the Marines in 1968.
Four D-7E bulldozers were destroyed in minefield clearing operations. The Khe Sanh airfield, consisting of a native
red clay base, XM-19 matting, and aluminum mat over-
lay, received its first four-engine transport, an air force
C-130. It had become an active combat-assault airfield.
The engineers also completed construction of a helicopter

tactical refueling area, capable of fueling thirty-eight helicopters at one time. It had a 260,000-gallon capacity.

The heavy helicopter lift, which permitted engineers to reopen both the road and airfield at Khe Sanh, was overwhelmingly successful. Four hundred twenty-five tons of equipment and supplies were moved without accident, injury, damage, or loss on January 31. It was the most ambitious engineer airlift to that date in the war's history. Khe Sanh had become an operational airfield. In the coming weeks new records would continue to be set by the pilots and crews operating out of Khe Sanh, but few would be set by choice or design.

## Camp Evans

A company meeting for the Phoenix officers had been called. Word was it would be a very serious meeting of the highest importance.

Maj. Jim Lloyd had only become the company commander two weeks earlier after a short term with the Redskins. He'd flown all types of airplanes in his career but he'd only finished the rotary wing qualification course for fixed-wing aviators in the past year. In his Stateside home, only a few months earlier, he'd received a call from a superior to notify him of his assignment to Vietnam. Lloyd knew the receding war effort meant enormous uncertainties for those in country.

That evening, Jim Lloyd told his story to the officers of the Phoenix. Laos was to be invaded by eight thousand ARVN troops. The Phoenix would lead the way. Concluding, he said, "I'll be there with you all the way, in the left front seat of the lead aircraft!"

The Phoenix had led the evacuation under fire from Ripcord the preceding July. Most of its officers were very experienced in Laos by virtue of CCN missions, picking up Green Beret teams under fire. Now they'd lead the largest helicopter assault ever staged. The CCN missions into Laos since November had been their training missions. They'd lived their lessons well. But Laos would claim its place in military history as Helicopter Hell.

WO Dean Grau, a Phoenix aircraft commander, was the son of a World War II bomber veteran who'd served over Europe. His father survived the worst of the European air campaign. Grau was to continue a family tradition of service, in the worst antiaircraft fire in helicopter history. WO Ricky Scrugham was the son of a C-47 pilot in World War II. He also continued his family's tradition of service.

### February 8, 1971

At seven A.M. on a foggy morning, the assault across the fence into Laos began. It followed massive B-52 strikes and artillery bombardment. The South Vietnamese armored division used the old French road QL9 to head westward, and American scout helicopter teams with gunships were destroying anything in sight. Because of the Special Forces experience with CCN, the 101st Aviation Group birds, including gunships from the Redskins and others at Eagle and Phu Bai, knew what to look for. The initial assault by the air cavalry elements was an overwhelming success.

Helicopters of the 158th Aviation Battalion, led by the Phoenix, carried paratroopers of the ARVN airborne division to their landing zones. There had been little antiaircraft fire and no losses during the initial phase in the morning hours. The second wave of flights continued shortly after noon.

The air cavalry units ranged widely. They inflicted massive damage on staging depots, antiaircraft sites, and troop columns. The North Vietnamese had a sophisticated, radar-guided antiaircraft system, which was mobile and accurate.

However, the low-flying attack helicopters, with Loaches designating targets, were highly effective. By the end of the day, the 101st's 2d Squadron, 17th Cavalry was fighting so many Soviet tanks that it was running out of ammunition before it could strike them all.

That afternoon, Kingsman One-eight Al Fischer (B/101st AHB) had a cassette recorder in his aircraft, Chalk Two-two in a thirty-ship formation into Laos. His crew chief, Joe Kline, had a panoramic view of the move under way. Capt. David Nelson, the 2d Platoon leader, was with Maj. Jim Lloyd, the Phoenix commanding officer. They were the lead, Chalk One, call sign Auction Six-five.

CW2 Paul Stewart was in the final week of his one-month extended tour with the Phoenix. The afternoon combat assault was the third major move the Phoenix had been involved in that day. Stewart was piloting Chalk Three, the third aircraft in the line of thirty helicopters involved in the troop move. As they passed over a wide section of Highway QL9, which ran from Quang Tri to Tchepone, Laos, Stewart's aircraft lurched.

A North Vietnamese antiaircraft gun crew had patiently waited for the first two aircraft to pass over. As Stewart passed directly overhead, they laced the Huey's tail boom with 23mm explosive shells. The shells fragmented the tail boom and severed the drive shaft of the tail rotor, leaving the Huey without tail rotor control and in danger of a fatal out-of-balance condition. If any portion of the tail boom fell off, the helicopter would tumble to the ground with no hope of survival. Stewart and Doody, along with the other pilots, were instantly aware of the mortal danger.

Paul Stewart called on radio, "Chalk Two going down." He was so upset he used the wrong call sign.

Despite the confusion of monitoring three radios, Maj. Jim Lloyd instantly recognized Stewart's voice. Knowing Stewart was Chalk Three today, he intuitively knew Stewart was critically hit. "Chalk Three, going down, where you going? Attention, aircraft going down, Chalk Three."

Stewart, "Chalk Three. Be advised, I'm going down. I'm shot down. I'm hit, have no left pedal. I'll try and get this thing back (to Khe Sanh)."

To the combat-experienced pilots, going down didn't always mean an instant crash. It did mean they were no longer capable of continuing the mission. They would attempt to return to friendly forces or put it on the ground safely.

"Chain Six-five (battalion commander, 158th, Lieutenant Colonel Peachey), Auction Six-five . . ."

"Okay, this is Auction Six-five, he's hit. He's got a stuck left pedal. He's turned back in down to Khe Sanh."

Chain Six-five, "Let's get the guns back out on station." The gunships weren't even with them at that point; they were waiting on standby at Khe Sanh. Things had gone easy in the morning missions.

"Auction Six-five, was he hit by antiaircraft fire?" called the mission command-and-control officer.

Another Phoenix in line behind Lloyd and Nelson called, "Lead, increase your airspeed, please." "Auction Six-five, Chalk Two, turning on final." "Chalk Two has thrown smoke out (marking a North Vietnamese antiaircraft position for the gunships to attack)."

Capt. Mike Teal called, "(Redskin) One-four is in hot on the smoke." The Cobra dove to the target, firing 2.75-inch folding-fin aerial rockets, each with the explosive impact of a 105mm howitzer shell.

Lloyd, "Chalk Three, did you get hit by antiaircraft fire?" "Chalk Three, Chalk Three, lead . . ." Lloyd called again, amid numerous calls of "taking fire."

"I don't know what I was hit by," Stewart said. "My tail . . . my drive shaft . . . my tail boom is gone. It was pretty heavy. I don't think it was .51-cal. It must have been pretty heavy stuff." Stewart had been hit several times with AK rounds and .51-caliber during his first twelve months. He had the personal experience to judge the type of hits to his bird, as well as how serious a predicament he and Doody were in.

"Okay, roger," Major Lloyd said.

Ever the warrior, Stewart continued, "If you want to put something on it, it's that big road intersection. That big road intersection is where I took fire straight up from below. It came right straight up underneath me."

Lieutenant Colonel Peachey, Chain Six-five said, "All lift birds, get more altitude, get more altitude. Let's make it a steep approach in there." Everyone climbed up to three thousand five hundred feet. "Okay, lift birds, get all the altitude you can get."

Nelson said, "Chalk One's on and off the LZ. LZ is cold." Those were reassuring words to the twenty-eight crews in line for the LZ. "How're you doing, Chalk Three?" he called.

Stewart, "Not bad, heading back Khe Sanh. Is gonna be good . . . right pedal," which meant the possibility of a violent spin at a hover, so it would have to be flown down to the ground without a hover. The aircraft would have to make a running landing on its skids.

"Just take it on back to Khe Sanh," Lloyd said. "They got the strip laid out, run it on in." A helicopter is capable of making a sliding landing without tail rotor control, similar to an airplane landing.

Two minutes later, WO Darryl Keith called, "Chalk Four coming off."

Then, in his last words, Stewart called, "Chalk Three, Chalk Three, I'm upside down!" Pilots monitoring Stewart's radio frequency heard an undescribable sound. Some instinctively knew it was Stewart's last breath, crushed from him as the Huey's main rotor blades sliced through the cockpit.

With that last radio call, Paul Stewart and Tommy Doody fell inverted to the ground, crashing in flames . . . a smoking hole. Twenty-three millimeter antiaircraft fire had lacerated the tail boom to the point that a portion eventually fell off. The drive shaft powering the tail rotor had been damaged to the point that a fatal out-of-balance condition sent it flipping inverted, exploding on impact. There was also speculation that it could have been a hydraulic hard-over caused by the battle damage. In either case, he'd had three minutes to put it on the ground and didn't. His refusal to put it on the ground immediately cost the 1st Platoon another crew.

Several pilots watched as Stewart's Huey crashed. The radios became chaos.

"What was that!?"

"Who was that?"

"Did he still have his troops on board?"

The recovery ship pilot said, "Break, I got the burning aircraft in sight, I'll be going down to see what I can do."

Lloyd, his voice filled with resignation, called, "Okay, mighty fine. Rest of you birds join back up on this flight. The recovery bird is on the way to that aircraft."

"Chalk One-two, coming out."

Lloyd had to order two Phoenix birds back into formation when they departed the LZ after dropping their troops then headed straight for Stewart's wreckage, hoping they could help. If one went down, another had to go get them!

The pilot of the recovery bird called, "There's nothing but burning wreckage. I can't see anyone to help, we're Charlie Oscar." "Charlie Oscar," continuing on—chilling words understood by the pilots. Despite the losses, the mission continued.

The Phoenix birds resumed trail formation behind Nelson, heading back to Khe Sanh. There they refueled, loaded more troops and did it all over again, slowly assimilating the shock of the loss of Stewart, Doody, the crew chief Bobo, and the gunner Robertson.

Many pilots took note, and the word was passed. When they took obvious, heavy battle damage, they'd put the aircraft on the ground and wait for a chase ship to pick them up. With the next three days of combat assaults, twelve Phoenix birds out of twenty took major hits. There was so much battle damage to the Phoenix Company that, in army parlance, they were combat ineffective. In other words, shot to hell. And they weren't the only ones. All units participating in the operation suffered hits and eventually losses.

The losses to the Phoenix and others would continue. The chain of command had, however, anticipated them and had replacement Hueys waiting. Within forty-eight hours of notification of a loss, replacement aircraft were in the company. The pilots and crewmen, however, had to endure the horrifying experience of taking replacement aircraft back into that hell, and two out of three would experience multiple antiaircraft damage incidents. But combat effectiveness was never lost for more than a day or two. Pilots and crewmen riding replacement birds had the distinctive sensation of cavalrymen riding steeds replacing those shot from under them. That awareness took a toll on nerves and stomachs, but it wouldn't stop them.

Although the 163d Aviation Company was designated a noncombat unit, we assumed direct combat-support missions, convoy escort, scouting, and reconnaissance as needed. Vandegrift had sappers at night, along with 122mm rocket attacks. The first American soldier had been killed there. The troops had also received a heavy barrage of mortars. There was an immediate, urgent need to get the North Vietnamese heads down. I had the feeling that I had landed in the right job at the right time. Most important, I had my very own Loach! They even let me have a machine gunner. What more could a young man want in a war! We were cleared to search out threats and attack them on sight. I Corps rules of engagement had become our game. If you see them, shoot them. None of that live-and-let-live crap in II Corps.

I landed at a small permaprime pad at Vandegrift and

met the major in charge of base defense. He was tired, dirty, and not particularly happy. His second tour of duty was getting rough. I asked him how it had been going there.

He replied, "Well, we thought we had an AWOL (absent without leave) case and it turned out to be our first KIA. The young spec-four was thrown by a 122mm rocket into the trees. Although he got hit yesterday, we didn't find his body until today. I helped bring him in. I can't get the smell off my hands." It was not a happy time for the major. I was surprised to hear they'd already had sappers (North Vietnamese Army commandos) in the wire attacking them at night. The 122mm rocket attacks and mortar attacks would become a timed daily event we referred to as happy hour.

With the major in my left front seat and no door gunner, we took off and circled the perimeter of Vandegrift. I then circled the hilltops surrounding Vandegrift. I contacted a FAC who had some aircraft returning from Laos without having expended their A-4 loads of 37mm cannon. I marked a ridge to the west of Vandegrift, which the major said had been a suspected mortar location. The A-4 Skyhawk was piloted by a Marine. We listened to the air force FAC brief him as I flew circling nearby, with an excellent view of the strafing runs, which ripped the top of the mountain west of Vandegrift from one end to the other.

After that, we returned to the Vandegrift pad, and I watched the mortars prep the mountaintop. I was going to drop smoke for the slicks taking in a two-platoon drop, which would walk down the mountain back to Vandegrift in an attempt to flush out any would-be attackers.

The mortar preparation lasted about a half hour. I stood on the small pad and took movies of the mortar crew firing, using my telephoto zoom to watch the rounds impact. A few minutes later, I took off with the major in my aircraft. He popped the smoke and dropped it on the

mountaintop. I backed off and climbed up one thousand
feet and took movies of the combat assault under way.
Hueys came in, one at a time, dropping their men and
doing a vertical departure with a 180-degree turn. It was a
helicopter ballet with the timing down to only a few seconds between aircraft. The insertion was cold, and the
troops made it down that night without contact. I took
movies of the entire operation.

## February 10, 1971

I flew three colonels up to Quang Tri and Khe Sanh. At
this time, Khe Sanh was as safe as Camp Evans or Quang
Tri. We overflew Khe Sanh at about three thousand feet.
The runway had been completed on one side, and a second
runway was under construction. Helicopters were parked
all along the finished runway, and a huge perimeter had
been created around the area.

I landed at Khe Sanh and walked out to the runway
under construction. Graders had been out grading the old
runway and clearing the debris from the 1968 runway.
Colonel Rodolph's engineering company was hurriedly
piecing together the metal runway, which was assembled
like a honeycomb on top of the graded dirt surface.
Things were really moving quickly. Bulldozers had dug
trenches for command-and-communication units that were
prefabricated into Conex containers.

I went to POL, and while being refueled, I watched a
critical emergency in progress. A slick was landing with
stuck pedals, which meant he had to fly it to the ground
without coming to a hover or he would enter a spin. He
had reported loss of fuel due to hits throughout the aircraft and had two badly wounded crewmen. He made a
beautiful landing to a stop and then, within three seconds,
a medevac Huey landed a rotor blade away off his nose.

The medics rushed around the damaged Huey and loaded the wounded crewmen. In less than a minute they were on their way to the hospital. Another battle-damaged company aircraft landed right behind him at the same time. A third smoking aircraft landed short of the first two. It was an impressive sight.

Army pilots were living proof of months of difficult training. Countless repetitive emergency procedures were put to reflexive use. I sat at POL and watched Cobras, Chinooks, and Hueys come and go. C-130s were being quickly unloaded on the ramp and activity was constant. It was quite amazing to watch C-130s landing, then flights of Hueys in between the C-130s, flying north, crossing over the runways and continuing on flight paths to the resupply pads and into Laos.

## February 11, 1971

I flew convoy cover between Quang Tri and Khe Sanh. Afterward, I flew general support for a company at Vandegrift. Was pretty interesting and got seven and a half hours flight time.

With only an unarmed major in the front seat with me, I heard a Mayday call from an F-4. An O-2 Skymaster, a forward air controller, called: "Mayday! Mayday! (Requesting) any helicopters in the Mai Loc area respond." I told the major what was going on. He did not have a weapon, and I only had my .38 pistol. So I handed him the pistol and said we'd hop over their ridgeline to see if we could pick up the pilot. The major calmly agreed to serve as door gunner with my .38.

The F4 Phantom, call sign Cobra Zero-four, had been based at Phu Cat near Quih Nhon. It was shot down by a 12.7mm machine gun during an air strike. It was a mile or two south of the convoy route I had flown morning cover for between Mai Loc and Vandegrift.

As I flew over the ridgeline, I saw the smoking hole where the Phantom had drilled into the ground. The pilot's orange and white parachute was draped over trees and he was safely on the ground. A Huey was hovering about twenty-five yards from him, the crew chief running through chest-high elephant grass to get him. I was amazed. In the forty-five seconds it took me to hop over the ridgeline from a mile away, eight helicopters were quickly over the spot. I know it must have made that guy feel good to have so much attention.

I was third, but as I looked around, it got real crowded, quickly. Within two minutes, there was a virtual air show of the army helicopter inventory along with Marine HH-53s.

Apparently the weapons-system officer in the backseat had failed to eject and was killed in the crash.

The Marine HH-53 pilots wanted the Huey to land and transfer the pilot to them. The Huey pilot did not want to land because of the possibility of enemy troops in the area so he flew the pilot to Quang Tri medevac pad.

In my letters home, I could hardly describe the complex activities going on at Khe Sanh. It looked like about ten square miles of nothing but artillery, armor, and helicopters. I was happy to be a part, involved in the operation.

Over the next three days, several armored moves and combat assaults would be completed. The ARVN 1st Regiment, 1st Infantry Division inserted two battalions on LZ Don and one battalion on LZ Delta I. A Ranger battalion was air assaulted onto Ranger North LZ, just southwest of the DMZ.

On February 12, I had what was described to me as an easy mission, ferrying. I had Specialist Five Jackson, the security-cleared courier, who was carrying printed orders from headquarters at Camp Eagle to locations along the DMZ and out to Khe Sanh.

We flew up to the DMZ. I made a landing at Alpha-2, where pilots were warned by a prominent sign: THIRTY SECONDS ON THE PAD OR RECEIVE MORTAR FIRE. I dropped Specialist Five Jackson off and dashed up toward the DMZ, just to look around. I took a photo and returned at one hundred knots with about three feet of altitude. That was just for fun. Most pilots wanted a glimpse of the North Vietnamese flag on the north side of the DMZ. I had seen it before with Cataldo. You could barely make it out from a distance. When the courier's business was completed, I was called. I picked Jackson up, and then we dropped off more papers at Camp Carroll, farther to the southwest. Then, I had to fly him down route QL9, south of Vandegrift, and westward to Khe Sanh.

It was a totally overcast and cold day, the clouds were barely above the mountaintops. The mountaintops north of Khe Sanh were 3,330 feet high. Along the Thach Han River (Song), which paralleled QL9, was a large mountain, Dong Ca Lu, just east of the Khe Sanh plain. The flight to Khe Sanh was uneventful.

After Jackson had dropped his papers, he hopped back in, and we began the return flight. I gained altitude to the point where I was just below the overcast cloud so I was, coincidentally, level with the mountaintops. As we passed a major bend in the river at Dong Ca Lu, heading northeastward, things looked pretty calm.

In the next second, neon-green softballs were floating through my cockpit. I then fully understood the term "lit up." In reality, the 12.7mm machine gun slugs were probably a few feet in front of us, but I felt as if they had passed an inch in front of my nose, coming in through the left door and out through the right door. It happened so quickly, I didn't even make a defensive move of the aircraft. I reached over to Jackson, grabbed him on the leg. "You okay?" I asked, expecting to find him wounded or worse! He had the biggest smile and widest eyes of anyone alive, barely nodding his head. "Yes! Sweet Jesus!

Yes!" He'd done it again: Magnet Ass had taken heavy fire, close misses. His amazing record of not being hit continued.

An experienced North Vietnamese Army antiaircraft crew had taken their best shot, a typical burst of 12.7mm fire. Enough to kill the Loach, but not long enough to reveal their location. They had barely missed. Had they not been so disciplined and fired one or two more seconds, I would have been another smoking hole in the ground. I imagined to myself that the spotters and loaders in the NVA crew were probably slapping the gunner on the head for missing the simplest shot!

I made a call on guard frequency advising other traffic of a hot .51-cal. An OH-58 pilot asked me to meet him at Vandegrift and show him where it was on a map. He'd had a near miss the previous day.

That night, I got back to the hootch and told Bill Gordy what had happened. He cracked up, laughing hysterically. "What's so damn funny?" I said.

He said, "Magnet Ass Jackson! He has that reputation. I don't know how it happens, or why, but everyone who has ever carried him has had near misses." Gordy said, "Let me tell you about the time I was going into Camp Evans."

I cried, "That was you!" realizing it was Gordy and Jackson who had come in during the rocket attack that barely missed my hootch at Camp Evans. So much for flying in I Corps. We laughed till tears poured.

Gordy then told me about his REMF mission. A convoy that he was flying cover for was mortared. He called the FAC for TAC air but was told the location was too close to friendlies. He then called division artillery to request a fire mission. They also refused. Gordy could see the smoke from the mortar tube. It was in a bunker opening, less than a mile from QL9. Frustrated, but not willing to ignore it, he landed and asked a ground unit for a volunteer and a case of fragmentation grenades. A specialist four quickly volunteered. Flying in the backseat of a Loach, tossing grenades, was much more fun than sitting in a foxhole being mortared.

Gordy returned to the mortar tube. After an M-16 clip was emptied into the opening to keep heads down, two frag grenades were dropped in. The war quickly ended for one NVA 82mm mortar crew. To Gordy, it was just another successful kill. He'd had many more his first tour of duty. Other similar actions would be fought along QL9 over the following days, going unreported in the shadow of spectacular achievements and losses over Laos. The many little skirmishes and fights along the DMZ and around Khe Sanh were uncountable. But they were deadly for those involved.

*Laos.* CW2 Arthur McLeod of Charlie Troop, 2d of the 17th Cavalry, 101st Airborne Division, was flying guns, covering another troop move in an AH-1G Cobra. The aircraft was at altitude, took antiaircraft artillery fire, exploded, and crashed in flames. Another WORWAC Class 70-3 member died, along with his copilot/gunner.

## February 14, 1971, Camp Eagle

On February 14, I flew again to Vandegrift to carry a major around on a perimeter recon and possible artillery adjustment.

However, the gravity of the mission changed dramatically. After witnessing the F-4 Phantom being shot down to the east of Vandegrift and feeling distinctly undergunned with only a .38 revolver, I realized that I needed to carry my own M-16 in addition. Several pilots began discussing personal weapons. We then agreed we'd better get really serious.

Gordy asked the CO to arm us with miniguns, but the CO refused; it was the wrong image for a REMF unit. We then decided to carry M-16s for each pilot, the crew chiefs carrying an M-60 machine gun or over-and-under (M-16 with attached 40mm grenade launcher). I opted for a crew chief with an M-60 machine gun along with a case of fragmentation grenades and CS (tear gas) grenades.

Our mission had expanded from carrying battalion and company commanders around their areas of operation to providing aerial armed convoy escort along the highway between Dong Ha and Khe Sanh. We were then providing direct combat support and reconnaissance in the form of white teams (two Loaches) all along QL9, ranging from the DMZ south to the river below QL9. An 0-2 Skymaster piloted by a forward air controller flew above us, staying on station most of the day. Gunships were available if needed. We were to request air strikes on suspected sources of artillery fire or any threat to ground forces and convoys.

The ground forces were being hit hard at night by infantry sapper (commando) attacks, as well as 122mm rockets and 82mm mortars. No convoy was attacked while I was overhead, and the waves and peace signs of the GIs on the convoy trucks showed their appreciation of us. We would buzz them frequently at eye level and eighty knots.

Despite the risks, the freedom from mission constraints allowed seat-of-the-pants flying. We'd zip between treetops along the mountain ridges, gliding over the mountainsides in search of any threat. It was exhilarating. We typically flew very fast at treetop or ground level as we initially covered an area. If we didn't receive fire, then we came back and went over it more slowly and repeated the process until we were slow enough, i.e., making ourselves very inviting targets, to be certain it was clear. The most important thing in my mind was control of my risk-level and exposure. I'd had valuable experience with the

4th Infantry and the Phoenix. I was ready to recon and had an air force FAC to back me up.

I was once again a man with a mission! Everything I'd longed to do in a helicopter, in war, was happening. My personal confidence and enthusiasm were buoyed by the massive military effort under way.

The lowest-risk mission was also the most fun, convoy escort from Camp Eagle to Da Nang. Da Nang was a rear area. Everything between Quang Tri and Da Nang was heavily covered by firebases. The flying, however, was sheer exhilaration. We had the opportunity to cover the hillsides of the Hai Van Pass, which separated Da Nang harbor to the south and Lan Co Bay to the north. It was exhilarating to fly over a mountain on its treetops, to cross the final ridgeline, and then have a five thousand foot vertical drop to sea level. The sensation of flying was akin to being Superman.

It was obvious that wars had been going on for years at the Hai Van Pass; the mountain paths were strewn with wreckage from World War II aircraft, French transports, and a number of CH-46 Sea Knight Marine helicopters. There were also remains of Loaches and Hueys scattered about. It was quite an interesting landscape that mirrored an ongoing war over many years. But we felt in control in our Loaches and enjoyed the landscape while reconning for potential ambush locations.

That night, I returned to Camp Eagle from Da Nang and convoy escort. The unbelievable had happened! Baby San had been shot down! The company commander called an immediate safety meeting in the officers club. The CO came in, told everybody to put their drinks down and listen up. He continued, "Number one, the war is still on. For those of you who think it ended back in December, wrong. Number two, the North Vietnamese are out there. They are more aggressive than ever, and they will kill you. Number three, antiaircraft fire is taking a toll on everyone. The Vandegrift–Khe Sanh area you fly is having just as many aircraft shot down as in Laos."

Then the commander recounted the experience of Baby San. He'd been flying his Loach over a North Vietnamese who'd been spotted walking on a hill north of the Rock Pile in an area known as the Razorback foothills. Baby San told his door gunner not to shoot the man and flew over him low and slow. He repeated the maneuver, just harassing the NVA, until the NVA turned around and fired with his AK, shooting Baby San out of the sky. The Loach crashed, vertically, in flames, and the door gunner pulled Baby San, semiconscious, out of the flaming wreckage. The other Loach, a mile away, came to the rescue and carried them out. Baby San was medevacked with severe burns and possible compression fractures. The CO had visited him in the Quang Tri hospital.

The commanding officer then ordered all white teams to stay together, closely coordinating with the FAC. All Loach pilots would carry additional personal arms with an armed crew chief or gunner in the back. Cobras would also accompany us. His last caution was, "This is still a very hot war. You can get yourself killed. Don't let it happen to you." Amazingly, our REMF unit had a combat loss, a Loach (OH-6A) downed by an AK-47!

Baby San, who had declared himself a conscientious objector and refused to fly Cobras at Camp Evans, was just playing with the North Vietnamese when the soldier shot him out of the sky. Baby San and his crew chief were incredibly lucky not to be killed after they were on the ground. There was an intense concentration of enemy soldiers in the area. We later learned that another Loach and a Cobra gunship were shot down within a mile of Baby San the same day, killing both crews. Four Americans dead.

We'd now fly as scout white teams, a pair of light observation helicopters, hunting to kill. The warrant officer Loach pilots had their dreams come true! They eagerly accepted the new mission despite the risk; it was the ultimate game of hide-and-seek. Hunt and kill. The excitement of the hunt. The pilot's requisite control of the aircraft . . . and the combat engagement. The long-awaited opportunity to pay back had come. Incredibly, we'd only fly the high-risk mission every other day. We'd alternate with lower-risk convoy and courier flights. The second-tour officers, however, understood the risks. They were thinking, oh hell, not me again!

After the safety meeting, I could barely contain myself. First, I had my very own Loach. After my experiences with the Phoenix, that alone was a dream come true. Next, they gave me a machine gunner—with orders to recon. The orders permitted us to hover along suspected enemy positions. We could drop frag and tear gas grenades, machine gun anything that moved. That was sport by itself. But it got better.

Remarkably, I'd also have two of my very own Cobra gunships, flying just above me . . . eager to pounce. In the air cav they called this formation a pink team—white (Loaches) with red (Cobras). And to top that off, I'd also have my very own forward air controller. He had the whole damn U.S. Air Force to call on!

I couldn't wait to get flying. Praying the little bastards would shoot at me! When hunting in a Loach, to have an enemy shoot at you and reveal his location was far better than having no enemy to attack. The NVA would suffer a very serious lesson. Messing with my tiny Loach would bring a terribly disproportionate world of shit dead center on them!

In the missions to Laos and North Vietnam with the Phoenix, I'd experienced the burdens of Duty, Honor, Service. With the Phoenix, I'd successfully completed life-saving extractions of Special Forces teams. After CCN missions, I'd been left with a sense of survival, not one of personal victory.

For me, the Loach missions in the Razorback foothills and the demilitarized zone were selfish. It was there I sought my very personal encounter with the enemy. I wanted my experience of victory, in hovering combat! The killer REMFs had been unleashed!

## Seriously Kicking Ass:
## A Day Between the Rock Pile and Razorback

Two days later, my wait ended. My prayers were answered. WO Stephan Cobb and I were assigned convoy escort duties between Vandegrift and Camp Carroll. We had an O-2 Skymaster overhead and Cobras were cruising nearby. We began our morning flight at ten feet above the mountain ridgelines, south of the Rock Pile. We saw no activity above the south side of the road. We then flew north of the Rock Pile because I wanted to see Baby San's wreckage. We found the crash site on a hillside with heavily used enemy trails crisscrossing the area. I slowed, circling with macabre interest above a pile of blackened white ashes. So that's what it would look like, if I was shot down. A pile of ash, a short length of tail boom. The only recognizable part of the Loach was the orange and olive vertical stabilizer. We then flew low level to a nearby hill just south of Baby San's wreckage, where American troops were lounging on Purple Heart Ridge.

We scouted a little farther east. Suddenly, cut into the top of a red clay hill, I saw a hilltop bunker in clear view of the American position and with a clear view of traffic on QL9, the road to Khe Sanh. Metal stakes supported a sandbag roof, three bags deep. At first, because it was so obvious, I thought it was an American position. I'd always figured the North Vietnamese Army only used highly concealed positions. I flew to the bunker and slowed in a circling hover just a few feet above it. To my amazement, I saw circular Chinese claymore mines, wires running from the bunker, set up in a circular defensive perimeter. None were pointing skyward. Had they been, my war would have ended there.

There was also a .30-caliber Czech machine gun on an antiaircraft mount just outside the bunker, in clear view. I hovered down, nearly touching the bunker. Below the sandbag roof, I saw the green fabric of a uniform and movement. I told my gunner, "Shoot damn it shoot!" He fired the M-60 directly into the opening, from less than ten feet. We saw blood. He threw in a CS grenade, and I hovered back twenty feet or so. Cobb was circling in his Loach, not fifty feet above me.

Before the grenade exploded, another North Vietnamese in green fatigues ran out of the bunker. Thinking we could get him to stop and capture him, I tried to follow him. He appeared unarmed as he ran wildly down the hill barefoot, his unbuttoned fatigue shirt flapping loosely as he ran. I was hovering a few feet above. He was dressed in green fatigues like the ARVNs, which startled me. I'd expected to see them in khakis, which was more common in the lower part of South Vietnam.

Cobb was circling above me. In amazement he radioed, "One-three, what the hell you doing?" The NVA ran down the hill and disappeared into a hole, obviously part of a bunker complex. I told Cobb the guy was unarmed. I wasn't really sure whether or not to open up on him. In the four or five seconds of his run to the bunker, it finally dawned on me. We'd just found a major bunker complex!

At that point, we hovered over to the American troops fifty yards to the west, wanting to tell them what we'd found.

I landed on Purple Heart Ridge, which was a long, narrow hill. It had barbed wire strewn around the sides and was pocked by infantry defensive positions for the GIs. The location was approximately fifty yards west-southwest from the hilltop where the machine gun was found. I landed and motioned for the platoon leader, a lieutenant, to come over to my helicopter. He wouldn't come. I sent my crew chief over, and he brought back an NCO. I shouted to him over the roar of my engine and rotor, pointing to the machine gun, clearly in view. "There's an NVA machine gun on that hilltop; why haven't you guys taken that out?" He looked at me, then looked at the machine gun. Obviously stunned, he then ran away. My crew chief hopped back in. The NCO came running back and gave me a radio frequency. He said they were sending four men over there and asked us to cover them. As I climbed up to fifty feet with Cobb, I continued to watch the machine gun, knowing it could take me out in seconds.

Four GIs immediately rushed over. They had to go down a steep hill thirty yards, and up another hill twenty yards, and then back down into a valley on the north side of the bunker.

We hovered over them as they found the bunkers. They had a firefight, killing one NVA with one American badly wounded. The soldiers on the ground asked me to call a medevac. They were taking the wounded man to the bunker on the hilltop.

I immediately radioed on UHF guard (emergency) frequency, "Any medevac, any medevac, vicinity of Rock Pile, come up guard, wounded GI, Woodstock One-three!"

Surprisingly, a Phoenix Huey was coming back from a CCN mission in Laos with a Green Beret medic on board. "Woodstock, aircraft, Phoenix (unintelligible), we're not a medevac, but have a Green Beret medic on board, two minutes out. Where you at?"

I gave him the location, told him it was cold (no enemy fire) at present. We'd be a pair of Loaches, hovering cover.

The Phoenix Huey came down to a smoke grenade, hovering with the right skid touching the side of the hill, just above the bunker complex. The mortally wounded GI was lifted aboard. I was hovering, circling the Huey, trying to offer protection. Two Cobra gunships had also responded to my call, circling overhead, eager to pounce.

The Phoenix pilot, recognizing me, remarked, "Marshall, I thought you were a REMF?" I'd been flying with him only four weeks earlier.

"Yeah, tell me about it," I replied.

The crew in the Huey thought I was absolutely insane, hovering around in a tiny Loach below them. I thought they were crazy to hover, exposed to God knows what. The Phoenix pilot didn't know he was hovering over a very large NVA bunker complex. Four F-4 Phantoms and two A-4 Skyhawks would bomb the hell out of it over the next six hours!

I was called by the Phoenix pilot and told that on the way to Quang Tri hospital the GI died five minutes after the extraction.

At that point, the other three soldiers had already headed back, taking intense mortar fire as they climbed up the hill to their position. Another GI was then mortally wounded by mortar fire. The remaining two men dragged the body of the dying man with them as they struggled to get back to the safety of their position. Without comment, WO Stephan Cobb hovered down to pick up the man, freeing the others to escape. Cobb hovered beside them, only the front tips of his skids touching the facing hillside. Then Cobb began taking rocket-propelled grenades, and mortars were exploding within a few yards of his Loach. Several well-aimed and carefully adjusted 82mm mortar shells bracketed Cobb. All in less than thirty seconds.

"They're hitting all around you, hurry!" I radioed.

He calmly replied, "Roger, he's almost on." Another warrant officer was doing whatever it took for men on the ground. His crew chief finally pulled the body of the man into the Loach, and Cobb climbed out as the other two soldiers scurried up the hill to their foxholes. Moments after Cobb departed, mortars exploded where he'd picked up the GI. He'd left barely in time. Cobb had acted bravely, calmly, under direct enemy fire. All for an unknown GI.

Cobb called, "I'm taking him onto Q(uang) T(ri), hospital pad, I'll call you on the way back."

"Roger." Then the command-and-control bird for the Americal Division came overhead. Six was a colonel's call sign.

The young second lieutenant, the platoon leader on Purple Heart Ridge who had not come out to meet our Loach, came on the radio. He called the colonel by rank and name, a clear violation of radio security procedures. "Can't you get us off this goddamn hill?" Then he sounded as if he were having an emotional breakdown. Literally crying into his FM radio, the lieutenant went on to tell his battalion commander, "We've been on this goddamn hill two weeks. I've had two men killed today, another wounded. We've lost four men killed and twelve wounded in two weeks. This is a fucking waste. Get us out of here!" What I heard was as close to mutiny as you would ever hear from an army lieutenant. It was obvious they'd been taking a pounding since the operation began.

I really couldn't feel sorry for him. The enemy position we had just attacked was in clear line of sight, less than fifty yards away from his perimeter, in broad daylight. I could still clearly see the .30-caliber machine gun on its antiaircraft mount while I sat in my Loach, on his hilltop. His platoon simply hadn't done its job.

The colonel came up on the radio and told him to "Get a grip and hunker down." They had all the assets in artillery and gunships that they needed. The lieutenant would have none of it. He wanted his men off the hill. They had suffered too many casualties, and there was no point in their staying. The colonel became furious. After his anger subsided, I heard him call another aircraft and steps were put in motion to replace the troops on Purple Heart Ridge.

With Cobb carrying the mortally wounded man to the Quang Tri hospital, I was left alone with the FAC overhead. I decided to scout farther to the east to see what was under way. Approximately one mile to the east, I saw a company of U.S. soldiers on the ground. They were sprawled out, taking a smoke break. There didn't even appear to be anyone on perimeter guard. I had my crew chief drop a piece of paper to them with my FM radio frequency. When they came on, I said, "Don't you know there are NVA all over this place? There are heavy trails ahead and dinks in a hilltop bunker (within) a half mile west of you." I then saw them scurrying around and beginning to organize themselves in a proper defensive posture. The platoon leader then asked me what the noise had been. I told him that it had been NVA mortar fire. It was obviously something they had not expected. Having warned them of the enemy to their west, I proceeded on to Mai Loc to refuel and meet up with Cobb. After refueling, we returned to the hilltop bunker area and checked in with the forward air controller.

The O-2 Skymaster FAC called in air strikes. Two air force Phantoms, F-4s, came in dropping 250-pound and 500-pound snake-eye bombs with high-drag fins. I put a smoke marker on the top of the hill where the bunker was and another below the north side of the hill, where the complex of bunkers was. The O-2 then fired white phosphorous rockets on each. On the first bombing pass, one 250-pound bomb hit within a few feet of the bunker on the hilltop.

On the second pass, a 250-pound bomb ripped the bunker open, revealing the body of a very heavyset, light-complexioned Chinese with wavy black hair. My crew chief had machine-gunned him before the bombing. He was obviously Chinese and not Vietnamese. He was also in a senior officer's dress uniform, which surprised the hell out of me. It had a collar insignia with red background and a gold star on a green woolen uniform. He must have been a senior officer in the Chinese Army, serving in an advisory capacity. We related what we saw to the FAC, who also found it hard to believe, but concurred. The jets then expended the rest of their ordnance to the north of the hilltop and opened up another bunker, which collapsed amid small, secondary explosions.

As the F-4s departed, I overflew the bunkers with Cobb. Before our eyes North Vietnamese were trying to crawl from the debris. They were obviously in shock, but they had their AKs and RPG rocket launchers up, still shooting! Our machine gunners opened up and for one minute, we circled. One NVA was loading an RPG launcher with one hand while holding an "entrenching tool" (shovel) to protect his head. It only delayed the inevitable a few seconds. The man beside him was firing an AK. Our M-60s ripped through them but more continued to climb out with AKs. The full wrath of my personal frustration, disillusionment, and loss of friends poured upon those North Vietnamese. That one, crystalline moment, transcended all my previous rage and sorrow. I was in total control. The exhilaration and release of those emotions was a high equaled only on the CCN mission I had flown with Nelson into North Vietnam. It was the defining moment of my tour.

We then backed off and watched our two Cobras work the area as more NVA crawled from the bunker complex, firing AK-47s and rocket-propelled grenades. Two pineapple-shaped RPGs streaked skyward at a diving Cobra, just missing. The two Cobras continued their runs, killing anything that moved.

We departed back to Mai Loc when low on fuel. There we met the Cobra pilots who were flying with us. One, a captain, came over and shook hands with me during refueling. We went back for two more rounds of two hours each, searching for bunker openings. We crisscrossed low in the area that was known as Helicopter Valley to the north of the Rock Pile. There we found even larger bunker complexes, and two more air strikes were called. Each time, Cobb and I crisscrossed through the area at eighty to one hundred knots barely above the dead treetops as the FAC called out fire that he saw from two thousand feet above us, through binoculars. He could actually see the men shooting at us. The NVA were well trained. They sat back in their bunkers until we passed over. Only then did they fire at us, when we could not see them or hear them.

Then the jets' bombing opened up another bunker, and the Cobras were making gun runs on it while wc hovered within a quarter mile. I watched as RPGs again darted into the air at the Cobra gunships. Fortunately, they missed. On the fourth refueling, we decided to go back out for one last look. At that point, we were mentally and physically exhausted. Eight hours of solo flying, mostly in enemy contact. The FAC had returned, and he could tell we were at the end of our strings. Even adrenaline has its limits.

At the end of the day, we counted nine North Vietnamese bodies and what we suspected were pieces of at least three others. Although some bunkers were collapsed from the bombing, the NVA had still not given up. As we made our last circle over the bunker complex, Cobb and I slowed it to thirty knots. I could hear the single shots of a pistol being fired at us. Cobb came on the radio, "One-three, you hear that?"

I replied, "I can't believe it, after all they've been through. I didn't think anybody else would be alive down there."

"Me, either." Our machine gunners both opened up with the M-60s then they dropped some extra CS just for additional discomfort. I called Cobb, "Let's just take it home."

"Sounds good to me." I couldn't help but admire the heart of the guy who'd just shot at us. Of course, I was glad he was a lousy shot.

Many years later, I'd understand that we'd destroyed the forward observation position of the NVA B-5 front. It included the NVA 31st and 27th Regiments. They were positioned to attack the line of communications and supply to Khe Sanh. The NVA infantry divisions were supplemented with the 38th and 84th Artillery Regiments, as well as the 15th Combat Engineer Battalion.

An hour later, Cobb and I made it back to Snoopy's Pad, our revetment area. We'd flown nearly ten hours (solo) and were exhausted. Of course, the mess hall had long been closed when we got back so we went straight to the officers club to have a beer. Everybody was cheering and celebrating the fact that we had confirmed kills. It was highly unusual for our REMF unit even to have combat activity not to mention a successful day hunting. All of us were, to some degree, flying much more dangerous missions than had been going on as recently as the week before. But that day we were the most aggressive REMFs in the 101st Airborne Division!

I'd finally experienced the personal encounter I'd sought in war! I'd hunted the enemy, found, engaged, and killed him. I had achieved everything I'd expected of myself.

It was a feeling unlike flying Special Forces missions with the Phoenix, after which I was left with the distinct feeling of a survivor, not a combatant. Today, I'd kicked some serious ass between the Rock Pile and the DMZ!

The exhilaration subsided to an intense sense of accomplishment, but not joy or happiness. Whatever inner hunger it is that compels men to combat, I'd satisfied. I'd met and clearly defeated my enemy for that day.

The celebration continued. There was a great deal of drinking and patting each other on the back. Celebrating as if we'd had a college football victory. We had directly accounted for the deaths of at least nine NVA and probably several more who could not be observed in the collapsed bunkers. By virtue of my finding the enemy, we were also at least partly responsible for the deaths of two GIs. A sadly sobering thought.

Very late in the evening, the battalion chaplain walked in and congratulated me upon my safe return. I then became aware of an inner conflict over what I had accomplished. I was physically exhausted, mentally fatigued.

I'd spent ten hours or so in solo flight in near constant contact with the enemy. I'd coordinated air strikes with the FAC, closely observed Cobra gunship runs, and arranged two medevacs of mortally wounded GIs. That day, I'd felt more alive and had more sense of the immediate moment than I'd ever experience again.

I had been very lucky, but I'd enjoyed the combat far too much.

The chaplain's presence made me aware that there was another aspect to the experience. Personal questions regarding deeper emotions and faith would have to be resolved. For the moment, I mentally filed the thoughts away. It was too much to handle in one night.

The next morning while I was asleep, Warrant Officer Schwab walked into my cubicle.

"Marshall, you stupid shit. Don't you postflight your damned aircraft? I had a hurry-up call this morning and rushed out to the aircraft—almost didn't preflight it."

I thought to myself, Well, that *would* be stupid. You *never* fly a helicopter without a preflight check.

He continued, "You ought to go take a look at your damn tail rotor, gear box, and vertical fin. You got it all shot to shit yesterday. If I'd flown that thing off, it might have disintegrated and killed me."

I lay there slowly becoming more awake and then began laughing. Schwab stormed away. I slowly got up then walked out to take a look at it. The fiberglass of the tail rotor was peppered with fragmentation from RPGs or mortars. There was a bullet hole in the vertical stabilizer and a bullet crease along the bottom of the tail boom. It was definitely a "red X," no-flying condition. The aircraft was unflyable until the entire gear box was checked and the tail rotor assembly replaced. It had been a close call. I had definitely taken enemy hits all over the tail of my aircraft. Bender had taken two AK rounds in the Plexiglas, but I had *really* messed it up! All my hits came near the Rock

Pile. It was obviously a tough little bird. I then took a photograph for my collection. I'd finally taken enemy hits and lost my cherry!

As I walked back to my room, I became aware of an endless stream of Chinook helicopters sling-loading Hueys and Cobra gunships. It seemed that every time a CH-47 was flying back to Phu Bai, where the primary maintenance area was, it was sling-loading aircraft that had been shot down. From that day forward, it became obvious that one hell of a lot of aircraft were getting shot down. It was also impressive to us that one hell of a lot of aircraft were being sling-loaded back for repair and reuse. Anyone who had any concerns about whether the war was back on had only to watch the procession of Chinooks and Skycranes sling-loading combat-damaged Hueys and Cobras.

The day after Cobb and I found the bunker, Weasel Saunders had convoy duty at the Rock Pile. In typical warrant officer style, he went north of the Rock Pile to find our bunker complex. He found the hilltop position and reconned the immediate area. No NVA. Having been shot down on Ripcord six months earlier, he was itching for payback. The NVA had either pulled out, taking the bodies with them, or gone deeper underground. After carefully reconning the area, he was excited to see the NVA machine gun lying on the hill. He landed at the bunker, and his crew chief grabbed the machine gun on the tripod. Unbelievably, a REMF unit had taken a war trophy. Lucky for Saunders and his crew, it wasn't booby-trapped. They didn't even take fire. There was no sign of the North Vietnamese Army.

Cobb and I had killed its crew, but Weasel captured it. It was quite a celebration that night. The North Vietnamese Army had learned the lesson. Don't mess with Loaches! We would not take enemy fire again while patrolling highway QL9 and the DMZ.

\* \* \*

A few days later, I finally got a day down from flying. Coming back from lunch, I ran into Darryl Keith at the division pad. He called, "Marshall, you REMF! What the hell you up to?"

I replied, "Man, just flying my Loach and enjoying life."

He retorted, "Are you kidding, with everything that's been going on in Laos? Have you heard what's been happening?"

I said, "Well, we get it secondhand down here, but it's not looking very good."

"Looking good, hell! It's goddamn grim! And if Laos isn't enough, we've had our problems. Didn't you hear of Mears and Davis going inverted in the (Phoenix) Nighthawk?"

I replied, "No." He started laughing and then I interjected, "Were they flying the damn thing without a spare inverter?"

"Well, that might have been part of it. They actually went inverted through a full loop or roll. Nobody knows. And pulled it out just in time to crash with some control. Mears screwed up his back . . . ended up in the hospital Stateside. Davis is back flying now."

I instantly remembered flying with Keith on Nighthawk and how terrifying it had been with me on instruments and him visual flight rules in the pitch-black, at one hundred feet above ground level.

"Guess you heard that Stewart and Doody went in," he said.

Even though they had died two weeks earlier, I did not know. The chill hit. "No," I said, "I'd heard a couple were lost, but I didn't know who." Keith knew the story of Larry Baldwin and his dad and he understood the reason I left the Phoenix. I just took a deep breath, shaking my head. My sleeping cubicle had been next to Stewart's. My mind was spinning. I asked, "What else is going on?"

"Well, you won't believe this, but we were combat

ineffective after about two days into Laos. Think we had fourteen birds that had taken serious hits. It's been a real mess." I shuddered with relief that I was no longer there, knowing that luck would not last forever. The Phoenix crews had daily been tempting death in the worst area of operations. The danger and the losses hadn't begun with the Laotian invasion; it was their AO (area of operations) and the mission demands of the Special Forces that routinely cost them.

I remembered in early January when Captain Hunt had Stewart try to talk me out of transferring from the Phoenix. Stewart was working off a thirty-day leave, near the end of his tour of duty with the Phoenix Company. Stewart was in the same hootch I was in. Our sleeping cubicles had been next to each other.

Stewart had said, "I'll probably die driving a slick." Now, Stewart was dead, along with one of the nicest guys I'd ever met, Tommy Doody. It was Doody I had photographed on the CCN mission and deer hunt. I was shaken. Keith held his head down, shaking it slowly from side to side. We shook hands and parted.

## February 17, 1971

On the seventeenth, I flew five hours for the engineer battalion commander, Colonel Rodolph, picking him up from the engineer pad at Camp Eagle and flying out to the eastern side of the A Shau Valley. Firebase Rendezvous was located just below the eastern mountain ridge, on the A Shau Valley floor. I thought of the infantrymen's poem, a blasphemed Psalm 23: "Yea, though I walk through the valley of the shadow of death, I shall fear no evil, for I am the meanest son of a bitch in the valley. My M-16 is my rod and staff . . ." While Rodolph was out, I kept the engine going at flight speed. I was prepared to leave after the first shot fired. I couldn't believe the men working were going to spend the night there. They truly were *combat* engineers. The colonel had everybody working intensely.

Bulldozers were clearing the one-lane dirt road from Camp Eagle for trucks. A dozer on Rendezvous was digging deep bunkers. Artillery registration was under way from Firebase Berchtesgaden, on a mountaintop overlooking them. Other artillery bases to the north and east could also support them. This was a major operation into the A Shau Valley or these guys were simply bait. Other engineering units had been air assaulted in to work eastward toward the other elements, speeding the road improvements. In addition to the road and drainage improvements, seven large helicopter landing zones were cut.

After finishing his business at Rendezvous, the colonel wanted a quick tour of the valley floor. We flew at one hundred knots with a slight zigzag up along the old Highway 548, which was a two-lane dirt road, obviously in heavy use. From our ten-foot altitude, we observed well-placed, corrugated culverts at small creek and drainage areas. I asked him why they were there, and he said simply, "The North Vietnamese maintain them. We go out and blow them up now and then, but they rebuild them." He then wanted to divert to Firebase O'Reilley, near Ripcord. A bulldozer was working on the mountaintop there. Then the colonel surprised me with a request for a low, slow flyover of Ripcord. Ripcord had been closed since the preceding summer when it was evacuated.

We did the flyover at Ripcord, low and slow. I thought of Jim Saunders six months earlier, shot down and evading NVA on the very hill below me. Flying there was an eerie feeling. I felt very exposed. We proceeded to O'Reilley, where I landed. I let the colonel off and kept the aircraft engine going at flight idle. The colonel spent several minutes talking to the people working. They were clearing mines and preparing new defensive positions. After a few minutes he hopped back in, and we departed.

He then pointed out a one-lane red clay road that ran from Ripcord to the A Shau Valley. It had been exposed by B-52 "defoliation" (bombing). I asked him when we built that. He said, "We didn't build that. The North Vietnamese built that last summer. They still maintain it." That was a shock. There I was in my little Loach, flying south of Ripcord. The North Vietnamese Army was maintaining and occupying the land and being resupplied by truck only twenty miles from Camp Eagle. Time to climb a little higher.

## February 18, 1971

*A Shau Valley.* The Comanchero flight of Hueys from Camp Eagle was attempting a hot extraction of a Special Forces team on the west side of the A Shau Valley near the Laotian border. CW2 Phillip Berg piloted the Huey to a hover for a hot string extraction, similar to my first CCN mission with Dave Nelson. They came to a hover, and the ropes were dropped as a 12.7mm antiaircraft machine gun riddled the aircraft, stopping the engine. The aircraft lost rotor rpm, rolled over, and crashed, killing Berg. Another WORWAC 70-3 class member dead.

### Ranger North, Laos

On February 19, the northern flank of LZ Ranger North came under massed human wave attacks, supported by field artillery and tank fire. Resupply to Ranger North, Ranger South, and Hill 31 had been canceled for three days. The few helicopters attempting resupply were shot up before even reaching the landing zones.

Sp5. Dennis Fuji, stranded on Ranger North after his helicopter had been shot down, was directing tactical air strikes for the ARVNs. If he hadn't been so effective, they would have been overrun the previous day. Plans were under way to extract him, regardless of the enemy fire.

Also on February 19, Dustoff pilot WO John Rauen had flown his Huey into Laos for an evacuation of wounded. On approach to the pickup zone, the aircraft was riddled with bullets, the hydraulic system was shot out, and flight controls were damaged. They attempted a running landing on return to Khe Sanh. Damage to the Huey prevented them from a normal landing to a hover. The aircraft crashed and burned on final approach, near the runway, killing Rauen, who was trapped in the burning wreckage. Another WORWAC 70-5 class member, John Rauen, dead.

On February 20, an emergency resupply of Ranger North and extraction of Specialist Fuji was commenced. A flight of twenty-one Hueys was led by a Phoenix Platoon. Capt. Dave Nelson was the lead aircraft commander. The company commander and flight leader was Maj. Jim Lloyd, flying in Nelson's Huey.

Sp5. Dennis Fuji was stranded on Firebase Ranger North, four miles inside Laos, west of the DMZ. The NVA was massing tanks and preparing to overrun it. Little time was left. In desperation, a gambling attempt to extract Fuji proceeded from Khe Sanh to Ranger North.

The Vietnamese Rangers had not been resupplied in two days due to intense antiaircraft fire. Lt. Col. William Peachey, the air mission commander, decided the flight could not make the approach. However, Specialist Fuji was still in radio contact.

An American was on the ground, in the most dangerous circumstances. Nelson and Lloyd agreed. They had to get Fuji out. With Peachey's acknowledgment, they dashed in low-level, flying between the trees, as fast as possible. They slid to a landing among mortar bursts, uncountable rounds of AK-47, .51-caliber, and 23mm fire. Fuji was hauled aboard, along with *seventeen* uninvited ARVNs who desperately wanted out.

As Nelson departed, the Phoenix Huey began trailing the white smoke characteristic of vaporizing fuel and burning oil. A few seconds later, the turbine engine belched a black-donut smoke ring, indicating catastrophic engine damage. Then fire erupted from the engine compartment, flames leaping back to the tail boom! Lieutenant Colonel Peachey radioed, "Fire! Get out! Get out!"

As taught, Lloyd reflexively reached to shut the engine fuel flow off to keep the Huey from exploding!

But Nelson, fearing they would crash-land to certain death with the NVA, slapped Lloyd's hand away from the fuel cut-off switch. Too late; the engine died. Nelson, alert to the crisis, calmly said, "Now we're committed." He entered powerless autorotation onto Ranger South, which, luckily, was in his flight path. Ranger South was also in the process of being assaulted by NVA. It was approximately eight hundred meters south of Ranger North. Nelson slid the flaming, smoking Huey to a powerless landing on Ranger South. But it was like Ranger North; he'd again landed among flying bullets, exploding mortars. Despite being grossly overloaded with eighteen passengers, shot up, on fire, and powerless, Nelson completed the perfect autorotation!

When they slid to a stop, everyone quickly evacuated but Nelson, who was calmly shutting down the aircraft as if it'd been a normal landing. Fearing an explosion, the gunner demonstrated his own minor miracle of coordination and physical prowess, simultaneously unlatching Nelson's seat belt and pulling him out of the aircraft. It could have exploded at any second. As he was yanked from the Huey, Nelson's only injury was the scuffed toe of his brilliantly polished boots. Most men running from the flaming Huey went left. But Nelson ran to the right and dove into the wood line. Ranger South was taking very heavy fire.

Overhead, the circling Phoenix pilots had a command-ing view, and the pilots grimaced as they watched friends running from the burning Huey. The fire and the heat were obviously intense as the aircraft's magnesium com-ponents flared; the tail boom sagged to the ground as the crew leaped into the jungle, away from the flames.

When they realized Nelson was down, without ask-ing permission, warrant officers Butch Doan and Pat McKeaney dove to get them. A Phoenix crew was down, they would retrieve them! Doan commenced a tightly spi-raling dive, nearly vertical, down three thousand feet to the left side of the burning Huey. Green .51-caliber tracers and fluffy white puffs of 23mm airbursts enveloped them during the descent. One 23mm struck the rotor mast, badly damaging the main rotor system vibration dampeners. McKeaney would later tell other Phoenix pilots of what could have been his last two thoughts, "Doan is fuck-ing crazy, and now we're gonna die!" When the action was safely over, laughing at mortal threat released some tension.

With Major Lloyd, the crew chief, and gunner aboard Doan's Phoenix bird, they departed under fire, taking many more serious hits leaving Ranger South. Doan and McKeaney, with their crewmen and passengers, barely made it to Hill 30. They'd taken a 23mm hit on the main rotor mast, which caused a horrible vertical vibration. The Huey's collective control actually bounced during the short flight. As Doan crash-landed at the larger ARVN position, they radioed the others that they didn't have Nelson on board!

The Phoenix had been lucky, one more time, but good luck was quickly being used up. Capt. John Bottman called Doan to see if they'd gotten everyone out. After a couple of minutes' confusion, the call came: Nelson was still on the ground. Covered by Skip Butler, Redskin One-five, with 2d Lt. John Henry Bond in the Cobra's front seat, came in, and Capt. Don Davis and Capt. John Bottman came in next.

Bottman descended the Huey east of Ranger South to approach low-level, trying to avoid the murderous anti-aircraft fire above the hill. Doan and McKeaney had barely survived. Don Davis saw the intense antiaircraft fire. As they raced a couple of feet above the treetops, Davis saw North Vietnamese Army troops everywhere he looked. The twinkling muzzle flashes of AKs were clearly visible in broad daylight. As they raced between the trees, Davis, the copilot, began calling out critical engine and flight instruments while Bottman kept his eyes outside the cockpit. Then, incredibly, Davis called out, "Airspeed 145 knots." In a desperate attempt to disrupt the North Vietnamese Army gunners' aim, Bottman had the empty Huey exceeding its designed airspeed limit.

They landed on the right side of the smoking pile of debris that had been Nelson's Huey. Only a piece of the tail boom remained. Bottman sat thirty *very* anxious seconds, under fire, waiting for Nelson, who finally came high-stepping out of the woods, running across the LZ under fire. He ran on his heels so he wouldn't scuff the toes of his legendary shined boots. Nelson dove into the back of the aircraft, rolling on his back, feet in the air, as he hit. He wouldn't scuff his boots further. While climbing out with bullets whizzing around them, Nelson tapped Davis's shoulder. Davis turned to find Nelson disgustedly pointing to a scratch in the black mirror-glaze toe of his boot.

Fuji spent one more night in Laos, at the safer ARVN position, but he was evacuated early the next morning. Bottman and Davis carried the Phoenix crew members home to Camp Evans. The second rescue bird had been the charm. The Phoenix lived their vow. When one bird went down, another went to get them. It continued until accomplished!

The Phoenix pilots' actions were memorialized with Silver Stars for the pilots. Specialist Five Fuji received a

Silver Star for his actions as a forward air controller, after surviving the helicopter crash on Ranger North.

The Phoenix crew chiefs and door gunners had excelled in their duties. Their personal courage and gunnery skills were acknowledged with Distinguished Flying Crosses, very rare awards for army aircrew. Sp5. Ronald Merek, Sp4. Ronald Starbuck, Sp4. Brian Fitzgerald, Sp4. Clarence Davis, and PFC Matthew Regner were the recipients. They made front-page news in the *Stars and Stripes*, as well as *The Screaming Eagle*.

When Bottman and Davis began their approach, Redskin pilot Skip Butler was out of ammo in his Cobra, but still dove on a .51-cal. machine gun firing at the Huey. Davis thought it was one of the bravest things he'd ever seen. Davis got a Silver Star for his actions; Butler was not recognized for his valor, just another day at work for a Redskin. The NVA gun crew ducked long enough for the Huey to escape. On the following day, Ranger North was overrun by North Vietnamese Army tanks and troops. The ARVN suffered horrendous losses.

*February 23, 1971, Laos.* Things stayed lively in Laos. Virtually every landing zone was hot. Every pickup zone was hot. The air between the Laotian border and Khe Sanh was the only place the helicopters weren't getting shot at. As a combat assault was under way, a Crossbows Charlie-model gunship, flown by CW2 James Miner, was turning out of a gun run and collided with a UH-1 exiting the landing zone under fire. The gunship rose below the Huey and lost its rotor system. In the ensuing crash, Chief Warrant Officer Miner was killed. Another 70-3/70-5 class member.

## February 24, 1971

I watched John Wayne in the movie *Chism* under the beautiful starry skies of the Nam. I'd just realized that the previous month passed faster in the 163d Aviation Company than any week at Camp Evans. Couldn't really believe it until I sat and started thinking. Lieutenant Hardin transferred down from the Phoenix. He said Laos is really bad. He was extremely happy to get down here. Hardin told us that the combat assaults in Laos were much worse than the missions we'd flown on CCN because the landing zones were preregistered by the North Vietnamese artillery and ringed with antiaircraft weapons.

On some firebases the Phoenix resupplied, the NVA were dug in just outside the wire. Even so, orders were that the door gunners could not fire their machine guns for fear of hitting friendly troops.

Hardin said CW2 John Michaelson packed an M-79 grenade launcher and used a couple of *cases* of ammunition per day. He was said to have made more NVA kills than any other Huey pilot just while sitting on the ground, unloading supplies in Laos. Michaelson told him it didn't matter if he hit the NVA or not, he just felt better firing back.

I could only shake my head in amazement, grateful to be in a Loach with the 163d.

That evening was eventful at Snoopy's Pad, or hover area. Warrant Officer Schwab and a nonaviation CW2 got drunk. They sang all night long, country and western music. They didn't cut it off until after 4:00 A.M. Then Schwab decided to give the nonflying warrant officer "hovering lessons" in a Loach. At 4:30 in the morning, Schwab and his friend, who had never been trained to fly anything, commenced to hover in the Snoopy's Pad hover area. Schwab gave his friend hovering lessons for about twenty minutes then landed in the wrong revetment and shut down facing in the wrong direction. They were appropriately corrected in the morning by the commanding officer, who called Mr. Schwab and his nonrated friend, obviously hurting puppies, very early that morning. A notice was immediately posted that any flying activities after dark and before sunrise would have to be cleared with the staff duty officer. Everyone got a laugh out of that.

*February 26, 1971.* Dustoff missions continued with the 498th Medical Company. During another extraction of wounded, WO John Souther took ground fire and became an aircrew casualty. Another WORWAC Class 70-3 member dead.

## February 28, 1971

My wife complained in a letter that my parents were acting poorly, worrying about me. I wrote her that it should have been expected. But I hated to hear it. Knowing I was there, they had been religiously watching news coverage of the Rock Pile and Khe Sanh areas. I'd learn later that there was a lot more TV coverage in those areas than in Laos; after several news-personnel deaths, cameramen weren't willing to fly into Laos with the VNAF, so TV carried lots of scenes of trucks carrying wrecked Loaches and Hueys. There were even horrifying scenes of dead pilots being carried away, facedown on stretchers, arms dangling. The graphic news coverage sickened those with loved ones committed there. But all I could do was write and let my folks know I had the safest job in I Corps I could get. I wasn't a hero nor a fool. I would simply do my job and come home.

## March 1971

On the first of March, at lunch, I walked out of the division mess hall and headed back to the company. On my way, I noticed a slick on the division pad and saw Ralph Moreira from the Phoenix Company. He yelled, "You REMF! What'cha doing?" I walked over, and as we talked of the people we knew, he told me of Nelson's flight with Major Lloyd and Sp5. Fuji's unexpected sojourn with the ARVN.

Moreira laughed as he told me of Nelson replaying the action that night in the Phoenix officers club. Nelson, who was the quiet, introspective type, had everyone in stitches. "There I was, NVA everywhere, the whole world shooting at us, eighteen packs (passengers), losing hydraulics, losing power, and the major gives me a fucking autorotation!" All present had laughed themselves to tears.

Moreira and I laughed about Major Lloyd's cutting the fuel off. Only a real live officer would attempt that. We shook hands, and I wished him well. I didn't know it was the last time I'd shake hands with a Phoenix in Vietnam.

# 9

# Lolo: The Worst Landing Zone

By March 3, ARVN movement in Laos had bogged down, and there were heavy tank battles between the North Vietnamese Army and the outnumbered South Vietnamese. A firebase on the northern flank was lost, and the 39th Ranger Battalion was overrun and wiped out. Another firebase held by an ARVN division was overrun and an ARVN brigade commander captured. Large-caliber artillery fire from North Vietnamese Army guns increased markedly. Intense antiaircraft fire made heliborne movement in the area costly and dangerous. The North Vietnamese Army units stepped up tank and infantry assaults. Individual tanks were used as mobile gun platforms and antiaircraft weapons.

Complications of political influences in the South Vietnamese government compounded the incapacity of the ARVN commanders to effectively control their troops in Laos. Operations capabilities were degraded by inefficiencies in tactical air support from the U.S. Air Force. Due to the lack of on-ground forward air controllers, things became desperate. In an effort to reverse the trend of events during late February, the original goal, Tchepone, was redesignated. The Tchepone assault would be smaller, as the site of a limited but effective delaying action to prevent North Vietnamese forces from pursuing the South Vietnamese, who were retreating to Khe Sanh.

On March 3, the 71st Assault Helicopter Company, the

Rattlers, led a combat assault into Laos that was to be a "piece of cake." The 71st had been temporarily posted from Chu Lai to Quang Tri in late January or early February to support LAM SON 719. They had flown some missions into Laos, but none as far as Lolo. In fact, they should not have been there in the first place. The pilots were under the impression that the company was standing down, and the unit had a shortage of pilots. The unit did have some experience flying Combat Control North (CCN) missions for MACV-SOG across the border, but was unfamiliar with the Lolo area.

Regardless of those facts, they were chosen to lead the assault onto Lolo. Planning prior to the March 3 combat assault suggested that forty UH-1Hs were required for the initial combat assault to establish Fire Support Base (FSB) Lolo. The name Lolo was derived from the name of Italian movie actress Gina Lolobrigida; Lolo was on fairly level terrain, forty-two kilometers west of Khe Sanh on the escarpment in Laos, overlooking the Xe Pon River. The map coordinates were XD 422375. Elevation was 723 meters above sea level.

The South Vietnamese strategic plan was to secure mutually supporting fire support bases along the escarpment that was the east-west high ground overlooking Highway 9 and the Xe Pon River as far as the abandoned town of Tchepone, show a presence in the North Vietnamese base areas, and then withdraw.

On the third of March, the 3d ARVN Regiment executed a series of airborne assaults to the west, along the southern escarpment of hills south of QL9. The 1st Infantry Division (ARVN) units air assaulted to successive positions at Landing Zone Lolo on March 3, Landing Zone Liz on March 4, and Landing Zone Sophia on March 5. The 2d ARVN Regiment assault to Landing Zone Lolo was the first step of the plan to enter Tchepone, the core of the Ho Chi Minh trail network. Landing Zone Lolo was thirteen kilometers southeast of Tchepone. By March 3, the assault had been postponed twice in two days because additional preparation (bombing by air force jets) was required to reduce the very strong antiaircraft defenses. Of course, the fact that the area had been prepped for combat assault for two days made clear to the North Vietnamese that a landing would be made there, so the antiaircraft network encircling the area was strengthened. Army aviation history would be made in the assault.

In the pilots' briefing the night before the assault on Landing Zone Lolo, the pilots were informed that a B-52 strike that night would prep the landing zone. They were also told that because of the B-52s' preparation of the landing zone, gunships would not prep the LZ. The crews from the 71st Assault Helicopter Company had so little experience in Laos that they even discussed the necessity of wearing the bulky chicken plates worn by all pilots active in I Corps. I Corps pilots "*never* left home without it." The men of the 71st AHC would soon learn the briefing was horrifyingly inaccurate. "Bogus" in the words of some young warrant officers. They would also learn they were the lead element simply because they were the largest unit remaining; everyone else had been simply shot to hell. Due to combat attrition, all the other companies were making do with from eight to twelve slicks instead of the usual twenty.

The helicopters assembled at Khe Sanh, then flew to pick up the ARVNs. From the pickup zone, they headed westward, deeper into Laos. Approaching the landing zone, still not in sight, the air mission commander directed them. The line of Hueys descended into the dust and smoke. The aftermath of the B-52 Arc Light strike reduced visibility to very poor visual flying conditions, less than a mile visibility.

Capt. Dan Grigsby, Rattler Two-six, was the lead ship, Chalk One, into the landing zone. On approach, all aircraft took continuous fire for at least two minutes prior to reaching the landing zone. One aircraft, a few miles behind the lead element, was shot down over LZ Brown. Before Chalk One even reached Lolo, other aircraft were taking hits. Two Charlie-model gunships were shot down just east of the LZ. Once in the landing zone, Grigsby took hits all over his aircraft from AK-47s, RPD machine guns, and mortar fragmentation. The fire was predominantly small arms, but also included 12.7mm antiaircraft slugs. Grigsby took off in a fusillade of fire and headed back to Khe Sanh. On departing the landing zone, he saw NVA running, crouched, to the left front of the aircraft. He also watched his copilot's head bobbing and weaving as if he were dodging bullets the way a boxer dodged punches. He called Red Oak Dragon Two-zero, and told him the landing zone was surrounded and under heavy fire.

Clearly the landing zone had been compromised, and it should have been moved elsewhere or the assault canceled. Red Oak Dragon responded, "Negative, negative, keep putting 'em in, keep putting 'em in." All hell continued to break loose.

As Grigsby climbed out, he tried to light a cigarette, keeping the cyclic between his knees, but his hands were shaking so badly he couldn't, so he asked his copilot to take over. After lighting a cigarette, he took the controls back and started to decelerate airspeed from one hundred knots back to the normal cruise of eighty knots. When he pulled back on the cyclic, it wouldn't move. He then told the copilot something was binding the cyclic. Grigsby looked back and saw bloodstained bullet holes in his cargo floor, in the area of the Huey's control push-pull tubes. He knew then that he could lose aircraft control at any moment. Heading straight back for Khe Sanh, he informed them that he had an emergency and could not slow below ninety knots.

Khe Sanh tower replied, "Roger, Two-six. You'll be emergency number three following the aircraft burning on short final."

When Grigsby was on short final, another aircraft declared a very frantic emergency. Grigsby then told the tower he could put his aircraft on the ground beside the runway. At ninety knots, that was not a wise decision.

The tower instructed him, "Two-six, put the fucking thing on the goddamn runway. That's what it's there for. We'll get you off." Patience hell, everyone had an emergency!

The Huey came to a sliding, screeching halt using a small portion of the runway. The instant it was stopped, an aircraft tug came over and hoisted the aircraft off with chains wrapped around the rotor mast. Grigsby found that a piece of shrapnel had lodged in the rotor system bell crank. In typical army aviator fashion, he got into another Huey and flew another seven hours of sorties into Laos.

Back at Lolo, Chalk Two, WO Gary Arne was call sign Rattler Two-five. He approached Landing Zone Lolo and also encountered the intense fire. Becoming low and slow in his final approach while waiting for Chalk One to clear the landing zone, he made an attractive target. In a hail of withering fire, Chalk Two had his tail rotor and hydraulics system shot out. The ship began spinning, and three ARVN passengers fell two hundred feet from the cargo bay to their deaths as other helicopter pilots watched in horror. The crew chief and door gunner frantically wrapped their microphone cords around the three remaining ARVN soldiers to stop them from falling to their deaths.

Arne departed the landing zone without dropping off his three remaining troops, but his engine was then shot out at one hundred feet above the ground. Then he watched his windshield explode as if in slow motion, while he took three rounds in his chest protector from an AK-47. Additional rounds continued impacting on the sliding armored plate at the side of his seat even as they crashed back into the landing zone. They evacuated the aircraft, and hid behind a log until things stabilized a few hours later.

* * *

WO Doug Womack, Chalk Three, watched the ARVNs falling from Arne's spinning Huey. To Womack, they looked like rag dolls falling from the sky. Grigsby was already on the radio telling command and control to call off the combat assault. Womack did a 360-degree turn and the aircraft behind him also commenced circling turns.

The command-and-control ship again refused to call off the combat assault. When asked by a fellow pilot if he was going in despite the carnage under way, Womack replied, "Yeah, I'm going in." Then, without hesitating, he continued his turn and went directly into the landing zone, taking hits all over the aircraft during the run in, short final, on the ground, and during the climb out. The gunmount post stopped one round that would have killed his door gunner, and several rounds just cleared Womack's head. Several just missed the crew chief but found the main rotor transmission. Fragmentation from RPGs and mortars struck the sides of the aircraft while it was in the landing zone and both main rotor blades took hits.

To an army pilot, a "defined risk" is acceptable exposure to the enemy, and may be well planned as part of a mission. However, risk without constraints, as in Landing Zone Lolo, is the ultimate, terrifying reality of control lost—naked exposure to enemy fire. Those who experienced the eerie sense of time expansion would later talk of time slowing to an unlifelike quality.

Womack entered the twilight zone of time expansion, mortal combat, in the presence of death.

With every revolution of the rotor blade, he could count the nicks and dents in the blades, while enemy tracers slowly wafted skyward at nine hundred feet per second. Words were spoken in syrupy slow voices. The question of mortality already understood, "Is this it, when time stops?"

In the heat of battle, Luck smiled on Chalk Three, if only for a moment.

On climbing out, Womack saw that his transmission pressure gauge was fluctuating wildly. He made a straight line for Khe Sanh and on final approach, lowered his collective to reduce power for descent. The transmission pressure plummeted to zero and the red warning light glowed "land now!" He barely made it back to Khe Sanh and safely landed. Suffering from shock, the young copilot was replaced by a copilot from another shot-up Huey, who'd lost his pilot and aircraft! In typical warrant officer fashion, Womack and his new copilot flew several more hours that day supporting the ARVNs.

The ship that followed Womack in was shot down in the landing zone and burned. Eleven of the next fifteen Hueys in the combat assault were shot down or shot up so bad they had to be replaced! One of the pilots in an aircraft shot down in the landing zone was killed by his own rotor blade while running from the burning helicopter under enemy fire.

Bob Morris was the aircraft commander of Chalk One-seven into Lolo. Seconds out from the landing zone, they started taking hits, and his crew chief called, "Uh, Mr. Morris, you do know we're on fire!" He then learned that it had gotten so hot in the crew chief's well that he had to move into the cargo compartment. There was no choice but to return to the landing zone. Morris landed in the landing zone, taking still more hits from small-arms fire as he touched down. They evacuated the burning helicopter and ran to a trench. Fortunately, Capt. Jerry Crews, a former Green Beret, now a pilot, had also been shot down on the landing zone. He borrowed a radio from the ARVN to direct air strikes. Crews was Comanchero Three-zero. He had plenty of experience on Special Forces missions in Laos. He knew exactly what the situation was and how critical it was.

Crews told the command and control to halt the assault until NVA on the south side of the landing zone could be removed. Crews pointed out that there was a fifty-fifty chance of any approaching Huey getting shot down. Another Comanchero ship, piloted by Steve Diehl, did try to get in to pick up the air crewmen, but Diehl took so much fire he couldn't land. Command and control finally decided to halt the assault and put more firepower into the tree line to the south of the landing zone.

Nineteen Hueys flew in. Eight Hueys managed to fly home, but they, too, were shot to hell. Useless after the engagement.

With the assault temporarily halted, the Hueys returned to Khe Sanh to refuel and check out their aircraft. Some aircraft were swapped for undamaged aircraft. Maj. Bob Clewell, Comanchero Six, was one of several aircraft commanders from the four companies involved in the initial assault who assembled at Khe Sanh. An ashen-faced crowd of pilots quickly assembled. The Comancheros had last lost an entire crew on the eighteenth of February on a CCN mission. They were well-acquainted with the fact that the war was ending—except, apparently, in I Corps. There were arguments about what to do. What would be the best way to go back to LZ Lolo, how to put more ARVN in and get the aircrews out? They compared notes and estimated how many ARVN were on Lolo and how many Americans. Chalks Two-zero and higher still had ARVN soldiers on the aircraft.

Clewell and the Comancheros were determined to go after their downed crews, and asked how many would go with them. Everyone was scared shitless, but all knew they had to go. If they left the guys grounded in Laos for long, the NVA would have them. Everyone present volunteered—all fifteen ships left flyable out of the flight of forty-four helicopters. For them, it was a turning point in that particular battle. There were no northern units with more combat experience from I Corps, and they'd long been shot to hell. Many 101st companies had only one-third strength at combat effectiveness. No one company and no one battalion could simply do it all themselves. There were only pieces of flight platoons, companies, and battalions left. The crews from down south quickly absorbed the experiences, and casualties, then they took their place at the lead. The northern I Corps helicopter units were then matched, loss for loss.

They reloaded the ARVNs, met up with the Cobras, and proceeded back to Lolo. All within less than two hours from the initial assault. They would approach low-level, between the trees, from the northeast, actually having to hover *up* to Landing Zone Lolo. The air strikes had helped suppress enemy fire, but the Hueys still took antiaircraft fire from entrenched positions. It began at the border of Laos and didn't stop until they reentered South Vietnam, west of Khe Sanh, courtesy of General Giap.

Two Charlie-model gunships had been shot down just outside the landing zone, and a total of eleven Hueys were shot down on Lolo or nearby. One was shot down over Landing Zone Brown, miles away. In all, forty-four helicopters took serious hits from antiaircraft fire. Chinooks bringing in two D-4 bulldozers dropped their loads from altitude under antiaircraft fire, destroying the bulldozers. It was not until the following day that the first regiment and second/1 Battalion had a battery of 105mm howitzers brought onto Lolo. At the end of the second day, Fire Support Base Lolo was established while a simultaneous operation created Landing Zone Liz six kilometers west-northwest of Lolo, near Tchepone. Next after Liz would be Landing Zone Sophia, four kilometers northeast of Tchepone, less than two miles from the announced objective.

But the helicopter crews were taking a beating. Everybody was taking hits, and it wasn't just one trip a day— for the lift birds it was eight to twelve trips daily into Laos, all under fire from twenty entrenched North Vietnamese Army antiaircraft battalions. In a three-day period in early March, 122 UH1s took serious battle damage, and many were DEROSed (shipped Stateside) as salvage. Twenty were destroyed.

### Evening of March 3, 1971, Phoenix Hootches, Camp Evans,

Door gunner Mike King finished a cassette-tape letter to his mother he'd begun three days earlier:

This is a recording, Mother, and I just want to see how the sound effect's coming in and uh, I think it's a little bit loud right now, and I'll stop and play it back . . . Roger out.

Like I'm saying, I'm trying to make a recording, and it's kind of hectic around here. You know, I don't ever have any real privacy, so I just kinda came outside here. It's near the flight line, anyways, Alpha Company, so, it's a flight line. Alpha Company flight line is, you know, right near our flight line. And, sun's just now going down. It's been a pretty nice day. Getting kind of hot over here though. Well, I'd say it's around one hundred today. But, you know, I'd rather have it hot like this than rain. I just thought I'd send you one of these tapes.

I know listening to a tape is much better than just writing letters. There, it sounds better. But, things here lately have been pretty hot . . . But, uh, things really got hot around February twenty-first.

On February twenty-first, my pilot got shot through the leg, and it got pretty bad. The crew chief and I managed to put him back in the backseat and, fortunately enough, he's not gonna lose his leg. He'll keep it. But he only had twenty days left in the army. That's the real bummer about the whole thing. He's a real fine person. And, we shouldn't even been going in that area, and he went back in. In this certain landing zone, they [the NVA] were mortaring the LZ at the time we went in, and it was really ridiculous. That damn colonel—you know the way colonels are. He was about six thousand feet above, in the air. He wasn't getting shot at, so he didn't really give a damn. He said, "Ah, you people go on back in there, and get your ass shot off," so we went back in, and we got hit. It was a real bummer. He's a real fine person.

And, let me see, what else. Oh, yeah, on February twenty-third, I got shot down. It was nothing more than a large piece of shrapnel, cut a fuel line, and we had to bring it in on an emergency landing at Firebase 31. Firebase 31 has really got a unique history. It didn't last but about a week. It was overrun by an NVA battalion of tanks and I think about five minutes after we left the ship there, on Firebase 31, our helicopter was destroyed by heavy artillery. But, this Laos thing is really a bummer. Really depressing. So many people getting killed.

Oh yeah, I sent you the door pin out of helicopter number 288, that got shot down on Firebase 31, and door pin [holds on] the door when you pull the door back . . . If you don't have that little pin in, [when] you get up high in the air, the wind will blow it off. . . .

You see, we got twenty helicopters, which is a normal strength of a Huey combat assault slick company. Right now, we don't have but six helicopters. You see . . . everyone is getting shot up, and pretty bad. Helicopters are really being damaged bad, and we have a lot of people over here to shoot at [us], but I think everything's gonna be all right. You know, you just gotta maintain my cool. And, you know, that's what I'm trying to tell you, Mom, just don't get worried. You know, this life's just a real sucker. I mean, you're gonna have the Green Machine on you, and sometimes you want to know what it'll finally evolve in to. This is no more than a little economical conquest for some fools who want to make a lot of money or have their names in the paper. It's got me to where I think, as much as I love my country, I hate my government with a hell of a passion, that's all I got to say about it. And, if you could've seen Firebase 30 and Firebase 31, you might have a little understanding of what I mean.

People think war is good. Hell, people think it's good when they're not in it. You get in it a while, and you see how good the war is.

Yesterday on Firebase 31, we hauled off enough damn dead people. They had 'em lined up out there like at a zoo. I've never seen anything like it. The ARVNs don't even know what they're doing. You CA 'em out into an area, and they're so damn scared, they won't even move. That's the reason they're all getting killed. They won't even move. And when we come to pick up, they hang on the damn skids to try to get out of there. They're like a human wave attack on your damn helicopter. You've got to kick 'em in the mouth, kick 'em in the head, kick 'em everywhere, to keep 'em off. A Huey slick won't carry but about nine ARVNs, and, hell, we have carried as many as twenty out, hanging on the slicks, grabbing 'em by the head and pulling them in to try to keep 'em from getting killed. But I still can't help but feel sorry for those people 'cause they really didn't want this thing to happen. Just minding their own business.

In fact, the people we CA'd in Laos didn't even know they were going there until we put 'em down on the damn ground. That's pretty bad in my book.

If you go into Laos, you have to do more than they're doing. I'm not saying it's the ARVNs' fault as much as it is the command's fault. The command doesn't even know what the hell it's doing. I mean, it throws them out there on the damn mountaintop and expects them to do damn wonders. It's just like throwing a bunch of dinks—eight hundred dinks—can you imagine, eight hundred ARVNs being attacked by six thousand NVA. I mean, you can see why they're getting their asses kicked. It's just that plain and simple. It's the United States' advisers and the Vietnamese higher-ups who don't know what in the hell they're doing. They're just dicking around with people's lives . . .

I'm kind of tired of talking about this war. The whole thing just kind of gets me down. All I want to do is get out of Vietnam and live my life and be left alone . . . I sure do miss home a lot . . . Sure would be nice to be back, especially coming up springtime.

Tell everyone back home I really appreciate them writing me. I've gotten a lot of mail. I believe a lot more mail than I got when I first came over here, you know, and I really appreciate it. It really helps things to come in out of flying and get a letter . . . Just kind of brightens up the day. In fact, that's really the only thing I really look forward to each day.

But, I really like working with these helicopters. I learned a whole lot, you know. They're really weird machines. In fact, I even got to fly one a little the other day. I didn't know what I was doing, but you know, I was just sitting in the copilot's seat, and this other pilot, he's a real crazy joker . . . you know, he just said, "You got it?" And I said, "Yeah, I guess I got it." I don't know, I guess I had it. But, I just floated along there, and I made one or two turns. Wasn't nothing spectacular. Course, I sure as hell couldn't land one or pick one up, I guess. But, you really gotta think a lot about the guys that fly these helicopters. To me, they're really brave, fantastic people. I would like to come back to the States and go to crew chief school and on a Loach. Loaches look like a little spider or something. And they're real small. They are used mostly for carrying generals or colonels around on some kind of recon mission. Just real light stuff, you know. But, you know, I'm learning a lot. I've still got a lot more to learn, and I plan on doing that. But, enough for helicopters.

When I say I work eighteen hours a day, that means I've put in about eighteen hours a day. I'm usually out at the flight line about 6:00, and I get through cleaning my gun at night around 9:00 or 10:00. Oh, that's not eighteen is it? That's just fifteen. Oh, that's not too bad. Oh, correction there. But, Mom, if you're worrying, I want you to cut that out. Worrying never did no good about nothing. . . .

I'm gonna go on back to the hootch and finish taping. I don't know why, I just have trouble thinking these days. But, I'll see you later. . . .

Here, we've got a young man here named Pineapple. We call him Magnet Man in our company. I think during the past week, Magnet Man was shot down once or shot up twice, three times. A total of three times. . . .

Well, here I am again the next night, which is around March 3, and everything is going good, I guess. Didn't even have to fly today. Oh yeah, I flew an hour and a half. Flew to Khe Sanh with the major. Major Lloyd, he's an outside guy. He's not like the rest of the majors in the army. He's a Cobra pilot. Cobra gunship pilot. He has pretty tough people. They have a very hard job. They really risk their lives every day. And he's just the kind of guy that just don't take anything off of anyone . . . He does stick up for you [even when] he doesn't have to. In fact, he's just about the best man I've ever seen in the United States Army . . .

I'm gonna continue to tape so you can hear my voice. I don't know if it's changed any or not. I guess I've changed in the short period since I've been gone . . . about a month and a half, two months ago. But, there's one thing. This crew chief I've got, Joel Hatley, he's from Iowa. He's a real good guy. He said there's one thing about life—no matter how bad it is, how bad the war is over here, you've always got to find something good about it. No matter how bad things are, if you can find something good about it, then it is bearable. I've learned about life over here; to live in this world, even back in the States, a person's got to find something good about it. Even something real small. Got to have some little thing he takes pleasure in. [Even] if it is nothing more than just being yourself. And I guess that's just what I take pleasure in, is being myself. I don't know even what I'm gonna do when I get out of the army. I'm thinking about going back to school. I might take a [course in] computers. I'll take up something; I'm really not worried about it right now . . . War puts people in strange moods and makes 'em think completely different. You know, everybody has his own little world, and just kind of lives in it. And there are so many different worlds in the whole world that it's really strange. Two or three years ago, I was going to college, and I had it made. Then I'm over here, but I believe I'm a better person, maybe, than when I was just going to college, having it easy.

I tell ya, it's a great pleasure just to be able to have a place like the United States to come home to. Have a mother like you, Mother. You're one of the finest people I know. Sure did a good job raising me and keeping my brother up.

Time to finish this tape up. I don't have too far to go.

Mike King, three years earlier, had been in college, and like many his age, sought adventure and the honor of service to his country, just as his brother and friends had. As a volunteer, he'd asked for the long hours of duty as a helicopter door gunner. He also helped the crew chief, Joel Hatley, in the daily maintenance of their bird. His opinion of the ARVNs and the operation was based upon his firsthand experience. Other crewmen and pilots generally agreed with his observations. The crewmen of the helicopters were just as aware of the dangers as the pilots.

They were equally committed volunteers who kept the machines flying.

He'd talked of religion and personal fears with the men around him, including Joel Hatley, who'd also been raised in a Christian home. Mike King's tape home was a message of frustration, laced with anger over the conduct of the war. He maintained his composure; he'd accepted his responsibility to those around him, remaining calm in the most depressing circumstances. Mike's brother had served in the Marines in Vietnam, losing a lung to an AK-47 round. Mike had written his brother, saying he "wouldn't be coming home."

His tape home was a graphic, genuine report of his observations and a loving message to his mother. She received it in the mail shortly after notification of his death. Elsie King, a Gold Star widow of World War II, became a Gold Star mother during Vietnam, an incomprehensible personal sacrifice.

## March 5, 1971, Landing Zone Sophia, Laos

The combat assault into LZ Sophia was the final stepping stone toward the objective of Tchepone, Laos. Gunships conducted a preparation on the landing zone as forty Hueys carrying South Vietnamese troops beat their way to the landing zone. The slicks kept up the procession, dropping ARVNs and returning to Vietnam to refuel and pick up more troops. There was pandemonium on the radios. Constant calls of "Taking fire! Taking fire!" The lush green landscape was dotted with clouds of red smoke grenades, thrown to mark enemy antiaircraft locations. Heavy fire was coming up from the roadways and the creek beds out of heavily bunkered, concealed positions. Antiaircraft fire included 12.7mm, 23mm, 37mm, and 57mm. Even the C-and-C ship at altitude was taking flak.

The slicks were taking fire even when they were twelve miles away from the hot landing zone. It was continuous antiaircraft fire from just inside Laos, all the way to the landing zone and after leaving it. Several helicopters were shot down with their ARVN passengers, and others were shot up so badly their passengers were wounded or killed. Nearly every one of the forty helicopters in the formation took hits. Fifteen more helicopters would be shot down combat assaulting Sophia.

The RP (release point) over which all helicopters turned to final approach was a river bend just west of a hill occupied by an NVA company of 23mm antiaircraft guns. They were nicknamed golden hoses because of their golden tracers and high rate of fire. Because of the very low visibility due to haze and smoke from nearby B-52 strikes, the lead aircraft missed the hairpin turn to final, so the other aircraft followed the lead over entrenched antiaircraft positions. The North Vietnamese Army gunners had a field day. The poor visibility meant that the lead Huey received no help in identifying the RP from the command-and-control bird above.

An air force pilot observing the action from above understood the gravity of the events under way. The combat assault was a nut wringer. In a discussion of the events with an army command-and-control helicopter crew, he complimented the army pilots by saying "they must have brass balls."

Capt. Don Peterson, flying with the 174th Assault Helicopter Company, put a cassette tape recorder into his cockpit and wired it to the radios, picking up FM, VHF, and UHF radio traffic. It was a complex aviation environment where pilots were monitoring two or three simultaneous conversations. In the first wave of the second day into Landing Zone Sophia, the 174th Aviation Company was assigned the honor of being the lead platoon. The assault was to reinforce Fire Support Base Sophia. Late in the previous afternoon, troops had occupied the firebase with little opposition and Chinooks had been able to land the 105mm howitzers. But the North Vietnamese had regrouped and created a high-intensity antiaircraft environment surrounding the flight path from the pickup zone near the Laotian/Vietnam border to Sophia, just northeast of Tchepone.

Peterson and his crew were in a Huey among the first ten birds making the combat assault reinforcement. The approach called for a flight path from the pickup zone, across A Luoi, Firebase Lolo, Landing Zone Liz to Landing Zone Sophia. The release point (RP) for the helicopters, requiring a turn from a northbound heading, was southwestward for a two-mile final approach into Landing Zone Sophia. Chalks One and Three made it into the landing zone despite taking fire and hits west of the RP. However, they let their flight path drift too far to the west, where they were subjected to all the entrenched antiaircraft positions.

Chalk Two elected to make a go-around because of antiaircraft hits to the tail boom and fixed tail rotor pedals. He couldn't hover. The aircraft could make only one landing, to the ground.

Chalks Four and Five were shot down by 23mm antiaircraft fire whose explosive air bursts could easily destroy a Huey. It was the same type of weapon that had laced Paul Stewart's tail boom and caused his fatal crash.

As it turned out, the entire ridgeline west of the RP (release point) and ridgelines northwest of the landing zone were covered with 23mm antiaircraft weapons. "Red Dragon Two-zero," the air mission commander called, "move your RP and flight path to the south. Move south of the RP." Chalks Four and Five, shot down, had crashed on a hill between the RP and the landing zone. One aircraft was burning, the other crashed next to it, but was not on fire.

With consternation and calm, Peterson and his copilot continued their approach. There was a loud *pop-pop-pop*. Peterson spoke to his crew chief in a calm voice, "Uh, I'm supposed to tell you guys not to shoot until you see something definite to shoot at."

The crew chief screamed into the intercom in a stress-filled, very high-pitched voice, "That wasn't me! That was them shooting at us! I just looked down and saw these huge, big red things coming at us. I didn't even have time to fire back!"

The copilot said, "Holy shit!"

"I've gotta get a camera for this," Peterson said calmly. Peterson then asked, "What was it?"

Crew chief, "I dunno! But these huge red things went by our tail boom!"

Peterson then calmly spoke to his copilot, "I noticed a fluctuation in the fuel pressure, sort of like the bump you get when the engine quits. But, we're stable now. I guess we'll have to check this out." By then other aircraft were calling out that they were taking hits. A well-concealed NVA 57mm antiaircraft weapon had fired at them from such close range they could hear it. The huge tracers had just missed them! They continued on into the landing zone, depositing their troops and returning for another run.

A short while later, the second wave was under way to Sophia. The release point had now been moved north-northeast of Sophia. The danger was that flying any farther west would put the flights in the heart of the most intense North Vietnamese Army antiaircraft capability. Hazards to the west included *heavier* antiaircraft fire, but there were also reports of enemy helicopters and fighter aircraft operating in the area. For that reason, there was a combat air patrol of air force F-4s above the operation.

Captain Dave Nelson was Auction Lead, heading a flight of ten Phoenix Hueys, with ARVN troops on board inbound for Sophia.

Dragon Lead called, "Auction Lead, what's your position?"

David Nelson replied, "Dragon Lead, I'm about three minutes out at this time. I'm just coming down between the road and the river."

Dragon Lead, "Keep me posted."

Nelson, "Lead, Roger. Just abeam Liz." A few seconds later, Dave Nelson's Huey was ripped by airburst and direct hits from 23mm antiaircraft fire. The fuel cell was riddled, causing smoking leaks. The metal floor of the cargo bay in the Huey erupted in shrapnel, taking a heavy toll on the ARVN passengers. The door gunner on the right side of the aircraft, Mike King, suffered a mortal head wound. Lost fuel made a smoky white trail. The danger of a catastrophic explosion was instinctively understood by all. The stability of the flight controls was in question.

Nelson had just entered his turn to long final, to approach Sophia from the north. He'd followed the lead ship, which had flown too far west, drifting above a heavily fortified ridgeline that bristled with antiaircraft weapons. Nelson turned eastward, away from the area of greatest danger. In accordance with standard procedures, Chalk Two began the turn to final, assuming lead; Nelson had already notified Two of his problems.

Chaos reigned. The formation dispersed in very loose trail (line formation) under fire but the other aircraft continued the assault. They weren't even at the LZ, but they were taking the most intense fire they had yet endured.

Command and control called, "Auction One-six, what's your status? Do you have the landing zone in sight?"

Nelson said, "Negative. I broke off the landing zone on long final. I'm heading in back to Kilo Sierra (Khe Sanh) at this time. I've got a gunner hit in the head, some of my troops are hit, and the aircraft's hit pretty hard. And I was losing fuel, but it stopped losing the fuel now. So I'm just heading back to Kilo Sierra."

Command and control, "Okay, who have you designated as your . . . (replacement)." Chaos erupted on the radios!

CWO Mike Cataldo was Chalk Three. He'd also commenced the fishhook turn to final behind Chalk Two. Farther back in the formation, WO Rick Scrugham was also commencing the turn to final. Constant calls of fire, constant calls of birds hit, and others reporting degrees of combat damage filled the radio. Cataldo, as he was turning final, thought he witnessed an SA-7 (a Soviet man-portable antiaircraft missile) hit Nelson's aircraft, causing an explosion. It might have been an extremely lucky RPG-7. And SA-2 SAMS were definitely being fired at the jets above them. As Cataldo turned final, he began taking 23mm antiaircraft fire hits.

Scrugham, in his turn to final, with his peripheral vision, glimpsed a catastrophic explosion in the air but became distracted by fire at his aircraft and looked away. As he looked back, he saw a fireball in the sky where Nelson's aircraft had been, a flaming, smoking ball, tumbling to earth. Years later, I would listen as he described to Nelson's younger brother and sister, "It looked a lot like the *Challenger* explosion." Ralph Moreira, the copilot, Joel Hatley, the crew chief, and Mike King, the door gunner, also died in the crash. King had sent his taped letter home the day before.

The ARVN troops on board the Hueys were carrying all types of explosives, including plastic explosives in addition to normal grenades, light antitank rockets, and armament. Although the H-model Huey had a self-sealing fuel tank, it was not fireproof. But we can only speculate about what caused the explosion—antiaircraft fire, an SA-7 missile, an onboard fire, equipment among the ARVNs exploding, the fuel cell exploding. In seconds, they were just another smoking hole in Laos. As the helicopter assault proceeded, smoking holes began to mushroom in

Laos. But the Hueys kept coming. Not for Americans, this time, but their allies, the ARVN, the South Vietnamese Army.

On final, the new lead aircraft, Chalk Two, took hits to the tail and fuel cell, which forced a go-around. Mike Cataldo, Chalk Three in the Phoenix formation, suddenly found himself the lead ship. He couldn't see the landing zone, which was obscured by smoke, dust, and the debris of shell fire. Then he observed a heavy volume of 23mm golden tracers and green .51-caliber tracers coming right at him. He reflexively made an evasive hard turn and through luck, found the landing zone in front of him. Turning on final, decelerating to the landing zone, he took very heavy hits, rounds stitching his aircraft. He lost power and made an autorotation to the perimeter of the landing zone, but not to the top of the hill. In his powerless descent, he hit a tree and then stabilized the aircraft, crashing on the skids with a twenty-degree slope downward from the rear of the aircraft.

Crew chief Robert Vial watched in horror as his Huey fell to the ground among Vietnamese soldiers, striking so fast they couldn't get out of the way. Vial saw the left landing skid crush a soldier's head, blood erupting from the poor man's nose and ears.

Not realizing it had been shot down, other Vietnamese began scrambling aboard the powerless Huey, hoping it would fly them to safety. Chaos and confusion, smoke and explosions, overwhelmed the ARVNs.

Despite taking hits, another Phoenix bird landed, and the copilot and door gunner scrambled aboard it as it lifted off while being mobbed by Vietnamese.

Cataldo was amazed that his aircraft stayed upright. There was just enough angle and just enough gravity to keep the aircraft in place without its tumbling backward or over on its side. Again, he'd called for his copilot to shut off the fuel (as he once had with me), again without response. He hadn't even called Mayday because, in the few seconds it took for him to go down, the radios were chaotic with calls of others "going down!" At the same time, a jet had been shot down above them, and a command-and-control ship had also been shot down as well as a gunship beside him, and the two aircraft in front of him had been shot down or badly damaged.

It took forty-five endless minutes for Cataldo and Vial to be rescued. The ARVNs in the landing zone were mobbing each ship that landed. They nearly trampled Cataldo and his crew as they exited his ship. Finally, Vial fired a burst from his M-60 machine gun into the ground in front of a landing Huey, which kept the ARVNs away from the next ship. Cataldo and Vial were then able to climb on and fly out. Heading back to Khe Sanh, Cataldo thought he would at least get the rest of the day off. Hell, he'd just had his bird shot out from under him. However, upon arrival at Khe Sanh, he found another helicopter waiting. Cataldo was upset that he'd lost his only flight jacket under the seat back on the LZ. With only thirty-five days left in country, he had been shot down. As he joked later, "That almost Laosed up my life!"

Phoenix bird 389, regarded by some crew chiefs as the best in the company, was destroyed by Cobra rocket fire. Kingsmen Zero-nine, an aircraft in the following wave, called the C-and-C bird, "Dragon, you better get these people under control down here. It's out of control."

Maj. Jack Barker, commanding officer of the Kingsmen, called on departure from the landing zone, "I've got about fifteen ARVNs on board, two fell off my skids, and I've still got three on my skids. It's bad down there, we've got to get the situation stabilized."

It would not get better.

The loss of Dave Nelson, the most competent, the most capable pilot, shook the men of the Phoenix. From that point forward, the Phoenix pilots understood how little control they had over their individual fates. Nelson's loss hit them hard, very, very hard.

That evening, Lt. Bruce Updyke, of the Phoenix 1st Platoon, remembered a conversation with WO Ralph Moreira on February 9, the day after CW2 Paul Stewart and WO Tommy Doody were lost. Moreira had the duty of crew scheduling for the initial assault into Laos and he'd scheduled himself to fly with Paul Stewart, but the night before the mission, Doody came to Moreira and asked to fly with Stewart. Doody said "something didn't feel right" about the pending mission. Doody knew Moreira had a son he hadn't seen, and Doody was single. Moreira had told Updyke the day after the loss of Stewart and Doody, "That [his own survival] had been real close." Fate, however, had given him only twenty-five days. Whatever the loss meant to the Phoenix pilots and crews, Ralph Moreira's wife was left to raise Angelo, a son Ralph never got to hold.

*March 6, 1971, Laos.* CWO John Hummel was piloting an AH-1G Cobra returning to Khe Sanh under instrument flight conditions. The aircraft crashed into a mountain, killing him and his copilot. Another WORWAC 70-3/70-5 class member died.

On the afternoon of March 6, Khe Sanh received twenty-two rounds of 122mm rockets and other artillery fire. Two U.S. troops were killed and ten wounded. This was the first major incidence of daytime artillery fire at Khe Sanh. A total of 120 U.S. helicopters were assembled at Khe Sanh to continue the assault to Tchepone. In addition, B-52s, U.S. tactical air strikes, and air-cover sorties were scheduled every ten minutes during the assault phase of the operation. Elements of the 2/17th Air Cavalry reconned targets and prepared landing zones and covered the assaults. The enemy attack by artillery fire on Khe Sanh had screwed things up, forcing the assemblage of U.S. helicopters to depart ninety minutes earlier than planned, but the assault continued, with slightly less disastrous results than Lolo.

* * *

I had twelve days and a wake-up call, until I left for R & R in Hawaii. I was about to go nuts. Time could not pass fast enough! I flew Lieutenant Colonel Rodolph, the engineer colonel, four and a half hours on March 6. We flew most of it along the eastern ridge of the A Shau Valley, visiting combat engineers working on the firebases. I had reacquired the simple pleasure of flying, something that had been missing since December.

*March 7, 1971, Quang Tri.* A Blue Ghost AH-1G Cobra with WO Barry Port on board was operating five kilometers southwest of Quang Tri. The aircraft took fire climbing out of a gun run, and the main rotor separated. The Blue Ghost gunship fell to a fiery explosion on the valley floor. Another WORWAC 70-5 class member died.

## Refuel Point, Khe Sanh Combat Base

Capt. Don Davis was copilot in a Phoenix Huey being refueled after another mission in Laos. As he sat there, he noticed an aircraft from the 238th Helicopter Company, the Gunrunners. Norm Miller, his West Point roommate, was flying with the Gunrunners. Davis asked the door gunner to walk over to the aircraft and see if the pilot or copilot knew of Captain Miller.

A few moments later, an individual left the cockpit, came over to talk to him. He was carrying something in his left hand. It was Norm Miller who walked up to Davis's side and stuck out his hand for a shake. Miller then held up the head of a cyclic stick. Miller told Davis that the cyclic had been shot off between his legs while he was flying the previous day in Laos. They had a good laugh over it. It was proof of the environment they were flying in. Davis laughingly told Miller of his landing in a Laotian LZ where he took several hits on the upper console and greenhouse.

The AK-47 rounds impacted in the twenty-four inches separating his head from WO1 Butch Doan's, and one round cut the headset intercom wire. After that he could only shout to Doan. Davis recounted that Doan just cracked up laughing, as if it were nothing but a joke, and kept on flying.

## Camp Eagle

I was flying between Vandegrift and Khe Sanh when I heard the emergency call on UHF guard frequency: a Kiowa had been shot down in Laos. The initial call was made by a Charlie-model gunship, which had overflown the area and nearly gotten shot down.

An argument began about whose bird it was and why it was in Laos. The 1st Brigade of the 5th Mechanized Infantry Division had no ground troops across the river in Laos; a presidential order forbade that. I was dismayed to hear the arguing between a bird colonel and a subordinate in different aircraft as to who had gone down. There was an immediate call to insert a security team. Citing the presidential order, the colonel refused to provide U.S. troops. Even to save an American crew, he would not put American soldiers on the ground in Laos. The ARVN troops were not well enough organized that day to make an immediate response. It was a typical army cluster fuck. I would later learn that the pilot was WO Randy Ard from my hometown of Pensacola, Florida. He'd only been in country a short time. Once he had stumbled into the smoky haze near the border, North Vietnamese popped smoke to draw him down to a landing approach. Then, when he was low and slow, they shot him out of the sky. He'd made the fatal mistake of approaching a smoke marker without radio confirmation. Two of his passengers escaped and evaded to friendly forces. The third died with Ard at the hands of the North Vietnamese Army.

**March 8, 1971**

WO Tom Aldrich had just arrived in country as a brand-new warrant officer, grade one, assigned to fly Chinooks out of Phu Bai. It was his first week in country, copilot on a Chinook. Their preflight instructions were to pick up a sling load of fougasse at Dong Ha: ten fifty-five-gallon drums of jellied petroleum, a derivative of napalm, a six-ton mixture of napalm and jet fuel in steel drums. They were instructed to contact a Loach and a pair of Cobras at the Rock Pile, west of Camp Carroll, where they would meet up with two Chinooks dropping four loads of fougasse on the Rock Pile. Aldrich was thinking, What in the hell are we doing bombing with Chinooks?

At the same time, virtually all air force aircraft were being used in Laos, where the activity had gotten increasingly worse. Troop movements in Laos required not only helicopter gunship escorts, but fighter-bombers to strafe and bomb simultaneously with the Cobra gunships. For the first time in the war, B-52 Arc Light missions were being used as close air support. As a result, the action in the Rock Pile, Vandegrift, and the foothill areas went without air-strike support. They had to rely upon artillery or gunships and make do. The Chinooks were making do.

Aldrich sat nervously in his seat as his aircraft commander flew in only one hundred feet above the seven-hundred-foot-high Rock Pile. As the pilot jettisoned the sling load, twelve thousand pounds of jellied gasoline and napalm splashed on the side of the Rock Pile. Simultaneously, the crew chief in the forward door window dropped white phosphorous grenades, igniting the mass in a roar of flame. Aldrich and his aircraft commander received Distinguished Flying Crosses for the mission. Aldrich had only been in country a few days.

I was flying command and control that day with Fitzgerald as a white team. We had a pair of Cobras on station and a FAC overhead. After loads of fougasse were dropped, I flew over to Mai Loc and met with the lift platoon flight leaders who were preparing to CA onto the very top of the Rock Pile. The soldiers from the Americal Division were going to be inserted at the top of the Rock Pile and would walk their way to the bottom, hopefully clearing any observers or snipers.

As the line of Hueys approached the Rock Pile, we hovered our Loaches over the mountaintop, dropping smoke grenades to provide wind information for the Hueys. We then circled slowly around them, trying to draw enemy fire. Fortunately there was none. Two Cobras circled a thousand feet above us, watching, ready to pounce if we called.

I had my crew chief/door gunner take movies of the combat assault. It was an amazing sight. Once the wind direction was established, the slicks began their approach. It was like a ballet. The first slick came in and touched only the tip of the right front skid to the mountaintop. The troopers jumped off behind the copilot seat in single file. As soon as they were clear, the pilot made a beautiful, climbing, left turn, then a steep dive away from the mountain. Within seconds, the second aircraft repeated the maneuver. Eight lift ships inserted five troops each, a reconnaissance team in force to clear the Rock Pile. Later we found out they made no contact. They did not find snipers, but they did find plenty of evidence of snipers, who'd retreated into the depths of caves or escaped.

Remember the catch in *Catch 22*? Anyone sane enough to want to be grounded was sane enough to fly. And if that wasn't enough, there'd always be another rule! Well, *Catch 22* was alive and well in the 101st. They lifted the 140-hour monthly maximum per pilot because everyone would have been grounded if they hadn't. I was very happily going on R & R. It couldn't have been a better time to leave.

**March 10, 1971**

Cobb and I continued to fly together on missions along the DMZ. We directed artillery fire and also marked positions that were later relayed by the forward air controllers to the jets. This time, I had my gunner take movies of the artillery fire and jets attacking the Razorback.

A major at Vandegrift was sick and tired of being shelled. He was convinced that the forward observers and some of the artillery launching positions for the 122mm rockets were located on the Razorback, a stone mountain outcropping northwest of the Rock Pile, running northwestward to the DMZ. A huge, granite-faced, white rock wall denoted the south end of the Razorback. Cobb and I flew with our crew chief/door gunners, the major in the front seat with me, armed. Cobb also had another armed passenger with a radio for artillery fire and adjustment if necessary.

Starting at the south end, we went along the top of the Razorback at a fairly fast seventy knots, right level with the top. We saw a lot of evidence of past fights and bombings, and there were obvious paths that were used by NVA. And huge rock outcroppings concealed caves used by the NVA. On our second crisscross, purple smoke appeared near the south end of the Razorback. Since neither one of us had thrown it, and we knew no Americans to be on the mountain, I immediately dove off the west side of the mountain to avoid possible fire. The smoke had been a deliberate attempt to draw me down low and slow. Instead, I was then caught in a mountain-ridge downdraft. It took every ounce of power from the little turbine engine to bring me to a hover, just above dead trees, the kind of obstacle you can't see until it's too late. As I slowed to a hover with an overtemp and overtorque strain to the Loach, I'd nearly lost it! The reserve engine power of the Loach had saved my butt. I then exited to the south at ninety knots, which, in my opinion, was not fast enough. I then told the FAC what had happened, and he immediately called in air strikes. For an hour, A-7s and A-4s dropped five-hundred-pound bombs all over the Razorback. We were close enough to see one large bomb, a dud, glance off the side of the mountain onto the valley floor. Once they found it, it probably would be used for making mines by the North Vietnamese.

During a mine sweep on the road at Vandegrift, a mine-sweeping truck hit a very large mine. It was destroyed, killing one GI and four ARVNs. Minesweeping was tedious, boring work, interspersed with the horror of sudden losses of the kind that left the soldiers particularly frustrated because there was no one to attack in retribution.

We continued the day cruising along the DMZ to the east-northeast of an area known as Helicopter Valley, north of Firebase Fuller.

At one point, I heard a hair-raising call on UHF guard frequency: "God on Guard! SAM! SAM! Channel One-zero-three (Dong Ha), two-eight-two Radial, two-two miles!" That was within three or four miles of where we were flying. Then I remembered that surface-to-air missiles weren't supposed to be a threat below two thousand feet. We were maybe twenty feet above ground level.

We flew into the DMZ northwest of Firebase Fuller and found a huge mortar base plate, which was obviously for a 120mm mortar. At that point, we marked the position and went back to Vandegrift and reported the location of the base plate. The major there believed that was the location some ground units were receiving heavy mortar fire from because the 120mm mortar had a four- to five-mile range. Eight-inch and 175mm artillery were used to blast the area.

Later that afternoon, we watched a line of eight Duster tanks with twin 40mm rapid-fire cannons as they sat on Purple Heart Ridge firing toward the Razorback, just lacing it with golden tracers and explosions. It looked like something I had seen in movies about Marines in World

War II at Iwo Jima. It made a lasting impression, the almost white, rock-face mountain, dense green vegetation, red clay, and golden streams of 40mm tracers.

On March 15, the troops based at Khe Sanh were introduced to the 122mm field guns of the North Vietnamese Army. The first of several consecutive artillery raids was conducted from concealed mountain tunnels, reportedly by railway-mounted guns. Rumors were, the tunnels, impervious to air strikes or counterbattery fire, had been built by the Japanese during World War II. But the simple fact was the NVA had learned how to tunnel their artillery and antiaircraft into nearly invisible positions. They'd learned it fighting the French at Dong Khe, before Dien Bien Phu, twenty-one years earlier.

On the fifteenth, I ran into WO Pat McKeaney, a Phoenix pilot, at the division pad. A real likeable guy, he always had a smile on his face. With his first words, I froze. "Did you hear 'bout Nelson's and Moreira's deaths?"

My mind reeling, "No!" I gasped.

"Yeah, they went down in Laos."

McKeaney repeating the words, "They're dead," shattered any of my remaining expectations of justice from fate. I wanted to believe that a good man, a leader, should live. It was a *right*, earned in service and battle, to return home safely to loved ones. The death was so wrong, God wouldn't allow it!

Being body-slammed to the ground could not have hammered me as badly as McKeaney's words. He then told me of Keith being shot up and of his copilot being critically wounded. Another Phoenix pilot was horribly wounded in the leg, with only twenty-one days till he ended his time in service. I was plunged into shock, overwhelmed by grief, anger. I just shook my head. We didn't shake hands. I wished him well, then walked away, my mind spinning. That was when I stopped shaking hands with Phoenix. I didn't want to jinx them. Survivor's guilt set in. I had chosen to leave them. The senselessness of it all. I would remember it as the day I refused to allow my own tears. I'd not cry again for nineteen years. The deepening grief and shock would eventually subside; the demands of flying would drag my mind from them.

Nelson was a platoon leader you'd knowingly fly into hell with, a man of experience and focus. He was viewed by the warrants and commissioned officers alike as the most capable, the most likely to complete any mission. We'd all been aware of our vulnerability, but the Phoenix who flew with him were totally confident in his ability. I'd flown with him into North Vietnam and Laos, my life totally dependent on his skills and good luck.

Captain Nelson's death was a travesty of fate. We all knew he'd been a first-tour warrant. He'd accepted a direct commission as an RLO and trained to fly the CH-54 Skycrane. He was supposed to have been assigned to fly Skycranes in a unit at Da Nang. But the Green Machine shipped him to the Phoenix. He'd accepted his leadership role and duties with enthusiasm.

The days would drag on, but the word of Nelson's and Moreira's deaths would resurface in my thoughts when the routine did not consume my attention. To me, Nelson was the most unlikely pilot to get killed: he was too experienced; too capable; too damn good! To me, Nelson had been the paragon of an army aviator.

For me, the missions suddenly reverted to REMF missions. Boring as hell, but very safe. It seemed as if there was no longer a war going on. That feeling would last for a short while. I had to carry a doughnut dolly (Red Cross worker) from Camp Eagle to Firebase Bastogne, where she would spend the day entertaining troops, playing games, bringing mail and Red Cross gifts. It was the first time I flew a woman passenger. During the flight out we took yellow tracers, .30-caliber machine-gun fire. That surprised the hell out of me because the firebase was only ten miles west of Camp Eagle. I was a single ship at two thousand five hundred feet and must have made a tempting target, but the yellow tracers were way out in front of us. The girl in the left front seat didn't even notice, and I said nothing. Four hours later, I picked her up at the firebase and returned her to Camp Eagle. The return flight was uneventful, at a higher altitude.

March 17 was a long day of flying convoy escort and general support. I spent it cruising the area north of the Rock Pile around the DMZ with Fitzgerald. We came across a few bunkers north of Firebase Fuller and came to a hover to drop fragmentation and CS grenades into them, but didn't find any enemy. I guess they'd learned that Loaches were only part of their problem. The FAC overhead could really make them hurt with the jets he had on call.

The DMZ was an amazing landscape. It looked like what I'd expect to see on the Moon or Mars. For at least two miles there was nothing but pockmarked craters from the continuous bombing. Red clay, water, and the debris of war. While scouting the mountain hillsides in the area, we ran across huge monitor lizards between six and eight feet in length. Obviously, with them out sunning, the North Vietnamese were not around. It had been a tension-filled day of convoy escort but, luckily, without contact. That night, I returned to Camp Eagle to pack. It was time for my long-awaited R & R week in Hawaii with my wife.

# 10

# Rest and Relaxation

On March 18 I caught a flight in a Loach to Freedom Hill, the airbase at Da Nang where the jets came in from Hawaii and the States. I went through out-processing and had to spend the night there prior to my flight for Honolulu.

The flight from Da Nang to Honolulu was long, but relaxing. In Stateside khakis I hadn't worn in seven months, I was sitting next to a second-tour warrant officer who'd brought along his own flask of whiskey because alcohol was not served on the government-charter flights. He gave me a lot of good-natured kidding about our arrival at Honolulu. He said, "You haven't seen your wife in seven months. She's changed her hair, her weight is different, everything is gonna be different. You're not even gonna recognize her! It gets so confusing when everybody jumps off the bus and rushes to meet their wives and girlfriends. Some guys end up with the wrong girls. Doesn't slow down the festivities though." This is going to be crazy, I thought.

So it was with some trepidation (and intense excitement) that I stepped off the bus and saw the long line of women waiting at the R & R reception center. But I instantly picked out my lovely blond wife. From then on, Heaven was on Earth. Since I only had a carry-on bag, we caught a cab to the Ilakai Hotel on Waikiki Beach. As we made our way up to our room, I was in a near state of shock. To touch my wife, hug and kiss her after not having seen or talked with her for seven months, was months of dreams come true. Less than forty-eight hours earlier, I'd been flying a Loach along the DMZ and the Rock Pile, dropping CS and fragmentation grenades, hunting the enemy. Two short days later, I was in a gorgeous hotel room on Waikiki Beach with my lovely wife.

Our personal reunion was as intense and joyous as one could dream, and was, I'm sure, simultaneously repeated by hundreds of other couples under the same wartime circumstances.

Later that evening, we had dinner in the rooftop restaurant of the Ilakai Hotel. Afterward, I called my parents to talk with them, the first time in seven months. The phone call was a very difficult time, at best, and not a whole lot could be said. The news reports obviously had them worried, and I still had five months to go in Vietnam. They did not understand the confidence and control I had over my risk. There was no way to convey how much safer I was now that I no longer flew with the Phoenix.

We spent the first night in Honolulu, saw the Don Ho show, listened to "Tiny bubbles." I was introduced to Mai Tais and Leilani Hawaiian Rum. Then we flew to Kauai and stayed at the Hanalei Bay Plantation, where *South Pacific* had been filmed. For a boy raised on the beaches of the Gulf of Mexico, it couldn't have been any more beautiful.

It was pure joy to have a room overlooking Hanalei Bay and the mountain waterfalls. The setting was perfectly romantic, but it stunned me when I realized that the mountains that created the Waimea Canyon, the backdrop of Hanalei Bay, looked remarkably similar to the Razorback and Rock Pile. The same dark green vegetation, white-face mountain cliffs, and countless wispy waterfalls under cloud-shrouded mountaintops. What was spectacular beauty in Hawaii was simply hell in Vietnam.

After the time at Hanalei Bay, we returned to Waikiki Beach and the SurfRider Hotel. Hanging over us was the fact that the six nights would end shortly, and I would be returning to Vietnam for five more months, my wife, Stateside, alone. We talked of friends lost but spoke little of what I was actually doing though I tried to explain how different things were compared to December. I had as good a flying job as existed in I Corps. I wanted to mentally remove myself from Vietnam as much as possible, and she simply wanted the year to end quickly.

We spent the days walking the shopping areas and lying on the beach. I bought a T-shirt with a picture of a Phantom on the front. It had the words, FLY THE FRIENDLY SKIES OF LAOS on the back.

We enjoyed our time together in a way that can only be made possible by seven months of separation, all the while living on the edge of hope, knowing I was involved in a deadly endeavor. At the end of the week, we laughed when I reminded her of Captain Anderson saying, "The reason they only give you six days of R & R? That's how long it takes to wear a couple out." However, the humor of his remark was overshadowed by Anderson's death in an instrument flight accident.

# 11

# The Worst Pickup Zone: PZ Brown

By March 20, a horrible toll had been taken upon the aircraft from the units that had begun the Laotian invasion. Many, many aircraft had been damaged and were being repaired. The lack of aircraft availability once again made necessary the transfer of assets, this time from the 116th and the 176th Aviation Companies from the lower part of South Vietnam. The veterans of LZ Lolo returned on the nineteenth to Quang Tri. They'd fly for three tragedy-filled days in the evacuation of Pickup Zone Brown, enemy-encircled, deep in Laos.

Fortune had turned so badly against the ARVNs that evacuation of their troops had begun in earnest. Pickup Zone Brown was the last major Laotian pickup zone still in ARVN hands. It was several miles west of the Laos/Quang Tri Province border. Brown was south of QL9, southwest of A Luoi, and east-southeast of Lolo. Lolo had been the site of the most devastating losses involved in a helicopter combat assault. The area west of A Luoi was still claiming aircraft on a daily basis.

But Pickup Zone Brown would assume its place in army aviation history as worse than the Ia Drang, Khe Sanh, and Ripcord. It was the most costly PZ for U.S. Army helicopters extracting South Vietnamese troops from a one-sided battle. The aircraft from the 116th and 176th, the mainstay during the extractions from PZ Brown, were supplemented by ten 101st Aviation Battalion aircraft, seven from the Kingsmen (Bravo Company), and three crews from Black Widows (Charlie Company). The emergency extraction was, in the commanders' eyes, to move out of danger an ARVN battalion in danger of being overrun at Fire Support Base Brown. Unknown to those in command, elements of other ARVN units were fighting their way onto FSB Brown in hopes of also being extracted. ARVN troops already there were dropping their weapons in fear. For three days, the South Vietnamese forces had been under continuous contact, the enemy making repeated probes. Finally a command decision was made: extract all the forces left in the area. The remnants of *four* ARVN battalions located in and around Fire Support Base Brown would be taken out.

March 20, 1971, would be remembered by the Dolphins, Kingsmen, Black Widows, and Minutemen as the worst-ever day of army combat aviation. Pickup zones around FSB Brown were the day's objectives. And as ARVNs were dropping their weapons, too panicked to fight, the North Vietnamese carefully hugged the perimeters, waiting for a shot at the army helicopters attempting to evacuate the ARVNs. It was a shooting gallery for the NVA, who were just yards from the landing zones. When a Huey came to a low hover, the ARVNs clambered aboard, many becoming casualties of AK-47 fire. It was a nightmarish, very real rout under direct enemy fire.

CWO Al Fischer, Kingsmen One-eight, had only a month left in country, of his twelve-month tour of duty. He'd flown many CCN missions in support of Special Forces, as well as many missions supporting Ranger teams throughout I Corps. Like most young warrant officers, he felt risking U.S. aircrew lives repeatedly for the ARVN forces was not justified because the ARVN were dropping their weapons and refusing to fight, which only made the PZs more dangerous for the air crews. Terrified of dying at the hands of the NVA, the ARVNs crowded aboard the helicopters as they landed, creating a volatile, lethal environment; an overloaded Huey could easily be stuck on the ground if too many troops leapt aboard. The Huey's single turbine engine had a carefully measured weight capacity.

Maj. Jack Barker, commanding officer of the Kingsmen, and Capt. John Dugan were flying the lead ship of the third ten-ship element of the morning rescue flight. Everyone was aware that all three pickup zones had been surrounded by enemy troops with antiaircraft weapons. There was no access or approach that could be used to avoid enemy ground fire. The pilots knew that they'd take fire on the approach to landing and while sitting in the pickup zone. And that enemy fire wouldn't stop until they reentered South Vietnam's air space.

Shortly after they launched and headed toward the pickup zone, radio calls informed them that the first five aircraft of the first wave had been hit by enemy fire. Six aircraft out of the first twenty had been shot down, and others completed forced landings after severe antiaircraft damage in the vicinity of the pickup zone.

To the south of the pickup zone, low-level visibility was less than one mile because of smoke and dust created by a nearby B-52 strike. Haze from the bombings mixed with the dust and fires from heavy combat under way on the pickup zones. In addition, in an attempt to mask the approach of the Hueys, there had been extensive use of white phosphorous smoke. But the smoke only added to the confusion. The reduced visibility created an instrument-flight-rules (IFR) environment where Hueys could only operate under visual flight conditions. It soon became apparent that anyone descending below two thousand five hundred feet was in deadly visual flight conditions.

Major Barker and copilot Capt. John Dugan led their element through the white phosphorous smoke in an attempt to conceal themselves from the enemy's numerous .51-caliber and 23mm positions dispersed throughout the area. Even worse, there were 37mm positions bunkered nearby. But as the Hueys broke through the smoke on descent to the pickup zone, they came under heavy automatic-weapons fire. As they came closer to the pickup zone, the antiaircraft fire became so intense they were forced to make a go-around. While they attempted a climb to a safer altitude, they confirmed that all aircraft in their element were still flying. Barker's aircraft received a round through the heater compartment and out the tail rotor driveshaft. A second round struck Captain Dugan's seat armor as they continued to approach, another hit the cockpit, leaving a hole just above the major's head and damaging one of the structural beams of the airframe. Due to the intense fire and damage, the aircraft was rendered unsafe to fly, but uncertain of the severity of damage to their Huey, they'd made a go-around and rejoined the flight.

Amazingly, Major Barker, Captain Dugan, and their enlisted crew members were unhurt. But the second attempt into the pickup zone was equally hot and unsuccessful. Another Huey had been rendered unsafe to fly.

Behind them during the first attempt, CWO Al Fischer was flying as Chalk Two, the second helicopter in formation. Fischer was thinking during the flight into Laos that the operation had to be ending; it seemed as if every pickup zone was hot, but some had heavier caliber weapons around them than others. The flight was very tense and very serious. On the flight in, smoke from a B-52 Arc Light bombing attack obscured the ground. As the element approached the pickup zone, the ships spread out into a loose trail formation, to keep a one-minute separation between aircraft. They would not sit the aircraft on the ground, but come to a five-foot hover above the PZ. The crew chief and the door gunner would then pull aboard enough ARVNs for a safe full load. They knew that if they set down on the ground they would be swamped by panicked ARVNs and would not be able to take off.

Fischer watched as Major Barker rolled in left off the smoke. It was hard for Fischer to keep him in sight. Fischer tried to maintain a one-minute separation, but visibility was less than a mile. Barker had taken heavy fire and hits on short final. He executed a go-around without picking up troops. Sixty seconds had expired with no word from Barker. Fischer dropped his collective and skirted along the smoke screen, descending to the pickup zone. He dived low, keeping his Huey's air speed at 120 knots, nearly 150 miles per hour. As he approached the ground, the landscape around the pickup zone was sparkling. Little gold muzzle flashes from AK-47s were everywhere.

Barker did not report his taking fire or hits in the pickup zone; he was too busy trying to keep his aircraft flyable through the go-around. Unaware that Barker had taken heavy hits, Fischer continued his approach, taking his own hits as he crossed the perimeter of the pickup zone. Because he was coming hot and fast, he stood the bird on its tail and pulled in all the power he could to stop it. As he leveled the Huey to hover, his first sight was ARVN soldiers. Through his chin bubble, he saw them crouching in the middle of the pickup zone. It was a demoralizing, disgusting sight to Fischer: none had weapons.

At the same time, all hell opened up inside the Huey as AK-47 rounds turned the Huey's underside into a magnesium Swiss cheese.

Fischer's copilot, WO Ed Cash, jerked back as both greenhouse windows above the pilots' heads were shattered. Through his flight suit leg, Cash then took a round that just missed his skin. A former Green Beret with two tours prior to his aviation tour as a warrant officer, Cash had an M-16 with a scope slung over his seat. But an AK-47 round had entered the eye piece and exited the side of the scope. More AK-47 rounds flew through the radio controls and instrument control panel.

The crew chief, Sp4. Lyle Smith, and door gunner Sp4. Roger Perales were shooting their M-60 machine guns while hollering to Fischer to "Keep moving! Keep moving! Still taking hits." Pulling in maximum power, Fischer rolled the nose over and climbed out. He radioed Chalk Three to take a different path. By this time, North Vietnamese were waiting on the very edge of the PZ. His climb out was made to the east under continuous fire.

To immediately assess the battle damage, Smith and Perales climbed onto the Huey's skids as it climbed out. They reported to Fischer that they'd suffered multiple hits through the tail boom. Some rounds had come through the critical tail rotor drive shaft housing. They were also streaming a white trail of vaporizing jet fuel, an explosive fire hazard.

Fischer called lead, Major Barker, and reported that he was climbing to altitude and heading back to Khe Sanh with the wounded bird. It would be unflyable on landing. Barker did not answer the call. It was simply more bad news. Barker had also suffered similar hits.

Fischer's VHF and UHF radios were shot up and unusable. For a Huey pilot, that is as close as a round can physically get, without hitting him. Chalk Three's aircraft commander, Gene Haag, and Chalk Four's aircraft commander, WO Tom Hill, safely flew in low level after Fischer's warning. They were both able to pick up troops and get out with amazingly minor damage. The young warrant officers of the Kingsmen, aided by three Black Widows, continued the extraction. All were under constant fire in the landing zone, taking hits. A few minutes passed, then Chalk Five, commanded by WO Bruce Sibley, was hit by something larger than a rocket-propelled grenade, perhaps a 57mm antiaircraft gun. Though wounded, Sibley and his crew survived a crash just short of the pickup zone. The crew was rescued by Capt. Willis Wulf, flying the Kingsmen's recovery ship. For Fischer, all of the excitement down below was not enough to distract him from the immediate problems on his bird: he had a mortally wounded helicopter. He continued to climb to altitude and picked up Route 9, the dusty, one-lane road that ran from Tchepone to Khe Sanh. He could fly right at the base of the overhead cloud ceiling and follow the road to Khe Sanh because visibility had greatly improved after he'd climbed above the low-level smoke and haze of ground combat.

Fischer reached the cloud base at four thousand five hundred feet above ground level. In South Vietnam that would have been a totally safe altitude, above the range of small-arms fire. But Fischer intuitively sensed that was not the case in Laos. And to some North Vietnamese antiaircraft artillery gunner, he was a prominent silhouette. Just another expensive, slow target, just below the clouds.

In a blinding instant, Fischer felt as if someone had punched him between the eyes. He was momentarily knocked unconscious. Although it was widely known there were 37mm radar-controlled weapons in the area, the pilots did not know that 57mm and even 120mm weapons were being used as antiaircraft weapons.

Moments later Fischer awoke. He was looking through the open front end of his Huey's cockpit. The helicopter's nose, pilots' windshields, and canopies had been blown away and the Huey was screaming towards the ground, nearly vertical, at 120 knots. In three or four seconds more the aircraft would have exceeded its design-to-load limits and broken apart in midair, but Fischer recovered soon enough to pull back on the cyclic and add power. He then realized most of the instrument panel was gone and the engine would only run at flight-idle; it produced *no* usable flying power. He was then in an autorotation, in a combat-damaged aircraft, still a target of antiaircraft fire.

Fischer's copilot, Ed Cash, was slumped over in his seat. Fischer feared he was dead.

Whatever hit them had been very powerful. Even the center metal post that separated the pilot and copilot windshields was gone. Wires were dangling and sparking from the overhead control panel. Fischer tried to talk to Smith and Perales but heard no results. The intercom was dead. He turned around to look at Smith. Smith was staring back wide-eyed and talking. Fischer motioned, pointing to his ears, he could not hear Smith. With the radios out, shouting was the only way to communicate. Fischer then looked back again and noticed a hole the size of a football in the transmission wall. That alone was a fatal wound to the Huey. Fischer then wondered if it would hold together long enough to successfully autorotate.

Perales had also been knocked out by the blast. Smith had been forced back against the wall and could not get forward during the dive. Below, in front of them, Fischer saw where they were going to crash. In a powerless helicopter, you can only look down and see where you're gonna land. Fortunately, it happened to be a hilltop that was also a fire support base, Delta 1. Unfortunately, Fischer confused it with Fire Support Base Delta. The confusion between Delta and Delta 1 would later cause a problem in their rescue because Fire Support Base Delta was being attacked by the North Vietnamese. There were only four hundred ARVNs on it. Later in the day it would be overrun by Russian-made tanks.

Fischer was autorotating with only enough power to provide hydraulics and electricity for his now useless radios. Perales came to as they approached the firebase. As Fischer crossed over the perimeter of FSB Delta 1, he started taking heavy small-arms fire. It was just as bad as PZ Brown. Once again, a base was totally surrounded by NVA, who were right up against the perimeter wires. As soon as the skids touched down, Fischer bottomed the collective pitch, slamming the bird to the ground. He didn't want any chance of being a slow-moving target.

The aircraft slid some, but the surface was level, and the bird quickly ground to a stop. They continued taking heavy fire from the right side. Cash and Smith got out very quickly. Suddenly, Fischer heard a burst from an M-16 right behind his head: ARVNs had rushed the bird from a bunker, onto the left side, and they were pinning Perales in the bird, but he was able to get them to back off by firing toward them, well over their heads. Cash had gotten around and helped Perales take as much M-60 ammo as they could carry.

The four of them headed to a bulldozed trench some thirty yards from the center of the firebase. While Fischer was crawling toward the trench, he remembered he hadn't pulled the self-destruction handle on the FM digital scrambler radio. He turned back to the bird and fired four or five times into the KY-28 radio with his M-16, then crawled for the trench. Under fire, he rolled in on top of a wounded ARVN soldier with a bandaged, bloody leg. The wounded man let out a horrifying yell. Cash had already gotten the crew chief and gunner set up with the M-60 on the western edge of the fifteen-yard-long trench. They began suppressing fire closest to the perimeter.

Fischer had his survival vest on with a portable emergency transceiver. He extended the antennae and the radio began to beep on guard frequency. But when he listened, all he could hear was the beeps from many other aircraft shot down. Of course, some of the beeps may have been jamming and deception from the NVA. The trench had fifteen to twenty ARVNs, none with weapons except for an ARVN officer who had a pistol and the only PRC-25 radio in sight. They had given up fighting and were simply waiting to be withdrawn by the helicopters or to die at the hands of the North Vietnamese. Even though Fischer did not speak Vietnamese, he convinced the ARVN officer that he was going to use the radio. Fischer thought he should take the officer's pistol too. The ARVN officer gave Fischer the impression he might use the pistol to get his radio back. Allies hell. Fischer called on the Kingsmen company FM frequency, but got no response. Then mortars started walking across the landing zone. It was easy to see they were working the hilltop, trying to destroy Fischer's Huey. It seemed a perfectly good target sitting there; the North Vietnamese didn't know it was unflyable.

After a few nervous minutes, Fischer received a response on the PRC-25 from Kingsmen Six-nine, CWO Bill Singletary, who was Chalk 6. He had crew members WO Joe St. John, with crew chief Bill Dillender, and door gunner PFC John Chubb. Singletary's bird had also been badly hit and could not make the pickup zone. Then Singletary and St. John learned that Fischer was down on Fire Support Base Delta, but they couldn't see the helicopter on the ground. Singletary asked for a radio line count and homed in on Fischer, finally locating him at Delta 1. The mistake was understandable considering the conditions. Fischer had been confused, having been knocked unconscious by antiaircraft fire, awakening in a near fatal dive.

Singletary and St. John decided, despite the damage to their aircraft, they would pick up Fischer and his crew. Fischer radioed Singletary and told him that Fire Support Base Delta 1 was very hot, was surrounded, and that he should not come in.

Defiant of the obvious dangers, Singletary chuckled. "I'll be coming in low-level from the north. Give me a mark." Singletary and St. John approached low-level, 120 knots, in the trees. As the Huey approached the edge of Delta 1, Fischer distinctly heard both the increasing sound of the Huey and the crescendo of AK-47s and .51-calibers. Just before Singletary broke over the edge of the firebase, Smith jumped out of the trench onto his knees, then held his M-16 above his head to mark a T for Singletary. He'd also become a perfect, motionless target for the NVA. Smith could not have been in that position for more than two or three seconds when the dirt around him exploded from AK-47 fire.

Fischer saw Smith fall to the ground in the fusillade. Thinking the worst, he sank into the trench floor. He believed Smith was dead or critically wounded. Fischer entered the mental zone shared by combatants facing imminent mortality. Time slowed as events around him unfolded. A sense of personal calm emerged from a spiritual presence. Fischer sensed this was not the end, regardless of the outcome. The calm empowered him to look up again.

Amazed, he saw that Smith had only fallen to the ground. Smith was again in a prone position holding his M-16 above his head. He hadn't been hit, but bullets were still flying.

Thank God! Fischer then believed guardian angels were working overtime. Lying in the trench under fire, he'd sensed a spiritual presence. He'd experienced the surreal peace that comes over many preparing to accept the inevitable end. It had empowered him to take the necessary steps to save himself.

St. John called the mark. As the Huey flared, shuddering in a violent deceleration, Fischer and the others sprinted to the center of the pickup zone, anticipating the Huey's touchdown spot. It was a twenty- or thirty-yard run at a crouch, weapons firing from the hip. Fischer would later recall it as a scene from a John Wayne movie.

Singletary stood his Huey nose-high, its tail stinger furrowing into the ground. He had decelerated from one hundred thirty miles an hour to a slow hover, in less than fifty yards.

Simultaneously, in a "John Wayne moment," Fischer and the others were running to the touchdown spot, firing underneath the flaring Huey at North Vietnamese on the far perimeter, trying to suppress fire. Singletary never had to stop the Huey as the four men jumped on. Fischer was the last one pulled aboard. They accelerated away from the landing zone as mortars were closely impacting on both sides of their flight path.

Fischer's chest had hit the floor of the bird, knocking the wind out of him. The very next thing he felt was crew chief Dillender grabbing his back and literally throwing him across the floor of the Huey. Fischer reached out his arm, luckily catching the back of Singletary's seat. He'd almost slid out the other side of the accelerating Huey as Singletary pulled in all the power he had and nosed it over, staying at ground level and accelerating away from the North Vietnamese. The four passengers in the back of the Huey were firing M-16s as the crew chief and the door gunner fired their M-60s.

Emotionally spent, they returned to Khe Sanh. They landed at the pad where other Kingsmen birds were sitting. After landing, Singletary's bird was red X'd for combat damage. Kingsmen Huey 492, the one flown by Fischer, was destroyed by Cobra gunships on Firebase Delta 1. Later in the day, Singletary's bird, tail number 185, would be claimed by Maj. Jack Barker to make one more attempt into Pickup Zone Brown because 185 had sustained fewer fatal hits than Barker's bird.

At Khe Sanh, Fischer learned that Chalks Three and Four had numerous hits on short final into PZ Brown, but elected to take the aircraft into the pickup zone. They each loaded troops but received severe automatic weapons fire on departure. They were able to evacuate the troops, but their passengers were wounded.

Chalk Five came on short final and, one hundred meters from the PZ, was hit by something larger than a rocket-propelled grenade and crashed in the trees short of the pickup zone. Amazingly, the pilot and copilot were the only casualties.

Chalks Seven, Eight, and Nine were forced to abort the landing due to antiaircraft hits prior to entering final approach. Battle-damaged, they all returned to Khe Sanh.

Chalk Ten was orbiting around Fire Support Base Delta 1 and went to the aid of Chalk Five.

Like the others, Chalk Ten received the same heavy automatic-weapons fire on final, but another desperate rescue was needed. Wulf hovered over the side of Sibley's Huey, which was resting on its side after a violent crash. The copilot and crewmen managed to get aboard the rescue Huey. They didn't know that Sibley had been wounded and could not help himself.

Then Wulf spotted Sibley motioning him to leave! Wulf was simultaneously taking AK-47 hits, and he could see North Vietnamese troops running toward them. In desperation, Wulf asked his crew chief to climb down onto the crashed Huey and retrieve Sibley. The crew chief succeeded in getting Sibley on board. Wulf had managed to pick up the entire downed aircraft crew, which had been surrounded by enemy forces. Chalk Ten successfully departed with the crew aboard but took heavy damage from automatic-weapons fire on departure. They made it back to Khe Sanh with badly wounded crew members. CWO Bill Singletary and Capt. Willis Wulf received Silver Stars for the heroic efforts that saved the crews of CWO Bruce Sibley and Fischer.

That afternoon, the evacuations continued. The morning flight of the Kingsmen had consisted of seven Kingsmen aircraft flyable, with three Black Widows from C Company, 101st Aviation Battalion. What had been a horrifying morning of close calls was going to culminate in an afternoon of courage, death, and heroism beyond the call of duty. Virtually all of the birds that participated in the Pickup Zone Brown affair were red X'd because of enemy antiaircraft hits. They were determined by maintenance to be unflyable without major repairs.

That afternoon, under the orders of Lieutenant Colonel Peachey, the company commanders assembled the remaining "flyable" birds. The evacuation of Fire Support Base Brown had been declared a tactical emergency, and they were to finish removing ARVNs from Laos by sunset. The Kingsmen had just one bird left that could fly, Huey 185. The survivor of Fischer's rescue, Singletary's bird.

Fischer had survived the attempted rescue of ARVNs from Pickup Zone Brown. He'd survived having his aircraft mortally wounded hovering in the pickup zone. He'd even survived the airburst over Delta 1 that had blown the nose off his Huey. Then he'd successfully completed a powerless autorotation onto an enemy-encircled landing zone, taking more antiaircraft fire during the descent. There he'd narrowly escaped under enemy fire after participating in infantry ground combat. Having been knocked temporarily unconscious by an airburst was grounds for an automatic medical grounding. But he was ordered to take another Huey to PZ Brown. With one month left in country, Fischer had lost friends and seen far too many wounded. Fischer told Major Barker it was worthless to try again; the pickup zone was totally encircled. The NVA were using the ARVNs as bait so that they could shoot Hueys out of the sky. The ARVNs needed to find another way out. His disgust was driven by his observation that the ARVNs had simply dropped their weapons and were just awaiting the encircling NVA.

By that point, Fischer had tested the limits of luck and fate. He was disgusted with the entire operation. He refused to be a target over PZ Brown again. He'd risked his life on behalf of the ARVNs in the morning and nearly died four times. CWO Singletary shared Fischer's feelings. At different times, both were called before Lieutenant Colonel Peachey.

First, Peachey threatened Fischer, to no avail. Fischer told Lieutenant Colonel Peachey of the ARVNs cowering on Brown and Delta 1. Fischer told Lieutenant Colonel Peachey that he wouldn't go just to extract ARVNs. Without them fighting, trying to defend their pickup zones, it was simply suicide. Fischer then told Lieutenant Colonel Peachey, that "If one American was stranded on

the ground, I'd go get him, and the sooner the better."
After the day Fischer had endured, he'd not go back for
the ARVNs. Lieutenant Colonel Peachey promised him a
court-martial, to no avail.

Sometime later, CWO Singletary was ordered to an
audience before Lieutenant Colonel Peachey. In separate
interviews, the same conversation was repeated. Another
flight would be a waste of American lives. Both men had
pleaded with Peachey not to send more aircraft into PZ
Brown. Peachey was adamant that the operation continue.

Fischer and Singletary were equally adamant that it
would continue without their participation. For both men,
it was the only time either had refused an order. It was an
emotionally charged, gut-wrenching experience. Neither
man had ever dreamed he'd be faced with an order to certain death. Fischer and Singletary knew any further attempt would be suicide, not only for themselves, but their
crewmen as well.

Maj. Jack Barker, the Kingsmen commanding officer,
was not rated as an aircraft commander. Neither was his
copilot, Capt. John Dugan. Prior to going through aviation training and returning for his second tour in Vietnam
as an aviator, Barker had served a first tour on the ground.
Barker told Singletary and Fischer that he and Dugan
would take the mission, with Singletary's flyable bird.
With crewmen Dillender and Chubb aboard, they'd join
the other remnants of helicopter companies, continuing
the evacuation of PZ Brown. Singletary went to Dugan
and begged him not to go. He said, "You're not only
gonna get yourself killed, but the others with you." Fischer also pleaded with Dugan, begging him not to go.
Dugan simply replied that "duty called" and continued
preparing for the mission. Fischer then begged Major
Barker, his commanding officer, not to go. It would cost
them their lives. Major Barker and John Dugan were
adamant. Dillender and Chubb had no reluctance to go

back with them despite what they had gone through in the
morning.

That afternoon they flew to a briefing for a final attempt
at PZ Brown. Leading a flight of only three aircraft, at
3:00 in the afternoon they again flew to the besieged
pickup zone.

The commander of the Kingsmen (Bravo Company),
Maj. Jack Barker, and Capt. John Dugan began their third
attempted sortie into Pickup Zone Brown to extract allies
on the ground.

As Barker began his short final approach to the landing
zone, the Huey was struck by a rocket-propelled grenade,
losing its tail boom. The main rotor then separated from
the aircraft, and the fuselage nosed over and plummeted
in an uncontrollable dive to the ground. It exploded in a
ball of flames, killing all aboard. Sp4. William Dillender,
the crew chief, and PFC John Chubb, door gunner, had
also volunteered for the mission, at the cost of their lives.

Maj. Bob Clewell was flying in extended trail formation behind Barker. Clewell listened in horror as another
pilot reported Barker's loss.


Sickened by the tragic and useless loss of Dugan, Barker,
Dillender, and Chubb, Fischer and Singletary returned to
Camp Eagle that night. They had shared a wretched experience, and it was the only time either would refuse an
order. They'd understood that Barker and Dugan were career soldiers whose careers were ended if they refused a
mission. Singletary and Fischer believed the mission to
be suicide not only for themselves but also for their enlisted crew members. Considering the day's experiences,
Singletary and Fischer believed they'd made the only
sane choice. Even so, they'd find no solace in surviving
the day.

Singletary and Fischer did not know what would face
them the next morning, but after defying Lieutenant Colonel Peachey's threat of a court-martial, they had no illu-

sions about making the army a career. Both young pilots were dazed. It had been unbelievably difficult just to stay alive. With the simple exception of not dying, it had been the worst of days.

The other combat-experienced pilots were also sadly relieved, to simply be alive.

At the five A.M. wake-up call the next morning, Singletary and Fischer were each given a Huey with an ash-and-trash mission list, resupply missions for U.S. troops in the beautiful but deadly A Shau Valley. After the previous day in Laos, it was as easy as a day could be for a slick driver. Neither heard any mention of a court-martial, and each attributed that to the deaths of Major Barker and his crew. Fischer and Singletary would not discuss the events until 1986. Only then would they learn of each other's being called before Lieutenant Colonel Peachey.

On the following day, attempts to lift out ARVNs continued, but the panicked soldiers swamped any aircraft that approached the pickup zone, packing twenty to thirty men into a Huey designed to carry no more than ten. This horrified the pilots and crew members, who knew the load limits of the aircraft.

The enemy fire continued to take a toll. On the afternoon of March 21, Major Bunting, commanding officer of the 48th Assault Helicopter Company, knew his men were physically exhausted, emotionally shot. All the remaining flyable aircraft were battle damaged. But the withdrawal was a trial of resolve and honor of the kind few ever experience in a lifetime. Major Bunting didn't climb up to altitude like some commanders, but flew the lead helicopter, down in the dirt, leading the army's charge. His leadership by example, with disregard for his own personal safety, had already gotten him shot down on two prior occasions. Knowing of Major Barker's loss the preceding day only added to the gravity of his decision.

During the evening briefing the night before, Bunting

had told his men of the mission. Warning them it would likely be a repeat of the disastrous one of March 20, he informed the men he needed ten aircrews, all volunteers.

In the morning mission, Major Bunting led his flight of ten Blue Stars as the final string behind thirty other Hueys. When they entered Laos, antiaircraft fire took its toll. As Bunting listened to those ahead of him, he heard horrifying commentaries of hits taken, wounded crewmen, and constant calls of "Going down!" *Every* aircraft in the first three flights of ten Hueys each was either shot down or damaged so badly it wouldn't fly again.

The debacle of panicked, unarmed ARVNs swamping hovering Hueys while the NVA took target practice was lunacy. Bunting realized that the pickup zone had to be moved. He called Lieutenant Colonel Peachey and asked Peachey to call it off until the PZ could be moved a short distance. Peachey was adamant. The extraction would continue.

For Major Bunting, combat risk had observable, carefully measured limits. Sanity had to set a limit. A month earlier, Bunting had been told by General Sutherland that a lift company was an acceptable sacrifice to maintain the diplomacy of the army support of the ARVN effort.

But Bunting had reached a rational limit. There would be no senseless sacrifice of his Blue Stars. He radioed Peachey, telling him they would not go in until the pickup zone was moved. Infuriated, Peachey ordered him to proceed. Again, Bunting requested that he move the PZ. A general of the 101st Airborne Division circling above, call sign Right Guard, overheard the conversation. He ordered Peachey and Bunting to meet him at the log pad at Khe Sanh.

Bunting ordered his Blue Stars back to Khe Sanh and headed for the log pad. Was he going to be relieved of command or worse? Bunting was hoping the general might back him up against Peachey, but thought that was highly unlikely. After all, it was Peachey who had ordered the continuation of the assault onto Lolo at the cost of seventeen Hueys. Then, in a moment of divine intervention or poetic justice, Lieutenant Colonel Peachey was shot down in Laos!

Bunting waited at the log pad, but neither one showed up. He returned to his Blue Stars and was informed the PZ was being moved. They were on standby for the afternoon. He then learned of Peachey's being shot down.

A short while later, another urgent call for evacuation was received. The Blue Star pilots were convinced the ARVNs were cowards, adding to the enemy threat by not defending their PZ. Most pilots said they'd not fly the mission. Major Bunting, instead of displaying emotion or threatening the young warrant officers, simply declared that he understood. In fact, he even agreed with the pilots' observations of the situation. However, as commander, he had his duty; he felt he had no choice but to go.

The gravity of the moment was no less serious than when Colonel Travis drew a line in the sand at the Alamo. Bunting walked away from the pilots and began the engine-starting sequence in his Huey. A wave of passion swept through the young pilots. The disbelief and profanity ended when someone shouted, "He can't fucking go alone!" The Blue Stars swarmed to their Hueys, saddled up, and followed Major Bunting back into hell over Laos.

Bunting led the Blue Stars through the antiaircraft fire, and the NVA threw everything at them. A few took hits to their Hueys. The Blue Stars, combat veterans with a highly experienced leader, came in at altitude. When they neared the pickup zone, they made a rapid descent to the treetops.

The final approach was an in-your-face treetop assault to the new pickup zone. Amazingly, though antiaircraft fire from bunkered emplacements was fierce, the NVA infantry were absent; moving the pickup zone had denied the bunkered NVA their fields of fire. In the worst mission, the last assault onto Brown, the Blue Stars prevailed victorious and extracted the beleaguered ARVNs. Unbelievably, by the mission's end no Blue Stars had been wounded or killed!

Major Bunting never heard a word from either Lieutenant Colonel Peachey or the 101st Airborne general.

*March 22, 1971, Laos.* A Minuteman UH-1H was flying at five thousand feet over Laos. At what would have been a very safe altitude in South Vietnam, the aircraft took heavy antiaircraft artillery fire and blew up. The flaming pieces slowly floated to the ground. Witnesses would remember the event, mentally replaying the haunting melody of James Taylor's classic, "Fire and Rain." The words "Sweet dreams and flying machines, in pieces on the ground" was a refrain never to be forgotten. Another WORWAC Class 70-3/70-5 member, Reginal Cleve died. Our wives had been good friends during flight school.

On March 23, daily artillery raids continued at Khe Sanh. Each time the first rounds fell, sirens wailed and aircraft scrambled into the air. At 2:30 A.M. on March 23, Troop D, 2d Squadron, 17th Cavalry, received a ground attack by commandos (sappers) of the 2d Company, 15th North Vietnamese Army Engineer Battalion. Forty men infiltrated to the perimeter. Then, under cover of 60mm mortar fire and RPGs, in an attempt to reach the helicopter refuel and rearm points, they penetrated the 3d Platoon night position.

The fighting, vicious hand-to-hand combat, lasted until 6:45 A.M. Fourteen NVA sappers died in the attack, and one NVA prisoner was taken, along with nine AK-47s, three RPG launchers, and one 9mm pistol.

U.S. losses were 3 killed in action, 5 with major wounds, and 123 minor wounded. Wounds were called minor if it wasn't you, and you didn't need hospitalization. Four days later, D Troop returned to its much more secure base at Quang Tri. One Medal of Honor was awarded as a result of the action.

## March 23, 1971, White House, Washington, D.C.

President Richard Nixon had a busy day with Secretary of State Henry Kissinger. At the midday meeting, H. R. Haldeman sat listening to a review of the action in Laos. As Henry Kissinger wrapped up his presentation to the president, he concluded with the statement, "It comes out as clearly not a success, but still a worthwhile operation."

Kissinger and the president both felt they had been misled by army general Creighton Abrams. The original evaluation of what might have been accomplished had obviously not been attained. Abrams continued with the plan to assault Tchepone, even though it was clear that the original plan wasn't working. Kissinger felt strongly that they should have followed Westmoreland's advice and gone south to cut off the Ho Chi Minh trail. Instead, they'd gone on to capture Tchepone. In the politician's eyes, the westward move toward Tchepone had turned out to be a disaster.

Had they asked the pilots who'd flown LZ Sophia and PZ Brown, the conclusions would've been far more certain. Secretary Kissinger then discussed with President Nixon the possibility of pulling Abrams out, of firing him.

The president thought for a moment. Pensively, he made a point. The Laotian invasion was the end of offensive military operations involving U.S. forces. In the words of President Nixon, "So what difference would it make?"

Abrams kept his job.

*March 24, 1971.* In Vietnam, Echo Troop, 1st of the 9th Cavalry, 1st Cavalry Division, supporting the 25th Infantry Division, fielded a normal daily operation, visual reconnaissance in an OH-6. The pilot, Steve Larrabee, was a warrant officer, of Class 70-5. Ground fire claimed his life.

On the morning of March 26, my wife and I left the hotel for the Honolulu International Airport. She would return to the States alone, and I would return to my unit in Vietnam. Looking around us, we saw many other couples in a similar predicament. There were few dry eyes in the room. The coming five months would seem like five years. I could not imagine how difficult it would have been to have taken a two-week leave, gone home to the States, and then had to return to Vietnam.

On the evening of March 27, I returned to my hootch, dropping my bags. I then walked over to the company officers club. I was surprised to see everyone enjoying themselves, sitting around, BSing. Few people had been around the club during the past two months due to the high hours of flying with long mission days.

I then heard the story of Mumby's being shot down while carrying a Vietnamese general, but without injuries. Fitzgerald had hit a tree, narrowly avoiding a midair collision with another helicopter, nearly losing his transmission/rotor system as a result. He barely made it back safely, but his aircraft DEROSed. Several other aircraft in the company had taken serious hits during the past week, but Khe Sanh had been closed. Mercifully, the missions in Laos had ended.

The demands and pressure had eased dramatically. I sat with Jim Saunders and others, laughing about all that had transpired in the previous two weeks. Saunders said, "You should have seen it. On the twenty-third, we had artillery shelling at Khe Sanh. Two hundred aircraft on the ground, and then the 122mm and 155mm artillery started hitting. It wasn't rockets because it was slow, constant fire. The kid in the tower told all aircraft to evacuate the base, and he was evacuating the tower. His last radio transmission was, 'This is fucking ridiculous!' "

Saunders continued, "As I took off, I saw the control tower exploding." Of the more than two hundred aircraft on the ground at Khe Sanh, all had departed during the artillery bombardment with no damage. Amazingly, there were no accidents in the melee. We joked about how we'd seen movies of C-130s being blown up in Khe Sanh during 1968. The only reason one wasn't blown up this time was that a C-130 had ripped up the steel planking runway during a very hard landing about March 9, and the runway was not back in service, so there were no C-130s going in and out to make big targets.

For Saunders, the admiral's son who'd nearly lost his life being shot down on Ripcord the previous July, the convoy escort duty was the last of his high-risk missions. His capture of the NVA machine gun was a memorable event.

Then everyone started ragging Mumby, a really likeable fellow, who reminded me of Tommy Doody, who'd been killed with the Phoenix. Mumby was flying General Phu, the top Vietnamese general in I Corps. They were at five thousand feet, flying command and control over a combat assault in Laos. Mumby simply couldn't believe he was flying so high he could barely be seen, yet he was taking flak, just like that in movies of World War II. Shot out of the sky, they successfully autorotated to a crash landing, without further damage or injury. Another aircraft picked them up immediately. They spent but a few seconds on the ground and immediately returned to Camp Eagle, got another aircraft, and went back out on station.

I was shocked to hear that Mumby had even taken fire, not to mention his being shot down. It turned out that several other aircraft in the 163d Aviation Company had also taken hits. Virtually everyone had numerous instances of taking fire, this in a rear-echelon outfit! All the Loach pilots had alternated missions flying VIPs one day, Loach white teams the next. They routinely flew aggressive reconnaissance missions, with an overhead escort of an O-2 forward air controller and a pair of Cobra gunships. The C-and-C birds took their hits over Laos at altitude. Saunders remarked that the North Vietnamese Army never returned to the bunker I'd found with Cobb. We'd made it far too costly to use. We proudly discussed the fact no convoys were ever ambushed, with us overhead. In fact, no one even took fire there after Cobb and I had directed air strikes on February 14.

### April 5, 1971, Camp Eagle

For me, April 5 was a zero of a day. I had the day down from flying. Didn't get mail from home. I calculated that I had one large tube of toothpaste and it would last until I DEROSed.

When I got bored, I went to the division officers club and started an early afternoon of drinking. I ran into a tall, white-haired kid from a slick company. We started swapping war stories. I made the near fatal mistake of telling him I'd flown CCN quite a bit with the Phoenix and had enjoyed my experiences. His mouth dropped, looking at me in absolute disbelief. His face flushed red, angrily. He said, "(I can't believe) you fucking *enjoyed* it! I say, you're a rear echelon motherfucker who never did it." A pissing contest was on.

I replied, "Well, we always had good missions, never had anything (bad) happen."

"I've had my ass shot down on CCN," he retorted. "We had four slicks go in, all shot down . . . lucky enough to be picked up by an air force CH-53, you fucking REMF!" At that point, I knew better than to argue. He was a man who'd experienced the absolute worst and lived to tell about it. He also had to continue flying those missions despite his personal awareness of mortality and fear. I'd experienced it, only seven straight weeks on CCN, which was the equivalent of four to six months normal rotation and exposure for some lift companies. He had been rotating on it for months and had months to go. I had chosen to leave it. He had no choice. The amount of risk servicemen faced in Vietnam was not balanced or fair. What your job was, coupled with where you were, determined heavy burdens for some, and very little for others.

For the moment, I was a convicted REMF. I was beginning to question my own sense of integrity. My friends in the Phoenix Company were still flying combat assaults in the A Shau and missions into Laos. I rotated between moderate-risk direct support of the combat engineers battalion along the A Shau Valley and convoy escort duties, and virtually no-risk courier trips to the land of freedom birds in Da Nang.

The work only made me appreciate more my decision to move to the 163d, but I was gaining an even deeper respect for those who served their entire tours with the Phoenix and the other assault helicopter companies. I'd keep my mouth shut and opinions to myself around the pilots in the clubs. I had plenty of combat experience. Not as much as those spending a year in the 158th or 101st Aviation Battalions, but a good deal more than pilots in areas south of Hue. From time to time, I'd witness angry pissing contests between pilots about their flying skills and degree of combat experience. Who got shot up most often or who'd been shot down the most was a truly ridiculous argument, when most people removed from the circumstances would agree once was too often!

I'd recover quickly from the insult. It did, however, increase my understanding of others' feelings, and remind me how damn good I had it. Would I have changed places with him? Hell no! I'd been there and done that! I knew better!

* * *

The following night, we had a Canadian show. Took movies of it. Vietnam style. Just a couple of dancers with their clothes . . . almost on.

The American band backing them up had two excellent singers. One girl sang Janis Joplin's, "A Piece of My Heart." It brought a complete silence to our rowdy, raucous drunks. But, when the next girl sang James Taylor's song, "Fire and Rain," the words, "sweet dreams and flying machines, in pieces on the ground," were met with a stunned appreciation, a whole new meaning to the song.

I was officially promoted to chief warrant officer, grade 2 (CW2). My indefinite status (lifer) was accepted. I'd have thirty-one months of duty remaining when I returned Stateside.

On the twelfth, I flew three hours, carried two American Red Cross girls out to Firebase Bastogne. Second time I'd carried women on my aircraft. In a letter home I wrote my wife, "Now, aren't you glad it takes both hands and both feet to fly a helicopter?"

I finally killed the big damn rat that made daily visits to my room. I baited a trap with C-ration chocolate (John Wayne candy bars). The big atomic rattrap didn't kill him, just stuck around his neck, but he couldn't get away. I held him by the tip of his nasty hairless tail, while he squirmed to get away, trying to bite me. I doused him in jet fuel and lit him. Guess I'm killing one large one a day. When you wake up in the middle of the night with them crawling on you, it's worse than a nightmare. The little black presents they leave are proof it wasn't a bad dream.

When I first moved into the 163d Aviation Company, I had a cubicle assigned to me while another warrant officer was on leave in Taiwan. The first night there, I woke up with a large rat sitting on my chest, licking my chin. As I threw him off, he left a few round black presents on my bed and me. I've loathed them ever since.

The next day, Bill Gordy came walking in. I told him, "I've had another rat in my cubicle. Have you killed the one after your food?"

"Yeah," he replied, "but I think we still need to do something. Why don't we use some mogas (gasoline) and clean out the graves around us, and the drainpipes? They're either living in those graves, or they're coming in through the drainpipe by the bunker."

"Okay, let's do it." So, out we marched. We picked up a five-gallon jerrican and filled it with gasoline at the maintenance hangar just below our hootch. Only a few feet from our back door, there was a large, round Buddhist grave, which was recessed about two and a half to three feet deep. It had a small mound in the middle, and was completely overgrown with weeds. We spread the five gallons of gas around it and a rat ran out. Then we lit the gas. To our amazement, we were then singed by a huge orange-black mushroom cloud. It billowed into the air, high above our hootch rooftop! It was an awesome sight.

At the same time, having dropped off General Phu and returning home for the night, Mumby was on final in his Huey. When he saw the orange-black mushroom cloud at Snoopy's Pad, he called Camp Eagle tower. "Eagle, it appears you have incoming at Snoopy's Pad. Executing go-around." Mumby initiated a flyby rather than coming to a hover and stopping. He thought he had just witnessed a rocket or mortar attack. Gordy and I were singed by the flames but we were laughing hysterically. It got even more silly as we flashed peace signs as Mumby flew by. We understood that he'd done the go-around because of us. As the fire continued, we heard popping sounds, and after it burned down, we found the remnants of probably twenty glass vials that had contained cocaine.

With that outstanding moment of success, we then took the jerrican and filled it with fuel again. This time, however, we went back to the drainage pipes that allowed the flow of rainwater out of our company living quarters. We doused as much gas as we could and then lit the drainpipes, and almost immediately, about twenty rats ran out on fire. However, there was a muffled explosion about twenty yards downhill at the adjacent company where people had been sitting around just talking and drinking brewskies until the drainpipe at their feet suddenly exploded in flames. Then rats on fire ran wildly among them. It was a scene from some comedic Dante's *Inferno*! Then a couple of officers came running up, demanding to know "Who did that?" Gordy replied, "Swamp gas," and I collapsed in cramps from laughing. A short while later, Mumby came walking up asking, "Where's the barbeque?"

In a letter from home, it sounded like my brother Steve had made his high school graduation party a memorable one. My wife told me his favorite saying is "Draft beer, not students!" I'll second that!

The Recon Team of the 3d Battalion (Airmobile), 187th Infantry, operating south of Firebase Fury, was attacked by the NVA. While attempting a hot string extraction, a Huey of the 101st Aviation Battalion was shot down on top of them. One Ranger survived the disaster and left to make contact with other U.S. forces nearby. After telling them of the situation, he returned to help his friends. He would, however, not return. He would later be listed MIA. Nearly three years later, he'd return as a former POW, unwilling to discuss his capture or the loss of his friends.

B Company, 2d Battalion Airmobile, 502d Infantry, was inserted to help in locating the downed UH-1. The company met fierce resistance from the NVA. Then A Company, 1st Battalion (Airmobile), was air assaulted in for additional strength. The aircraft was found. The wounded were recovered at a high cost, ten U.S. killed, twenty U.S. wounded, and three missing in action.

The Kingsmen Company was just across the hover pad from our company area, and several of our pilots had transferred in from the Kingsmen. But there were personal friendships that didn't end simply because acquaintances transferred to a nearby unit.

Cobb was a very good friend of one pilot killed. Cobb had personally survived our daylong engagement north of the Rock Pile, cruising the DMZ in a Loach, and countless other risks flying convoy escort between Vandegrift and Khe Sanh.

Fitzgerald had flown similar missions with me in the DMZ. He nearly died hitting a tree in a Loach, while trying to avoid a midair collision with a Huey outside of Vandegrift. He flew it back to Quang Tri, but the aircraft was DEROSed.

A 101st pilot was drinking with us last night. Only had three months left in his tour. Today, he's dead, his Huey shot down by an NVA .51-caliber while inserting ARVNs on the east side of the A Shau Valley, near O'Reilley. Fitzgerald and Cobb were both sickened. They were close friends. Some complain, "What's the point? We're leaving." The fucking war really was over, for some.

We had been celebrating the end of DEWEY CANYON and LAM SON 719. For us, the closing of Khe Sanh was the end of high-risk missions. Their deaths jerked us back into the grim awareness and admiration of the assault helicopter companies who continued combat assaults until the units DEROSed.

*April 29, 1971.* CW2 Ronald Evans, serving with Bravo Troop, 7th of the 17th Cavalry, became the next casualty by enemy fire for Warrant Officer Rotary Wing Aviator Class 70-5.

CW2 William Hasselman was working with the 155th Assault Helicopter Company at Da Nang. During a maintenance post-flight inspection, he walked into the tail rotor of a Huey and was killed. Another WORWAC 70-3/70-5 class member was dead.

On April 29, I got my pay slip. Two other guys and I downed a quart of gin and two quarts of lemonade during the movie *Love Your Wife* with Elliott Gould. I'm told it was a real funny show, watching us lead the movie.

## May 3, 1971, A Shau Valley

Special Forces Recon Team Asp consisted of staff sergeants Klaus Bingham, James Luttrell, Lewis Walton, and three Montagnards. They were dropped into the jungle near the big valley's north end to investigate NVA road-building activity. Ten minutes after they were on the ground, they radioed a "Team okay." It was their last transmission. They were believed captured since no call for air support was made. They would be listed as missing in action.

## May 4, 1971, Stateside

Police and military units were used to arrest twelve thousand antiwar protestors who tried to shut down the Pentagon and Capitol. They were detained at the Washington Redskins practice field.

## May 10, 1971

Ninety-eight days to go. Still a long time but sure sounded better than three hundred. Army Secretary Resor came to Eagle, and I didn't even know it. VIPs were commonplace because the 101st Airborne was the largest combat division remaining in Vietnam and with them came hordes of newsmen. After what I'd seen of newsmen I felt it would be hard to find a network I would believe. The ones I crossed paths with appeared out to make a fast buck on a big war story. I thought most of them were prohippie, antiwar. I felt I could be called antiwar, but certainly not in the same way.

# 12

# Recon Team Alaska
# and the Phoenix Vow

**May 17, 1971**

May 17 would never be forgotten by Capt. Skip Butler (Redskin One-five) and Capt. Don Davis with the Phoenix Company (Phoenix Two-six), as well as others involved.

Butler was to provide gunship support for UH-1 companies in the 158th Aviation Battalion, which were supporting SOG's CCN. Butler had trained as a Green Beret prior to going to flight school, so he was specifically requested by SOG personnel to support their missions.

Don Davis began what he thought would be a normal day of flying. As a platoon leader in the Phoenix Company, he was monitoring the flying assignments for his platoon. Early that morning, one pilot, WO Dale Pearce, was sick and unable to fly, so Davis took his logistics mission to support one of the brigades in the field. The aircraft commander was WO David P. Soyland, who was also the platoon's standardization instructor pilot (SIP). Soyland was unhappy that the assigned pilot was unable to fly. Phoenix pilots were expected to fly with anything short of *very* serious illnesses. Pearce, however, was one of the newer Phoenix and was still learning the ropes.

Soyland's day was supposed to be a routine day of ash-and-trash resupply, a piece of cake.

Due to the mission report time and change in crews, Soyland had to wait and learn the reason later. So between the hours of 7:00 A.M. and 3:30 in the afternoon, Warrant Officer Soyland and Captain Davis flew several resupply missions in the flatlands east of the mountains between Camp Eagle and Camp Evans.

Butler, in the meantime, had been monitoring the efforts of Special Forces Team Alaska, which had been inserted west of the A Shau Valley along the Laotian border. The team had reported numerous NVA in the area. Butler suspected that the team would be discovered by the enemy. That afternoon, upon return from the resupply missions, Soyland's aircraft was put on standby, and the crew went to wait in their hootches at the Phoenix Nest at Camp Evans. In the meantime, Soyland met with Pearce, who said he would be able to fly if the aircraft was recalled. Davis agreed and proceeded with another flight that was on standby for an infantry extraction.

Butler was busy leading a team of two Cobra light-fire teams to assist in the insertion of another eight-man reconnaissance team. While the first insertion had been successful, the team already in the field had been compromised. Butler received a call that the CCN eight-man team was in contact, pinned down. They quickly suffered two dead and several wounded. He immediately scrambled four guns, and CCN control launched the lift aircraft, Comancheros from Alpha Company, 101st Assault Helicopter Battalion at Camp Eagle. During the flight out, the forward air controller, in an air force plane overhead, briefed them of what to expect.

Butler decided that it would be best to extract the dead and wounded with one slick and the remainder with a second lift ship. Butler directed guns three and four to put a heavy prep on the wood line to the north and northeast where the concentrated enemy fire was coming from. The pickup zone, which had been predesignated, was slightly below the top of the highest point in the area. Butler held everybody three kilometers to the northeast at an altitude of five thousand feet to avoid small-arms fire.

Enemy fire was so heavy, they decided to make low-level approaches following a river into a valley draw where they could fly level straight into the pickup zone. It was, however, going to be below the enemy antiaircraft positions on the hilltop. As they approached the pickup zone, decelerating to fifty knots, Cobras were flying beside the Hueys to provide protection. They were so low and slow that to fire a rocket, Butler had to dump the nose and then readjust his aircraft to resume his position alongside the slick. The first Comanchero approached the pickup zone and began flaring to the approach when a heavy volume of enemy fire hit the ship, wounding two crew members. He aborted the approach, dumping the aircraft nose to gain speed quickly, and exited the area.

The second Comanchero Huey, thirty seconds behind him, circled so gunships three and four could put heavy fire on the enemy fire. The second Comanchero then commenced his approach and quickly aborted after several hits by enemy fire. His hydraulics system was shot out, critical instruments in the cockpit were destroyed, and two crewmen were wounded. He went on to Quang Tri where he made a successful running landing. By then the gunships were out of ammunition and needed to refuel. They also had to rethink how they would attempt to get reconnaissance team Alaska out.

It was obvious that the team was in deep shit. They'd unknowingly been deposited near the North Vietnamese Army 66th Regiment Base Area, a heavily developed supply dump with underground living facilities. The North Vietnamese Army troops in the area had been strengthened by a *Binh Tran*, a logistical unit, comprised of twelve hundred combat engineers with their own 12.7mm antiaircraft company. The odds against the eight men of the Special Forces team were beyond comprehension.

In Quang Tri, Butler and the others met up with the two remaining Comanchero slicks. Additional slicks were called in, along with two more gunships. On the third attempt, the second set of guns made two passes on the enemy location as the Huey began his approach. With four remaining guns ready for heavy suppression, it did no good.

The NVA then shot up the next slick, wounded the copilot, and badly damaged the aircraft. The Comancheros thought they were having a bad day, but it would get worse for the Phoenix. As the Comanchero Huey was climbing out, white smoke was pouring out of the belly. Capt. Steve Cook flew beside it in his Cobra and saw that it was fuel. Although there was an immediate danger of a catastrophic explosion and fire, the pilot elected to continue flying back to the forward combat base, Mai Loc, where he could at least land in the safety of friendly troops.

The forward air controller then called jets into the area to drop snake-eye bombs and napalm. A second flight of F-4 Phantoms was used to saturate the enemy with cluster bombs. Then the gunships continued putting rockets as close as they could in the vicinity of the team. One of the team members on the ground called, "Some of the stuff is exploding at the top of the trees, falling on us, but keep it coming!" While the fast movers were working over the area, the helicopters returned for fuel. At Quang Tri, Butler requested an additional fire team of two Cobras from the Redskins.

A call was then made by the Redskins for any available slicks to assist in a Prairie Fire (hot extraction). It was a chilling term understood by those with CCN experience: an American team had been compromised and was in immediate danger of being overrun. WO1 David Soyland of the Phoenix, with WO1 Dale Pearce as his copilot, were called by Phoenix operations to respond. The Redskins would have a total of eight Cobras. They rearmed and headed back to the area and were joined by another set of guns from the Redskins and three slicks from

Charlie Company. David Soyland was in the lead Phoenix
with WO1 Dale Pearce. What had been a long day of ash-
and-trash now turned into a hot extraction of Green Berets
in a running battle. It had already been a long day, yet
Soyland was in the lead. Americans were on the ground.

With the air strikes ending, Soyland commenced his
approach. He'd been carefully briefed on the flight path,
altitude, and enemy fire. With Cobras flying beside him,
Soyland called, "I think I can get in there!" Of course, Soyland knew of the three aircraft that had been badly shot up
with wounded crews prior to his attempt. He also knew
how desperate the Special Forces team had to be to ask
for a hot extraction: they would die if he couldn't get
them out!

During the approach, the team on the ground asked that
the crew chief and door gunner be prepared to get out and
help load the bodies if necessary. The pickup would be
made on a mountain slope, one skid on the ground, the
other held in midair at a hover. The door gunner, Sp4.
Gary Allcorn, unclasped his safety harness, in anticipation. Soyland commenced his approach flying low level
up the valley while two Cobras with aerial rockets were
prepping the area. Two Redskins were flying alongside
him at the same speed. It was the best possible cover.
With guns blazing, Phoenix Two-two commenced the hot
hovering extraction.

Soyland brought the Phoenix bird to a hover above the
recon team. Allcorn saw the camouflaged Special Forces
team holding white palms upward to reveal their locations in the dark jungle of the pickup zone. He told Soyland the team was at their 6:30 position, i.e., behind them.
Simultaneously, the Phoenix took heavy antiaircraft fire.
An NVA antiaircraft company with 12.7mm machine
guns was located on the hillside above them, and at least
two of its heavy machine guns were shooting the hell out
of the helicopter. The instant it came to a hover just above
the team, the 12.7mm rounds began destroying the air-

craft. The canopies were exploding, the engine cowlings were shot off, the rotor blades were disintegrating.

Rounds flashed through the cockpit windshield and door. Allcorn saw Pearce's hands jerk upward to the skylight as he was hit. The aircraft shuddered and died. Allcorn, the door gunner, was ejected as the Huey rolled violently on its side to the right, rolling, bouncing, and grinding down a steep hill. In that tangled mass of metal, Dale Pearce was crushed to death. The crew chief had been knocked unconscious, held within the wreckage by his seat belt.

As Skip Butler and Steve Cook broke off their Cobra passes, two other Cobras joined up right behind them. Just as Butler began his break, he saw Soyland come to a hover and simultaneously heard him call, "Taking fire, heavy, heavy fire!" Butler saw pieces of the Huey flying through the air, and the aircraft began to roll to the right.

Steve Cook, Redskin One-six, Butler's Cobra wingman, watched as it happened. He observed enemy rounds impacting and pieces of the aircraft being torn off. The aircraft yawed violently to the right. Hit by an RPG, the entire tail boom separated from the fuselage, the aircraft inverted, rolling to its right, impacting on the side of the ridge. It then slid and bumped down one hundred feet of ridgeline and came to rest in a deeply vegetated area.

CW2 Ricky Scrugham was circling, watching Soyland "go in." The euphemism exploded him into unthinking reflexive action! He peeled in, diving to retrieve Soyland and his crew. He did it without a call to the command-and-control ship, which was not a Phoenix bird. The others above Scrugham understood his selfless bravery. It was a defining moment of personal character. They all intently watched, wondering if they'd be next.

Scrugham had less than two weeks left in country, the end of his tour. An hour earlier, Scrugham had thought to himself, *Americans on the ground is the only acceptable reason for this mission.* His copilot, a newbie, grabbed

Scrugham's arm and shouted into the intercom, "Control said call it off! Listen to your radio!" He was horrified but relieved.

Jerked backed into the moment, Scrugham aborted the approach and climbed away. At that sickening moment he realized there was nothing he or anyone else could do for Soyland. A personal friend. A Nam buddy. Another hootchmate gone.

The two Redskin gunships dove into the target area, circling low and slow. They reported that Soyland's aircraft was immersed in thick vegetation and couldn't be seen. Due to critically low fuel, all of the gunships expended their ordnance and returned to Quang Tri for fuel and rearming.

While the gunships and other Phoenix birds returned to refuel, an SOG Bright Light team was inserted nearby in an attempt to link up with the reconnaissance team and reinforce them in their ground fight. The NVA suddenly found the Bright Light team attacking them. The Redskins had departed the area to refuel and rearm. Gunships from the 101st Aviation Battalion now supported the team. With a kilometer (.62 mile) separating the Bright Light response team from the team pinned down, the Cobras were called to support them.

The Cobras placed rockets as close as possible to the team. Butler and Cook quickly returned, observing the other Cobras working out. Suddenly he heard screams on the radio. "Check fire! Check fire! You're hitting us!" The Cobras broke off.

The report from the ground was one U.S. killed by friendly fire, Sgt. Dale Dehnke, who died coming to the aid of Lt. Danny Entrican, Sp4. Gary Hollingsworth, and the other Special Forces RT Alaska members. The linkup did not occur due to darkness. A first-light extraction was scheduled for the following morning.

Special Forces officers with multiple tours on CCN

would later speculate on how events had happened. David Soyland had been stunned by the crash and wandered semiconscious out of it. Soyland was believed captured shortly afterward by the North Vietnamese as they swarmed over their conquest. He was marched up the hill and told if he tried to escape, he would be hunted down and executed. They then took his boots and socks off, along with his green Nomex shirt, leaving him barefoot in his Nomex green pants and white T-shirt. The T-shirt left him an excellent target in the shadowy jungle.

Sometime later, just before darkness, Gary Allcorn slowly regained consciousness. He became aware that he was lying on a very sharply sloping hillside, his head pointed downhill. He couldn't see out of his right eye. His weapon and helicopter were nowhere to be seen. Needing to conceal himself, he crawled over to a dense stand of brush. Along the way, he found a flashlight from the helicopter. It would be his only survival tool for the next twenty-four hours.

The North Vietnamese were noisily working on the ridgeline above him. The noise and level of activity was scary. Swarms of NVA were searching the hillside around him between air strikes.

Later that night, after dark, he heard an AC-130 gunship and helicopters overhead. He took a banana palm leaf and wrapped it around his flashlight, trying to focus it upward like a strobe. He pointed it toward the AC-130, which saw it just as an SOG team at the downed helicopter was also signaling. Luckily, he stopped the signaling because the AC-130 thought he was NVA and was preparing to shoot him up.

Lapsing in and out of consciousness, Allcorn again concealed himself in the jungle vegetation. He awoke at first light and decided to attempt to find the Huey. As he climbed up the hill, he heard noises on the opposite ridge-line. He saw a figure in a white T-shirt running as fast as possible, down a hillside, using palm trees to propel him faster down the hill. He was astonished to see large numbers of NVA on the ridge. Moments later, he heard a burst of automatic-weapons fire. Shortly after that, a single shot echoed through the valley.

Allcorn then moved downhill until rockets started impacting in front of him. He then went down the mountainside, half jumping, half flying, to a stream below. Rockets and bombs exploded nearby as he ran from the explosions, down the stream to a large open field of elephant grass where very tall blades of grass formed a natural tunnel for him to run through.

As he struggled to get away from the firing, an air force B-57 Canberra jet came by at eye level, dropping napalm. A wall of flames approached him but stopped short of engulfing him.

Exhausted, having suffered a concussion and loss of blood, he sank to his knees in the elephant grass, sobbing a final prayer. Then he clearly heard the voice of his grandmother, "It'll be all right." Unbelievingly, he heard it a second time, "It'll be all right." With those words, he regained his composure and moved away from the flames. His grandmother had been dead two years.

He ran farther across the field and climbed into a tree to escape the onrushing grass fire. Then Vietnamese Air Force A1-E Skyraiders dropping bombs ahead of the wall of flames passed by him at eye level without seeing him. In an effort to attract their attention, he ripped off his white boxer shorts and waved them at the planes, to no avail.

Exhausted, he climbed down the tree, hopped through the passing wall of fire, and collapsed on the hillside. Staring into the sky, he wondered if everything was going to turn out all right. As he stared into the sky, an O-2 Skymaster with a forward air controller began to dive at him.

Startled, he waved the shorts again and the plane banked away. A few minutes later, a Huey picked him up and flew to the Quang Tri hospital.

During the night before, the rescue force, which had been inserted late the previous evening, was struck by enemy rocket-propelled grenades. One Special Forces soldier was killed, and several others were wounded. Shortly afterward, they found the remains of the original ground force, Team Alaska, which had been in contact and overrun by enemy forces.

Later that day, at 12:45, there were three more air strikes and a second rescue team was inserted to sweep through the area of the contact and crash. Receiving sporadic enemy fire, the second rescue force succeeded in locating two survivors of the aircraft. Specialist Five Parker, the crew chief, and Specialist Four Allcorn, the door gunner, were recovered. The recovery team also found three bodies of the ground force. The leader of the second rescue team informed the commanding officer that there was another body in the downed aircraft, but he was unable to extract it. From the rescue team's description, the casualty appeared to be heavier than Soyland and was believed to be Dale Pearce. The body was otherwise unidentifiable due to injuries sustained in the crushing of the cabin.

The downed helicopter was upside down and pointing uphill from the bottom of the steep ravine. The tail boom was broken off, as were both of the rotors. The side of the aircraft was badly damaged, and the right front seat had been almost completely ripped out of the aircraft. The seat belt and shoulder harness had been completely ripped out. However, the left seat (Soyland's) was intact, as was the left side of the Huey. The armor plate on the left side of the aircraft was moved back and no blood was found on the pilot's side. All indications were that the pilot exited the aircraft under his own power. There were footprints in the mud on the left side of the aircraft where someone had exited or entered the aircraft.

At that point, all that was certain was that crew chief Specialist Five Parker was alive and being treated for a wound in the upper leg, along with a fracture. Specialist Four Allcorn would recover quickly. The unidentifiable body was believed to be that of copilot Warrant Officer-1 Pearce.

Based on the physical evidence of and around the wreckage, and on Specialist Four Allcorn's description of an apparent chase, Special Forces officers later surmised that David Soyland had attempted an escape, was hunted down, wounded, then executed. In the penultimate fraud of war, as with the case of over two thousand other Americans, the truth would never be known. Team Alaska's Lt. Danny Entrican was believed captured; he was never heard from again.

The next day, I ran into Ricky Scrugham at the division pad. It was good to see him. He had survived everything in Laos. We briefly discussed those who were killed. I was still finding it hard to believe that Nelson had been killed. He then told me of Soyland's and Pearce's being shot down near the Laotian border. I didn't know Pearce, but I knew Soyland. He read J. R. R. Tolkein and science fiction. He'd been meticulous. He'd stored his Nomex flying gloves in their original plastic bag.

The word of Soyland down and believed killed was another kick in the gut. It was pain piled on the pain of Stewart, Doody, Nelson, Moreira, Baldwin, and Finn. But, if it could happen to Dave Nelson, it could happen to anyone. I couldn't believe that the Phoenix were still having aircrew casualties in combat; the fucking war was over at Camp Eagle.

I wished Ricky well. He was a quietly courageous man who'd endured the worst. But, he was a Phoenix, and I would not shake his hand. He was DEROSing shortly, and I simply didn't want to jinx him.

More Phoenix casualties, when the "war was over" elsewhere. The final Phoenix casualties came from the Phoenix 1st Platoon, where I'd been. Including Stewart and Doody in February, Nelson and Moreira. All preceded by Finn and Baldwin in the preceding September. Eight Phoenix pilots (seven in 1st Platoon), had died in nine months. Three had slept in the same cubicle I'd lived in. The worst imaginable events that I'd feared in December 1970 had culminated in a series of horrifying accidents and combat losses. Soyland and Pearce had the unwanted honor of being the last Phoenix combat casualties.

I could only shake my head, sadly, thankfully. It hadn't been me.

## May 26, 1971, Phoenix 1st Platoon Hootch, Camp Evans

The hopeless search for David Soyland and Dale Pearce had ended. All search operations were pulled out, and no further attempt would be made. The air cavalry unit that normally worked the area would remain vigilant.

Soyland's and Pearce's effects had been carefully gathered, organized, and prepared for shipment home. The most abhorred duty for officers who knew them was completed: the letters to relatives, their survivors.

Soyland's cubicle was then nailed shut, never again to contain a living 1st Platoon pilot. Soyland's call sign, Two-two, would not be used again by Phoenix.

It had been Paul Stewart's call sign also before his loss in Laos. WO Dean Grau accompanied Soyland to their instructor pilot course earlier that spring, and Grau had asked Soyland about his intention to reuse the call sign Two-two. Soyland told Grau he wasn't superstitious and had no reservations using it. Two-two, double deuce, no slack! The call sign had rolled rhythmically from the lips of many in the Nam, as easily as drinking water. In the Phoenix it had evolved to a totally different understanding. Three Phoenix pilots with the call sign "Two-two," all in first platoon, had died in combat action.

Nineteen years later, Skip Butler still wore a POW-MIA bracelet with Soyland's name on it. Dean Grau, the other instructor pilot in the Phoenix, also wore one with Soyland's name. Crew chief Larry Frazier would also remember. There were men who'd not forget him or Dale Pearce in their lifetimes.

In terms of combat casualties, the Phoenix earned the reputation of being the hard luck company in the 101st Airborne Division, but its record simply reflected the danger of the missions its helicopters and crews flew. The 158th Aviation Battalion earned the reputation of being the Flying Cross Battalion because of their combat awards.

## May 29, 1971, Camp Evans

WO Phil Rutledge had just arrived a day earlier in the Phoenix. He was lounging in his bunk, slowly assimilating the environment. He'd already seen the company mission board, where Soyland and Pearce were listed as missing in action. That was an ominous sign to a newbie. He'd also endured CWO Butch Doan's DEROS party the night before. Some said it was Doan's 364th such party, in country.

A ground-shaking *KA-BAAM!* threw Rutledge to his feet as dust rose in the air. Butch Doan came running by, grabbed Rutledge by the shirt, "Come on, Newbie!" They dove into the bunker just outside the door of the hootch.

After several seconds, there were no more 122mm rockets. Doan stood up, dusted off the orange-red clay of

I Corps, then, without speaking to Rutledge, went inside the hootch and picked up his bags. Doan then headed down to the flight line, catching a flight to DEROS. Doan returned to the States after an action-filled, heavily decorated tour. He'd served in the last two major actions in I Corps and was one of very few who'd flown both the Ripcord evacuation and the LAM SON 719 invasion. Rutledge, like all newbies to the Phoenix, could only shake his head in wonderment.

# 13

# June 1971

## June 1, 1971

CW2 Don Wan and 1st Lt. Jerry Majors were piloting a Cobra gunship for the Redskins. A combat assault was being attempted on Hill 1051, west-northwest of Khe Sanh. Nearby Special Forces Outpost Hickory overlooked it from one thousand meters away. Sp. John Caviani, a Green Beret on Hickory, was commanding the outpost, monitoring communications with Green Beret teams in Laos and North Vietnam. Caviani had been reporting seeing one thousand NVA soldiers a day. He'd been calling in helicopters to shoot them up. However, the intelligence staffs in the 101st Airborne and areas south did not fully believe him. They had been setting up a network of electronic sensors all across the northern part of South Vietnam and Laos, and those sensors weren't indicating the level of enemy activity that Caviani was seeing. To Caviani, it was obvious that the North Vietnamese were manipulating the sensors and were knowledgeable of the impact that would have on command decisions. Caviani kept hearing from intelligence that "Our assets don't show anything out there." Caviani's retort was "You don't have any assets out there."

As helicopters of the 101st Airborne tried to land on the top of Hill 1051, Caviani sat on top of Hickory, watching the gunships work out and the Hueys making their approach. As the Hueys left under fire, the gunships began another run.

High above Hill 1051, CW2 Don Wan and his gunner, 1st Lt. Jerry Majors, began a dive, and Caviani watched the Redskin Cobra diving. He also saw a single North Vietnamese kid stand up with a rocket-propelled grenade launcher, slowly put it up to his shoulder, taking very careful aim. Caviani was amazed as he watched the ground exploding around the kid, torn up by the minigun fire. But the kid simply stood there, taking even more careful aim, while 12.7mm machine guns were also firing at the Cobra.

Caviani grabbed for his rifle, hoping to take a shot at the kid. He was right at the sniping range of one thousand meters. But before he could get the rifle up, the RPG flashed upward, into the cockpit of the diving Cobra. Both crewmen probably dead, the Cobra continued its dive, exploding on impact with the mountain.

Caviani had only two more days before he would nearly lose his life when Outpost Hickory was overrun by the North Vietnamese. Then he'd have to endure the horrors of living as a POW for twenty-two months.

Wan and Majors were the last losses of a Redskin crew and aircraft. There would be one more tragic fatality as the war ended, but it was the last Redskin Cobra lost.

I spent June 16 carrying combat engineer officers to firebases southwest of Eagle, near the A Shau Valley. Tricky flying, in and out of the fog on mountaintops. Got six hours despite rain. I realized I'd have over one thousand hours flight time in the Nam. I continued carrying a paperback book in my lower leg pocket. I finished *The Frail Ocean* and *The Pyramid Climbers*. I was halfway through *The Andromeda Strain*. I'd read anything to get my mind Stateside.

It had been just like the monsoons for the past three

days, but I was happy knowing I'd never have to go through another knock-on-wood period flying CCN or reconning the Rock Pile AO. I was happy to receive orders for Fort Rucker, Alabama. They could as easily have been for Fort Bragg, North Carolina, or Fort Hood, Texas. But I got 120 copies of my orders that said Fort Rucker. That did make it official.

## Camp Evans, I Corps

WO Dean Grau had been thinking of his friend, WO Randy Hines, who was an O-1 Bird-dog pilot down south in III Corps. Grau had the day down from flying, and he wanted to call his basic-training buddy who was also a friend of Tommy Doody who'd been killed in February. It was a personal call to a friend with a deceased common friend.

Grau went to Phoenix headquarters and had the call placed on the cumbersome landline telephone system. After a couple of hours passed, with the usual mixed-up landline connections, a duty sergeant answered the phone at 221st Aviation Company. Grau identified himself and asked to speak to WO Randy Hines.

The NCO responded, "Sir, Shotgun One-two died this morning (June 19) in a jeep wreck on the flight line." Grau was hammered with emotion, in disbelief, said, "What?"

The NCO repeated himself. Continuing with "An ARVN deuce and a half (two-and-a-half-ton) hit his jeep on the flight line."

Of three buddies who shared time together in basic training and flight school, Grau had become the survivor, with two months left on his tour. Shaken by word of his friend's death, he quietly tried to assimilate it all.

The survivors' club had another member.

**June 25, 1971, Camp Evans**

On June 25, a Redskin Cobra crew responded to a call for support below Firebase Fuller, overlooking the DMZ. In the rush to launch, the captain serving as the gunner in the front seat of the Cobra gunship for some reason left his chicken-plate chest armor positioned behind his seat.

The Cobra team departed Camp Evans and twenty minutes later was in contact with ARVN ground elements, directing them toward the same enemy fire.

Once in the area, the pair of Cobras began their cycle, one diving, firing rockets and minigun at the target. As the first turned away from the target, the second commenced his dive, also firing.

In the mountainous terrain below, an NVA cut loose with his AK-47 rifle in the direction of the Cobra diving toward him, then ducked belowground. Unknown to him, he'd accomplished a one-in-a-million shot. One AK-47 round ripped through the Plexiglas canopy of the Cobra and pierced the heart of the gunner.

Sickened by the loss of his gunner, Redskin One-six, Capt. Steve Cook, flew the Cobra gunship directly to the Quang Tri hospital pad. Cook was angry at his gunner for not wearing his chicken plate, disgusted at himself for not having forced him to wear it. The armor still hung behind the dead gunner's seat. The gunner had only been in country since June 10.

Two hours later, Sp. David Carline was cleaning up the blood and mess of the fatality. He had also been instructed to find the bullet that killed the copilot. After cleaning the copilot's area without finding it, he decided to check the weapons bay below the seat. As he searched under the copilot area for the bullet, he shifted a panel and, as he was looking up into the bay, what seemed like a quart of the dead pilot's blood flooded into his face.

# 14

## July 1971

On July 14, I flew seven hours for the engineers. Told my wife to stop writing on the fifth. That made me feel short. I only had twenty-five flying days left. I would leave the division three days prior to DEROS, and I'd have to quit flying a week before that. I thought the worst part of leaving would be the wait for the plane at Cam Ranh Bay.

As the 101st began to stand down, more and more missions were oriented towards the Da Nang area. WO Mike Goodman had transferred into the unit and finished his in-country checkout. I took him on his orientation ride around the area of operations, and we flew out near Vandegrift and the Rock Pile. He told me of his best buddy, Steve Hansen, who was a warrant officer with a unit at Quang Tri. Hansen had gotten married just before he came to Vietnam. His wife, Eleanor, and Mike's fiancée, Carol Burdeshaw, were best friends. Mike had been best man in their wedding.

That night, Mike and I did more than a little drinking; we both got pretty messed up. The guy who slept in the room next to him was a second-tour CW2, new to the company. I took a big cement-filled sandbag and threw it on the corrugated metal roof above him. When hit by a large rock, the sheet-metal roof sounded like a 122mm rocket going off. We then stumbled in his room and found the guy hiding under his bed waiting for the next one to hit. I hadn't laughed so hard in six months. I was a short-

304

timer, so I messed with everyone; my turtle (my own personal replacement) was in, Capt. Tony Moorehead.

A few days later, Captain Moorehead, my brand-new platoon leader, decided I was too short to fly. He decided I needed to spend my last month in Vietnam, safely sitting on my ass in the company motor pool as assistant motor pool officer. I was furious. I pleaded with him. Anything but that! I knew nothing about jeeps or trucks.

I had no experience in mechanical repairs and didn't want any. My attitude may have been bad, but I knew I had no business in a motor pool. I told him I'd rather fly *any* mission the company had to offer than sit on my ass in the motor pool. Moorehead was an infantry captain. His platoon-management attitude was unacceptable to one very short warrant officer. He wanted to run the flight platoon like a Ranger unit. It was his way or nothing. He ordered me to accompany him to the CO's office.

We met the CO in his office. I pleaded to the CO to let me fly or just work on my college correspondence course. The routine for short warrants had been simply to skate their last two or three weeks in country. Earlier the CO had depended on me alone for the five-minute standby for Lt. Col. J. C. Bard's G-3 (operations) at the division headquarters. Some lazier warrant officers were slow in responding to those missions, resulting in a general chewing out from the major. I had been the one he relied upon to prevent those problems. I had been totally dependable for six months, with no complaints, accidents, or incidents. Not to mention seriously kicking some NVA ass north of the Rock Pile. That in mind, the major conceded, permitting me to fly up to seven days prior to DEROS.

Moorehead was not happy with the CO overriding him. As we walked out of headquarters, he smiled. "Mr. Marshall, if that's what you want, that's what you'll get. Tomorrow, you'll get the mission in the Ruong Ruong

Valley, south of Firebase Pistol. There's a recon team out of contact with their operations. You get to find them."

Of course, Moorehead knew it might be that a simple emergency resupply of radio batteries was needed, but the team might have been overrun by NVA who'd set up an ambush for me or anyone else who came calling.

"Check in with operations at 7:00 A.M., and they'll give you your gunship escort frequency."

Smiling, I thought, Well, hell. Beats sitting in the motor pool.

The following morning I woke up and completed pre-flight inspection. Then I went to operations and picked up my gunship escort frequencies. I returned to my Loach, placed an M-16 with ammunition bandolier next to my seat, cranked up, and departed Snoopy's Pad. I met a pair of Hawk gunships en route, heading south from Camp Eagle down to the Ruong Ruong Valley. The platoon was out of contact deep in the bush. A very unfriendly place, the area south of Firebase Pistol. It was in the middle of Indian country, northwest of the Hai Van Pass, southeast of the terminus of the A Shau Valley.

With an artillery observer in the front seat and my crew chief in the back with an M-60 machine gun, we began the search. We were given the last known map coordinates of the platoon. We had a radio and fresh batteries to drop off. Luckily, they heard us coming and fired a pen flare to get our attention. As we flew by, I mentally marked their location. The gunships high behind me also saw them. Determined to be a fast-moving, low-level target, I was zipping between the treetops, lightly zigzagging at eighty knots (100 miles per hour).

As I continued past them, decelerating, just over the next ridgeline, I passed twenty feet above a huge tiger with a vivid pattern of gold, red, black, and white stripes. It was the most beautiful animal I had ever seen in the wild.

I called the Hawk gunships, "Hey you guys, wanta see a lion?"

One of the Cobra pilots came back laughing. "You've been here too long if you're seeing lions. They're only in Africa."

I said, "Whoops! I think you're right. What are those big gold and yellow things?" I turned back and hovered over the tiger. He just walked slowly, stopped once, looked up at me and my door gunner. Then slowly, deliberately, walked on.

He looked as big as my Loach.

I said, "If you guys want to see him, he's right below me." So the Cobras made low, slow passes. One of them wanted to shoot him, but I told him to leave it alone. No need to bother him. Besides, if he was casually walking around, there probably weren't any NVA in the area. We then dropped off the radios with the unit on the ground and returned home. The team was able to establish contact and get resupplied. I think they were pulled out later that day without incident.

All the way back, I was laughing at Moorehead. The worst mission the 163d Aviation Company could give me. It was fun, memorable, and I had a photograph of a tiger in the wild.

Short! . . . and still lucky!

## August 2, 1971

August finally arrived.

At lunch in division headquarters, I met WO Steve Hansen, Mike Goodman's buddy. Mike was best man in his wedding before he came to Nam. Steve told me about his wife and Mike's girlfriend being best friends in Dothan, Alabama. His father was an army chaplain, and Steve asked me to look them up when I got back.

On August 16, I finally out-processed the 163d Aviation Company. The big event that week involved an eight-foot-tall treelike shrub in front of the entrance to the headquarters administrative office. Over the months, I had noticed enlisted men walking up, picking a leaf, and walking away, chewing them in good humor. It was meticulously cared for while the rest of the company area was littered with ancient Vietnamese graves that were routinely ignored and overgrown with weeds. Then a new second-tour officer had come into the company, studied the shrub carefully, and pronounced that the tree was simply a marijuana plant which had been nurtured to treelike size. Everyone had a good laugh. It was chopped down and ceremoniously burned. The officers got to stand downwind in the smoke.

After a two-day out-processing wait at Qui Nhon, a beautiful Boeing 707, appropriately from American Airlines, was taking me home.

On the morning of the eighteenth, I boarded and sat next to another warrant officer. The plane was filled. It was stone quiet until we taxied out onto the runway. Then, the instant the nose wheel lifted off, there were cheers and shouts. Sheer jubilation! Most of the passengers on board were enlisted men, a large percentage were draftees who had never wanted to be in Vietnam in the first place. They had successfully ended their year, i.e., they were alive. On the other hand, I was a volunteer from the first day of military service. I'd eagerly wanted to serve, flying helicopters in the war.

For me, there was an odd sense of calm as we lifted off the runway. I did not shout or cheer. I simply felt as if there was a lot of unfinished business. Although I was personally satisfied with my service and combat experience, we were withdrawing, without victory. That understanding raised questions about the last years of the entire operation, our military command, and our political leaders. The public attitude we were returning home to was "Who cares, it's over." I felt that surviving, even enjoying parts of my tour of duty, was a monumental achievement. However, I was already aware of the equally monumental indifference I'd face in the World.

Thoughts of those who'd died, some I'd known well, and even flown with, would not be forgotten. The memories of specific actions had been burned indelibly into my mind. As the jet climbed out, I began to understand how people could come back to the States and then, within a few months, request a second or third tour in Vietnam. I thought of Jimmy Thornburgh, who as a Green Beret had served five and a half years in South Vietnam before becoming a warrant officer to fly Cobras. I began to understand his attitude.

I realized one very important accomplishment of flight school. My army aviation training had been more than adequate for the task. During the twelve-month tour, all of the emergency procedures I'd been taught had successfully been put to use by me or my aircraft commanders. As an army aviator, I personally felt I'd had an undistinguished tour. But I'd crossed paths with heroes, and participated in history. In my missions on CCN, I'd experienced duty and honor as I'd never have guessed it could be. In the Loach mission with Cobb north of the Rock Pile, I'd experienced a sense of personal accomplishment I could never have equaled outside of war.

On the evening of August 19, I arrived Stateside at Seattle-Tacoma Airport. I'd been through customs and checked my baggage for my flight to New Orleans, where I would meet my wife, Pat. That evening, I got on a Continental flight, a multiple-stop red-eye from Seattle-Tacoma to New Orleans. There were three intermediate stops.

I arrived in New Orleans at 9:00 A.M. the next morning. As I rushed to get off the plane, five nuns paraded in front of me. All had heavy handbags and were taking their slow, deliberate time getting off.

Pat was waiting at the gangway. I watched for an eternity, maybe three minutes, as the nuns slowly made their way forward, blocking my way. Then I rushed off the gangway into her arms! We embraced, together again, after one very long year over. We claimed my luggage and took a cab to the Royal Orleans Hotel. Late that afternoon, I called my parents, assuring them I was really back, safely. Later, we began to enjoy the sights, sounds, and a taste of New Orleans. I found very quickly that I was not used to real food. The stores along Canal Street were really interesting to me. Double knit clothing was the fad. I had never seen anything quite like that before and promptly bought casual clothes and a sports coat, since I had none. After three days in New Orleans, we continued on to Pensacola. Then we rented a beach cottage on Santa Rosa Sound for a week's leave, with a lot of family activities.

During that week, I realized not much had physically changed, but dramatic changes had occurred within me. It would take quite a while to sort them out. I had longed for a sense of return to the world that was before I left. But I soon realized that would never be and decided to get on with the business of the rest of my life. That meant getting into a new flying job at Fort Rucker, which would allow college night school.

## September 24, 1971

In September, we moved into a rental trailer in Enterprise, Alabama. Eleanor Hansen and Mike Goodman's fiancée, Carol, came to visit us after a POW/MIA rally on post at Fort Rucker one Friday night. Eleanor was very concerned about her husband Steve, and the job he was doing. Carol's fiancé was Mike Goodman, whom I'd given an orientation ride two months earlier. Although I wanted to reassure Eleanor, I sensed something wrong.

Then she asked me if what he was doing was dangerous. When she said he was flying a Loach in Quang Tri Province, I knew he was hunting the enemy on a daily basis.

I wanted to say something encouraging, but how do you tell a man's wife how unbelievably dangerous his work is? Before I spoke, the chill hit, don't lie to her! I wanted to say no, that he was safe. Jolted by the chill, I then said, "He does dangerous things, but he is with the best people and has the best possible support assets. Everywhere he goes, he has people with him." That was the truth, but it gave her little comfort. I'd unthinkingly reverted to the very words Ken Mayberry had used with me, conceding the danger of Phoenix missions, the previous November at Camp Evans.

They returned home to Dothan late that Friday night.

Twelve hours later, on Saturday morning, I answered the phone, only to hear Carol choking back sobs. Then she took a breath and, momentarily composed, continued. Eleanor had just been visited by an army chaplain. Her husband Steve was dead. He'd died while trying to escape the enemy after his helicopter had been shot down in Quang Tri Province. In a desperate attempt to extract him, a rope was thrown from a Chinook. He tried to hold on as he was lifted from the jungle, but the rope broke and Steve fell to his death. Carol then asked if I'd serve as a pallbearer.

I instinctively replied, "I'd be happy to help in any way possible." Moments later, I put the phone down, cursing myself for the unthinking use of "happy." Why couldn't I have used a more appropriate word! I'd had no training or experience for this! But I was sadly relieved I'd not lied about Steve's duties, the night before.

The funeral was five days later. Escorting Steve's body, Mike Goodman came back on emergency leave. The funeral parlor was in Dothan, Alabama, the church just a short distance down the street. The funeral ceremony was a place and a time I didn't want to experience. As a pall-bearer, I sat next to Mike Goodman. We were both in dress uniform. A girl sang a beautiful rendition of "To Dream the Impossible Dream," the theme music from *Man of La Mancha*. My mind kept bouncing back to the day I'd met Steve at lunch in the division mess hall at Camp Eagle. It had been less than two months. Mike was holding back tears as I was. Then he began to cry. I gripped his knee in an effort to help him restrain the tears. The words of the minister passed by unheard; we did not want to hear them. I felt as if a well-known foe, Death, had followed from a war on the opposite side of the earth to taunt me in Dothan, Alabama.

The burial, with full military honors, was completed at a small cemetery several miles north of Dothan. Steve was buried in an area reserved for military veterans who would not be joined by their wives. Everyone hoped that eventually Eleanor would remarry. A reception was held by Eleanor's mother after the ceremony. There I met Steve's mother, father, and his younger brother. I found it hard to believe that an army chaplain, who had officiated at so many funerals during his life, now had to endure his son's.

Eleanor's mother made an exaggerated performance of how pretty Steve's Purple Heart was. I was filled with revulsion, bordering on rage. The way the women carried on about the medal, as if it were a piece of jewelry! My wife didn't understand my feelings. She had no real understanding of what I'd done during my tour. She was working at a bank where most of the men had joined the Alabama National Guard or air force reserve to avoid service in Vietnam.

The indifference to lives lost in military service was found even in Dothan, Alabama. Those who'd joined the army and air force reserve or National Guard made no apologies. They'd gladly serve six years as weekend warriors to avoid one year of duty in Vietnam. People

working with Pat told jokes ridiculing Vietnam vets. I'd
hear them repeated to me at home, without revealing my
disgust.

At the end of the reception, Mike and Carol came to us
and said they wanted to get married immediately. They
asked us to drive them to Georgia. That evening, we
drove them to Bainbridge, some forty miles southeast of
Dothan. There they applied for their marriage license and
took the required blood test. The next day they were married. Two days later, Mike returned to the 163d Aviation
Company at Camp Eagle.

Mike's return to South Vietnam had to be hell. After
burying his best friend, getting married, and returning to
South Vietnam from Stateside, he had to be bouncing
between the widest emotions.

## October 1971

When I'd reported into the warrant officers' personnel
branch at Fort Rucker, I spent a few minutes with my
placement officer, who asked me if I was staying in the
army for twenty years or what plans I had. I replied, "I'd
like to try and finish as much college as possible, at night.
I'd really like to finish a degree during the three-year
tour." He said, "I've got just the place for you! Flying
OH-58s in the Rotary Wing Qualification Course. You
have in-country 58 time, which is a plus. You'll be transitioning fixed-wing rated pilots into helicopters. It's the
easiest job for a college-minded young man." I said
thanks and waited outside his office while my orders were
cut for instructor pilot training in the little Jet Ranger.

A few days later, I reported to instructor training. In
ground school, I learned that two 58s had had fatal
crashes over the previous three months, caused by the tail
boom's buckling and falling off. What I'd known as a

very safe aircraft had since been revealed to have an engineering weakness. The downed aircraft were suspected of having hard tail stinger strikes during practice autorotations. These had supposedly caused the crashes. While engineering studies were nearing completion to cure the problem, I began instructor pilot training without touchdown autorotations.

A test pilot had interviewed the very lucky survivor of one of the accidents. The pilot's practiced response, when an aircraft begins spinning to the right, was to attempt a left-compensating pedal or a coordinated left-cyclic turn. However, when the tail boom buckled, the standard response merely accelerated the departure of the tail boom, inverting and destroying the helicopter. Helicopters were incapable of going upside down without catastrophic destruction. We were then taught that if the tail boom or rotor was damaged, we would have to override trained reflexes, and turn into (with) the right turn of the aircraft, flying it to the ground in a descending, accelerating left spiral.

Just one more thing for a highly experienced helicopter pilot to brood about! Preparation H was heavily used for the next month, until the pilots were convinced the engineering and training modifications worked. In November, we were permitted to continue autorotations to the ground.

I finished my transition as an instructor pilot in the Rotary Wing Qualification Course for previously rated (airplane) aviators. I'd also begun studying at Troy State University at night. I had a very full schedule, flying from 6:00 A.M. until noon, then relaxing, studying, and going to school from 4:00 to 9:00 at night.

My call sign was Recon Six-one at Fort Rucker. My first student in Rotary Wing Qualification Course (RWQC) was Endashaw Endiri, an Ethiopian flight student with an excellent command of the English language. Unlike most of our students, who were jet-rated air force or army fixed-wing aviators transitioning into helicopters, Endiri had only 450 hours in a Cessna 172. I had my hands full, but it turned out to be a successful transition for him and me.

There was an interesting group of pilots in the RWQC course. Maj. William L. Robertson, our commanding officer, was from Mississippi. He was a good commanding officer, but subject of a lot of humor because of his southern attitudes. He once described his time taking master's courses at Mississippi State University. There, he observed all those thousands of students just walking around daily, with "no one in command."

I knew I was getting out of the army, it was just a matter of finishing college as quickly as possible. Chief warrant officers Dennis Patterson and Bob Williamson were good buddies, who had flown Charlie-model Huey gunships together in Vietnam. A number of very fine aviators, all combat-experienced, were in the company. The Rotary Wing Qualification Course instructors provided the core of pilots for the army's Silver Wings flight demonstration team, which performed at the Paris Air Show in 1973.


## Da Nang, I Corps

In late September and early October 1971, the Chu Lai PX started to have some glaring shortages. Because of the impending standdown, the logisticians decided to use everything up through intentional shortages. Fresca was everywhere, but not a Coke could be found for miles.

The 174th Aviation Company, with Capt. Mike Sloniker, was assigned CAs near Da Nang. At the end of a combat assault, Sloniker made a run on the PX at Freedom Hill. He landed at a permaprime pad at the base of the mountain, near two Chinooks. One was from the 159th ASHB, 101st Abn Div, the other from the 178th ASHB, Boxcars, 23d Inf Div (Americal) from Chu Lai.

Mike had to bum a truck ride to the PX; walking had been banned due to drug sellers and pimps. Mike found his way into the USO, which was staffed by a doughnut dolly selling tacos.

There were two aviators, one from the 101st, sitting at the adjacent table in the USO. They were two young warrant officers, Chinook pilots, who had either attended flight school or the CH-47 transition course together, and had not seen each other in quite a while. A serious conversation was under way. The one from the 101st mentioned how pilots in their unit were damned if they did, and damned if they didn't.

The somber discussion regarded a CH-47 aircraft commander who'd responded to an emergency call from a downed Loach pilot, west of Quang Tri. He heard on the radio an emergency beacon activated on UHF guard frequency. He responded, "Beeper, Beeper, come up voice." Apparently, the Chinook was the first one on the scene. The pilot had been shot down, was alone, and heard NVA pursuing him. The Chinook pilot instinctively understood that he had to get the Loach pilot out by any means possible or the fellow would quickly be dead. The Chinook pilot instructed the crew chief to extract the downed pilot by securing a rope to the aircraft floor. The crew chief dropped it down through the hole in the center of the Chinook floor. But as they were lifting the CH-47 to clear the pilot out of the trees, the rope broke and WO Steve Hansen fell to his death.

The young 101st warrant officer was particularly upset. There was open discussion that the Chinook aircraft commander would be court-martialed for his attempted rescue. Mike's first reaction was disgust. Then he began thinking of the heavy responsibility an aircraft commander has in a combat environment. Damned if you do and damned if you don't. Having spent a year on the ground in a prior tour, he would always respond to a call

for help, damn the rules. Ask any pilot who served in
I Corps. Ninety-nine point nine percent would have taken
the rope, accepting whatever risk, in light of the very certain option at the hands of the NVA. Damn!

### November 29, 1971, Camp Evans Combat Base, I Corps, Republic of Vietnam

The Phoenix Company, Charlie Company, 158th Aviation Battalion, 101st Airborne Division, Airmobile, was
being stood down. The unit was being deactivated, and
the pilots were being transferred into other units or shipped
home. Some would eventually leave Vietnam earlier than
their scheduled twelve-month tour. The retreat from I
Corps was nearing its end, and Camp Evans would soon
be turned over to the ARVN. There was an uneasy feeling
among those at Camp Evans, the last Americans north
of Phu Bai. The North Vietnamese Army was out there,
still making its presence known with 122mm rockets and
82mm mortars. A "Corregidor mentality," that of the last
American outpost in a collapsing effort, was obvious in
the conversations of the young warrant officers.

In the Phoenix officers club, a small group of pilots
gathered around the Phoenix Company emblem, a wooden
plaque that had adorned the stage since 1969, a large,
three-foot-by-three-foot carved wooden plaque with a Vietnamese Phoenix that had been carved into it by an early
Phoenix veteran in 1969. The base was being evacuated
in days. A decision had to be made: what to do with the
Phoenix emblem? WO Phil Rutledge and several others
began discussing what to do. Individual officers wanted
to keep it themselves, but they were booed down. In short
order, one of the Phoenix recommended the mythological
answer—flames!

Rutledge and the others decided a slight change was

appropriate. The warrant officers began to write on the back of the emblem the names of all the Phoenix pilots they could remember. When they ran out of names, they continued writing Phoenix call signs. Phoenix Six and others were added in succession. There were more drinks, toasts in remembrance of those lost, peppered with stories of actions unbelievably survived. The plaque was then carried outside.

The group included Warrant Officer Rutledge, Lieutenant Brea, Lt. Eddie Stafire, and several others. They irreverently offered a profane toast, as the Phoenix emblem was set ablaze in the time-honored warrior tradition, with lighter fluid.

Mythology blended with reality.

In the twilight landscape of Camp Evans Combat Base,

the Phoenix ascended,

resurrected in a swirling ascension,

flames, ash, and smoke,

freed from the tribulations of I Corps . . .
the rite completed.

So ended the Phoenix presence at Camp Evans . . .

and the Republic of South Fucking Vietnam.

# 15

## 1972

### March 1, 1972

One year after the Lao invasion, Lee Fairchild, the former door gunner, was once again a civilian. WO Bobby Gentry had been mortally wounded during the combat assault at Landing Zone Hotel the first day of LAM SON 719, one year earlier, on February 8, 1971. Gentry's copilot was Warrant Officer Burch, the crew chief was Pat Wade, and the gunner, Lee Fairchild. As the aircraft lifted off the landing zone, a two-man NVA machine-gun team at the left front of the aircraft fired. Several rounds impacted the cockpit, hitting Gentry, destroying his cyclic stick and the radios, and severing the hydraulic lines. Crew chief Pat Wade killed the two NVA with his M-60 machine gun. Meanwhile, Burch was just able to regain control of the ship an instant before crashing. Luckily, the aircraft was over a very steep incline and took no more fire. Wade and Fairchild lowered Gentry's seat back and pulled him to the floor of the cargo bay. There they administered first aid. Fairchild stayed with Gentry, while Wade crawled back into Gentry's seat to assist Burch with the pedals. Gentry lost a lot of blood during the short flight back to Khe Sanh. Due to the destroyed radio, Burch had no contact with the Khe Sanh tower or other aircraft. After avoiding several near midair collisions over Khe Sanh, Burch was able to put the aircraft down, without hydraulics, at POL, a major accomplishment for a young pilot. Gentry, by then near death, was placed on another aircraft and flown to the Quang Tri hospital. After the crew secured the damaged aircraft, they were flown to Quang Tri, where they learned that Bobby had died. The young door gunner, Lee Fairchild, would not forget WO Bobby Gentry.

In 1972, Lee Fairchild had served his nation, ended his time in service, and returned Stateside. One year after the action, he commemorated Gentry's loss in a poem of loving memory.

Writing the poem allowed Lee to place the memory of Bobby Gentry to rest. But it would not be until the summer of 1989 that Bobby Gentry's father would hear the poem. A federal building would be named after Gentry, in his hometown of Orlando, Florida.

*A Song for Mr. Gentry*
Lee Fairchild
1972

The wind screamed loud, that one fateful day.
When young Bobby Gentry went walking away.
Young flying warrior of the sky
Strong as the lion's roar
quiet like the snowfall.
Flew in from the west
to that green grass valley,
to a flowery field, landing
in a strange foreign battle.
Then the lightning flashed
and God had his say
as the flowers turned red
and the valley went grey,

and the valley went grey,
and young Bobby Gentry
went walking away.
Like a warrior of the skies
he was too proud to cry
as he looked to the heavens
and quietly slipped away
to the land where slain warriors
of battles do play.
Oh, I heard his mother cry
and his father drop to his knees,
his brothers and sisters
all screamed toward the sky
cursing the wind
that one fateful day
when young Bobby Gentry
went walking away.

## Fort Rucker

In 1972, I continued taking college courses. I had constantly sought a sense of normalcy after my return from Vietnam. In late 1972, the army required all aviators to have a standard instrument ticket. In addition to flying as an instructor pilot, I had to fly as a student pilot in the afternoon to earn my standard instrument ticket. I continued finishing college at night. I was obsessed with finishing college as quickly as possible and getting out of the army.

I successfully completed requirements for the army's standard helicopter instrument ticket and then, using my VA benefits, continued flying as a student in civilian aircraft. I finished a bachelor of science degree in business administration at Troy State University, paying for it with the army tuition assistance plan. While I was on active duty, the army paid 75 percent of my tuition. By 1973, I'd completed a fixed-wing, commercial, multiengine instrument rating using VA benefits as well. I'd tried to obtain the maximum educational benefits from my enlistment.

In March 1972, I watched on television the fall of such familiar places as Camp Carroll, Mai Loc, and Quang Tri City. Phil Rutledge, then out of the army and back home in Bakersfield, California, also watched the evening news in amazement as Camp Evans was destroyed by North Vietnamese Army artillery. He'd only been home three months. The previous November, he'd discussed with others at Camp Evans the Corregidor mentality that pervaded daily activities. They knew the NVA were capable, and would choose when. The Easter Offensive in March 1972 was when. Fortunately, it was well after the departure of the 101st Airborne Division.

# 16

# Exit

From 1965 to 1968, the U.S. Navy and Air Force lost ninety-seven aircraft unsuccessfully attempting to bring down the bridge at Thanh Hoa, the primary rail connector to China, which was the source of supplies and safe havens then just as it had been against the French. The Thanh Hoa was destroyed on the first run in December 1972 by a single, "smart" two thousand pound bomb. At the time, the effectiveness of the smart bomb was noticed only by those in the service, but it would change the way wars would be fought many years later. The American public would understand them after the 1991 Persian Gulf War.

In the bombing period of December 18 to December 29, 1972, the air force and navy flew 724 B-52 sorties, und 640 fighter-bomber sorties, dropping some twenty thousand tons of bombs. In addition, there were 1,384 sorties in support of attacking aircraft (chaff flights, refueling flights, fighter cover, SAM suppression, and electronic countermeasures).

On December 29, 1972, 150 U.S. aircraft roamed the Red River Valley at will, virtually unopposed. It was the first and last time of the war that American air power held supremacy. Just twenty-three unguided surface-to-air missiles were fired at the attackers, and none of the missiles were even close to constituting a threat. The SAM guidance facilities had mostly been destroyed. There was little left of the North Vietnamese stockpile. Of 150 U.S. aircraft attacking, all returned safely.

At the completion of the twelve-day campaign, North Vietnam's military potential, industry, and economy lay in ruins. Finally, the United States' unrestricted raids had destroyed North Vietnam's ability to defend itself against further attacks from the air. Its airfields had been destroyed, and it had expended all of its surface-to-air missiles. During the last three days, United States aircraft were virtually not fired on.

Unrecognized by the uncaring American voting public, a semblance of military victory had finally been attained by the air force. At the time, only 24,200 American troops remained in South Vietnam.

In response to the North Vietnamese Army Easter attacks, B-52 bombers had been first used in North Vietnam during 1972. By year's end, approximately 20 percent of South Vietnam had been conceded to the North Vietnamese Army. However, the round-the-clock bombings of North Vietnam in December 1972 forced the North Vietnamese leaders to agree to an American withdrawal and repatriation of prisoners. Until then, they'd had no need to negotiate anything. The air force bombing and President Nixon had finally accomplished the goal of getting North Vietnam's undivided attention.

On December 30, 1972, President Nixon halted the bombings.

On January 23, 1973, an agreement was signed permitting repatriation of American prisoners of war.

Lyndon Johnson's decision not to run for a second presidential term represented a tragic watershed. Years later, former Defense Secretary Robert McNamara would reveal his purported belief that Vietnam was an unwinnable war. More U.S. servicemen and women died in the war after Johnson's decision than before it.

On March 29, 1973, President Nixon, then reeling

under Watergate pressures, announced that "no American Prisoners of War" remained in Southeast Asia.

Five hundred ninety-one prisoners of war were released by North Vietnam and the Provisional Revolutionary Government. However, the families of 2,383 Americans still listed as MIA were stunned. Included among the relatives refusing to give up hope were families of men I knew. In their minds, their loved ones either remained in captivity in Southeast Asia, under the worst of circumstances, or were dead. The phrase "Killed in action, body not recovered" left gaping wounds in the hearts and minds of thousands of loved ones, as well as those who served with them.

In the words of Neal Pointer on the Texas Vietnam Veterans Memorial Monument, "In the harsh reality of war, the wounds that run deepest are the wounds of uncertainty. . . . These are the wounds that cannot heal." The emotional wounds over MIAs would fester for years not only in the hearts of their loved ones but also with many who'd served with them.

The stories of the NVA not taking prisoners of war in Laos would eventually be proven fact. The army helicopter crews, as well as air force, navy, and Marine aircrews supporting operations in Laos, knew the risks. The extra personal weapons and ammunition carried by Phoenix crewmen on CCN missions reflected that understanding. However, the worst fears were no longer nightmares, simply proven fact. And there would be no retaliation, no vengeance, no payback.

The Defense Intelligence Agency listed 354 missing in action in Laos, pilots and crewmen *known* to have survived their crashes in Laos. On March 10, 1973, seven military prisoners and three civilian prisoners were repatriated from Laos. The North Vietnamese offered no explanation or comment concerning the other 344. A "grieving nation" could simply conclude that they had been executed, died of injuries, or killed during escape and evasion.

The French had lost 36,979 men as prisoners during the Dien Bien Phu defeat. Only 10,754 were returned alive. Over 60 percent of French Legionnaires and Union Forces died in Viet Minh captivity. Starvation, brutal treatment, disease, and executions were the rule, rather than the exception. The Viet Minh had learned the methods of their Japanese captors during World War II, and ratcheted atrocities to an even higher level. Even the infamous atrocities worked on the American Lost Battalion early in 1942 cost "only" 40 percent killed at the hands of Japanese captors.

The B-52 bombings, jet fighter attacks, artillery raids, and Special Forces booby traps gave them no reason for mercy or compassion. The rules of war had been simply kill or be killed, just as we were briefed prior to our first CCN mission. The little bastards simply killed those they captured in Laos. Years later, the North Vietnamese would blame the Communist Pathet Lao. But Americans knew who occupied, controlled, and operated the Ho Chi Minh trail . . . the North Vietnamese Army.

The South Vietnamese government did not collapse until two years after the prisoner release, not until April 30, 1975. General Phu, whom I'd flown as copilot for in 1971, killed himself with a hand grenade as the North Vietnamese Army overran Saigon. Swarms of South Vietnamese attempted to reach American ships and escape. Most did not succeed. The panic and anarchy were well documented on television.

On May 17, 1975, the American freighter *Mayaguez* was captured by Communists off a Cambodian island. One of the fifteen Americans killed in the combat assault to free it was a former army warrant officer with Vietnam experience, piloting an air force CH-53 helicopter. A rocket-propelled grenade killed him as he touched down on the beach during the combat assault. His second tour of duty claimed him, just as it had Capt. David Nelson and so many others.

News reports would remark those as the last casualties of the Vietnam War, not mentioning the deaths of twenty-three other Americans whose CH-53 exploded midflight over Thailand, en route to the *Mayaguez*.

The *Mayaguez* rescue operation was a bizarre ending to our losses in Vietnam, the last casualties tragically dying in Marine and air force H-53 helicopters. Of fifteen Marine and air force CH-53 and HH-53 aircraft taking part in the operation, four were destroyed and nine were badly damaged. The one that exploded in midair over Thailand, while en route to the operation, killed more men than were lost in the combat assault. The other helicopters were destroyed by enemy fire after touchdown in the hot landing zone.

Although the *Mayaguez* action was a military victory, it had taken a far greater cost in lives than expected. Twenty-three deaths by accident exceeded the fifteen killed in combat. The merchant ship and its crew were freed.

The tragedy of the Vietnam War experience had been replayed in the last major combat assault. It was on an island off the coast of Cambodia. A military victory, retaking the *Mayaguez*, was achieved at far too great a cost. The Vietnam War had sapped the national spirit, leaving too many desperately wanting to forget.

The feelings of futility, shattered beliefs and abandonment of virtue were accurately abridged in Don McLean's popular song of the time, "American Pie." In quadraphonic stereo, we'd sing along with the passage, "the Father, Son, and the Holy Ghost, they caught the last train . . . to the coast . . . the day . . . the music . . . died."

# 17

# Veteran

I ended my time in service with the army in April 1973.
As I reentered civilian life, I had a distinct feeling of
accomplishment, as if I'd already completed one lifetime
and career. In June, I graduated Troy State University
with a B.S. in business administration. I then entered the
real estate appraisal business in Dothan, Alabama, and
began a program to attain membership in the American
Institute of Real Estate Appraisers. From time to time, I
would run into people I served with. On May 8, 1978, I
achieved my Membership, Appraisal Institute (MAI) designation after five years of long hard work and political
opposition. Achieving the designation in the minimum
time, five years, and at the minimum age of twenty-eight
years was my personal and business goal. I was one of
less than fifty members under the age of thirty, out of over
five thousand members nationwide. The week of that mo-
mentous professional accomplishment, I received a POW/
MIA request for donations from a retired major. In his
letter he'd cited David Nelson as a surviving POW, still
missing in action. The unwanted but intimately familiar
metallic chill wracked my body.

What had been a singular accomplishment in my business life was suddenly overshadowed by the possibility
that Dave Nelson had survived his crash in Laos, lan-
guishing in a filthy bamboo cage for seven years.

The difficulties of personal business accomplishments,
or unhappiness in a questionable marriage, were nothing

compared to the rage I held for my government. I, too, perceived the government as uncaring, for not seeking men like Nelson, to free them after years of a living hell. I was equally disgusted with myself for not having done anything to help. It was an attitude and perception shared by many veterans. But it was one based upon the deepest emotions, not facts.

The following Thursday night, I went to a Sertoma civic club party at Seville Quarter in Pensacola. I drank until I crashed and burned. I attempted to drive home, but succeeded only in wrapping my car around a telephone pole, narrowly escaping my old enemy, Death.

Later, carefully unconfirmed television news reports continued. Dave Nelson had been reported on national television, as seen by refugees. Alive. In Laos.

The stories would not end . . . until October, 1990.

In 1988, Lt. Col. Mike Sloniker, then assigned to the Pentagon, attended his first Vietnam Helicopter Pilots Association reunion at Fort Worth, Texas. Sloniker met veterans of one unit he'd served with during his second tour as an aviator in 1971, the 174th Assault Helicopter Company, the Dolphins and Sharks. When he'd joined the unit in July 1971, many LAM SON 719 veterans were there, and they passed on their cockpit experiences. In the spring of 1972, during the Easter Offensive, he'd successfully put their teachings to test. His company from the 229th Assault Helicopter Battalion, 3d Brigade, 1st Cavalry Division, supported the South Vietnamese defense of Loc Ninh and An Loc. Like Laos, it was a "mid-intensity" antiaircraft environment. But this time replete with *Strela* (Russian for "arrow") shoulder-fired surface-to-air missiles used against helicopters. For helicopter pilots it was as bad as Laos had been, but with a more effective helicopter-killer. And it seemed as if every private in the North Vietnamese Army had at least one *Strela*.

A year after his first VHPA reunion in June 1989, after

exercising in the Pentagon Officers Athletic Club (POAC), Sloniker met Col. Joe Schlatter, then director of the Defense Intelligence Agency's POW/MIA office.

Sloniker learned the DIA was still working on Vietnam-era cases, some over twenty years old. He was impressed with the professionalism they displayed in a totally thankless, highly stressful job. The office was constantly responding to congressional inquiries, investigations, and highly emotional allegations. But, as far as Sloniker could tell, each case was handed professionally, utilizing every resource available.

Sloniker mentioned that he had served with the 174th Aviation Company from June to October 1971 before transferring to the 1st Cavalry Division to finish his tour. Schlatter then invited Sloniker down to review documents they had regarding that era, mentioning that two Cobra pilots' remains had been recovered. They'd been shot down on April 5, 1972, south of Loc Ninh. The aircraft commander was CW2 Joe Windler and the gunner was Capt. Hank Spengler. A memorial service at Arlington was being planned for the family of Captain Spengler in August 1989.

Sloniker had flown Hueys with the First Air Cavalry in combat during those times. In 1972, Mike lived and carefully observed the toll of stress endured by Huey pilots assigned missions into An Loc. Some army pilots had to puke by the tail boom before saddling up. Others drank themselves into oblivion each night, after surviving horrifying missions. Some calmly accepted the missions and quietly endured. All performed their missions admirably, under the worst of combat and political environments.

Mike Sloniker decided to attend the funeral service at Arlington in honor of the men who'd provided his gunship cover. He'd known them by their call sign, the Blue Max. Sloniker knew he'd survived his tour of duty not merely because of his personal skills and good luck but because of the gunship support getting him in and out of some horrifying landing zones. The skills, courage, and professionalism of Blue Max pilots were unquestionably part of his survival equation.

Sloniker attended the Arlington funeral for Captain Spengler. There was a family reception afterward at the welcome center of the national cemetery. Spengler was a 1968 West Point graduate, and thirty or so of his class-mates attended in uniform. When Sloniker was intro-duced to Spengler's mother, she mentioned that she did not remember his name in her son's class. He responded that he wasn't a West Point graduate, but was there paying personal respects, representing those who'd been pro-tected by the Blue Max. She immediately introduced him to the other family members.

Sloniker attended the VHPA convention in Chicago during the July 4th weekend, 1989. There, he chanced upon a Phoenix minireunion where thirty Phoenix pilots had a well-organized meeting under way. It was obvious a great deal of personal effort was made to organize and get veterans there. They had their own meeting room with a slide show, movies, and beer. Obviously, many were extremely close even after eighteen years. The camaraderie impressed him.

Mike returned to his job at the Pentagon, where he worked in the office of the secretary of defense, special operations staff and was involved in special operations aircraft acquisition. He continued his discussions with Col. Joe Schlatter. The fact that the Phoenix had been very active on CCN missions, to the point of even being requested specifically for some missions, was not lost on Mike. Those were formative missions of the Green Berets, evolving to the Special Operations Forces of today.

He then began reviewing documents concerning Phoe-nix KIAs. Mike realized that the Phoenix had sustained one of the heaviest tolls of those killed in action of the lift companies in the 101st Airborne Division. In November 1989, in an effort to assist the DIA in locating some of the remains, Mike spent time reviewing the tapes provided to him by Capt. Don Peterson in 1971. The tapes described the action involving the loss of Paul Stewart and Tom Doody, near A Luoi. They also described the downing of David Nelson and Ralph Moreira, southeast of Sophia. Both were commonly misinterpreted as at other locations in after-action reports. While going over these documents, he also came across the report on CWO David Soyland, a Phoenix pilot still listed as missing in action in 1989.

Colonel Schlatter's staff asked Mike to contact Lt. Col. Skip Butler, a former Redskin Cobra pilot, in hopes he would meet with the DIA staff. Butler's witness statements to the Soyland incident were kept on file in hopes of eventual resolution of his case. The keeper of the files asked Sloniker if he could persuade Butler to visit with them so they could update as much of the data as possible. DIA recovery teams had been searching for the crash site since early 1989, without locating it.

On November 27, 1989, Butler, coincidentally working in the Pentagon labyrinth, came to the Defense Intelligence office. He sat down with retired CWO Bob Destatt, an intelligence analyst in the Defense Intelligence Agency's Prisoner of War/Missing in Action Office. Destatt had been personally touched as he studied the after-action reports describing the heroism of the army air crews attempting to rescue Special Forces Team Alaska. It was during the end of America's involvement, with many units withdrawn, returning Stateside. Destatt questioned Butler in a very careful manner, intentionally not showing Butler's own handwritten statements of 1971 to him. Those present were awed by the detail of his recall. On December 16, 1989, Butler had not seen his statements since he wrote them. He recalled every minute detail from May 17, 1971. The aircraft armament, the weather, the sources of ground fire, types of fire, the terrain features they flew around, the names of the Special Forces team on the ground, the approaches by the different aircraft. He also recalled the direction of attack and the effect of the air strikes called by the FAC. He even recalled the make-up of the flight crews that poured in around him. Butler's personal flight records recorded thirty-one hours on May 17 and 18. Pilots and crew members understood the gravity of those numbers. Butler's memories enabled the American recovery team to return and confirm the crash site in early 1990. All that remained were tiny pieces of the aircraft. They could not possibly identify it as the particular Huey, but the fragments were pieces of a Huey. Obviously a crash scene, but most of the metal and fiberglass of the Huey had been salvaged and removed by the mountain people living nearby.

Sloniker understood Butler was sharing very personal memories of the failed rescue attempt. Butler had been an experienced Redskin who had lived the I Corps school of bad weather, the unforgiving mountain terrain, and deadly combat environment.

Trying to cover Soyland during the unsuccessful rescue attempt, Butler had hovered his Cobra up a long, enemy-controlled valley. Eighteen years later, he still wore the POW/MIA bracelet with David Soyland's name. Despite all the successful actions in his career, the tragedy of Soyland's and Pearce's loss was the one thing that hung in his mind. Butler, like most helicopter veterans, had reluctance to discuss the stories without someone in attendance who understood their meaning and gravity. The fears, frustrations, and vulnerabilities learned in one's combat tour are not easily shared with those who have not shared combat experience and acquired the proper vocabulary.

## June 1989

The December 1986 Federal Income Tax Laws initiated by President Reagan had dramatically changed real estate investment taxation, beginning a decline in demand for real estate services, including mine. The October 1987 stock market crash, Black Monday, further worsened matters by extending losses into the savings and banking business, culminating in nationwide banking closures. My appraisal business reflected the national trend. It was down, way down.

In June 1989, a year and a half after my divorce was final, my business hit rock bottom. Emotionally and financially, I was at an all-time low. While driving in Pensacola, I saw a billboard advertisement for the Vietnam Helicopter Pilots Association reunion in Chicago. Jim Cronley, a successful contractor and developer, had encouraged me to join. Jim had been a warrant officer a few years ahead of me. Jim had also introduced me to Robert Mason's book *Chickenhawk*. I decided to go to Chicago as a gift to myself.

I'd saved enough frequent flyer miles to trade in on a round-trip, first-class ticket to Chicago. Not knowing what to expect in my first VHPA reunion, I arrived at the Hyatt Hotel and cautiously observed the festivities under way.

I quickly discovered a patriotic Fourth of July setting. Any sense of decorum was destroyed by the gregarious reunions. Flight jackets, T-shirts, cavalry hats, and beer were everywhere. Any somber or subtle feelings were instantly swept away in the color and camaraderie.

When I entered the lobby of the Hyatt Hotel, I realized there was a Charlie Company, 158th Aviation Battalion, minireunion. I remembered vaguely of having served with them. I had my book of photographs underarm. Eighteen years after my service, I walked slowly into the room. I was instantly dumfounded to recognize the names and some of the faces. I then met Ken Mayberry and Pat McKeaney, who both denied I'd ever been in Charlie Company, since they did not remember me. I pulled out my photographs and showed them a picture of me sitting below the Phoenix 2d Platoon flag, with the bra on the wall in the hootch. They nearly passed out in disbelief!

Those of us attending our first reunion were in an absolute, profound state of shock. It was amazing to me that after eighteen years, the events which had been such an important part of my psyche were reaffirmed in common experiences. A week rarely passed that I did not think of something that happened during that long year. The memories were not just dreams or nightmares. They had been real events, which could again be shared with living people.

In the Phoenix minireunion with Charlie Company, 158th Aviation Battalion, I found myself reacquainting with Mayberry, McKeaney, and Scrugham. We had shared the experiences and emotions during a very difficult time in our nation's history. It was with a sense of pride that I left for home from Chicago. On the flight out from Chicago, Sean Moore, a Phoenix pilot from Houston, came on the plane and shook my hand as he passed by. A minute later, he walked back and asked me, "Were you there, really there in that deep extraction in Laos, where we took flak?!"

"Yes, I was." Another shared experience and memory that was so unreal, we mentally questioned ourselves whether we'd truly experienced it. The affirmation of those experiences made the trip worth it.

In the unspoken terms of personal honor and patriotic duty, the Phoenix veterans understood where you'd been, what you'd done. For most of us, few chose to talk about combat experiences. People in the World simply did not understand and could not relate to our experiences when we returned.

We were men who had chosen to serve, a rational, conscious choice made during a period in our nation's history that saw a reversal of a war and a withdrawal begun. All done in the face of political opposition at home. We'd shared fear, fatigue, and exhaustion, yet experienced together the sense of being alive that can only be realized in the eerie time-expansion of combat. However, a very small corner of my mind reminded me of "unfinished business," just as I'd felt in the American Airlines jet lifting me back to the World, many years earlier.

The weekend of July 4, 1990, was another Vietnam Helicopter Pilots Association convention. The Sheraton Hotel in New Orleans was the scene. New Orleans was an appropriate location for a bunch of heavy-drinking pilots. On Saturday morning, the minireunion for the Phoenix Company was held in two adjoining rooms, consolidated into a party room. David Wolfe, from California, showed up with his wife and sons. Dave Rayburn again made it in from Atlanta. Ken Mayberry and Dean Grau were in attendance, along with a dozen other former Phoenix.

The celebrity at the event was Layne Heath, who'd recently finished a novel, *CW2,* and was autographing copies of it. Those present were autographing each other's copies of *CW2* and *Into Laos*, just like high school or college class yearbooks!

Heath's novel involved a character, Billy Roark, a warrant officer who'd served with the Phoenix in his first tour of duty. Roark then returned for a second tour of duty, during the wind-down of the war, at An Khe in 1972. I discussed with Layne the striking reversed sequence of my one-year tour, beginning with the standdown at An Khe, then moving to the Phoenix. I gave him movies of the An Khe golf course described in his character's second tour.

He signed a copy of his book, *CW2*, "To Tom Marshall— who traveled the same ground, but backwards!"

I'd enjoyed reading *CW2*, which intensely described the actions and frustrations of a warrant officer aviator in Vietnam during the ending of the war. I quietly wondered why Heath had written a novel. Most of the book, excepting the last chapter, accurately depicted the internal rage and sense of unfinished business.

My girlfriend, LuAnne, was startled by the anti–Jane Fonda bumper stickers (We're Not Fonda Jane) and T-shirts in abundance at the meeting. Although they were not apparent among the Phoenix pilots, they were prominently displayed throughout the convention sales floor. In LuAnne's eyes, Jane Fonda was the idol of a liberated woman. At twenty-eight years of age, highly successful in communications marketing, she could not understand the resentment many veterans held toward Fonda. But we remembered Jane Fonda visiting, with former Attorney General Ramsey Clark, prisoners of war in Hanoi during the antiwar demonstrations of 1968 and 1969. They'd caused additional torment for those she visited and even worse treatment of those who'd refused her. Fonda even posed sitting behind a 12.7mm machine gun, after calling the POWs war criminals. To those of us who'd been on the receiving end of an NVA heavy machine gun, that was unpardonable.

When Dave Wolfe came into the Phoenix party room, I immediately recognized him and introduced myself. He said he didn't remember me and didn't believe I was a Phoenix. I instantly told him that I remembered a Christmas present he had received while I was in his hootch at Camp Evans. Wolfe, typical of vets at their first reunion, was somewhat bewildered and amazed at our minireunion.

At the meeting in New Orleans, I finally began to have the sense of being part of the Phoenix again. I'd begun the slow process of unlocking the mental compartments where so many vivid images were kept. I made the commitment to myself to continue the process.

# 18

# Hail and Farewell

In late 1989, the remains of a Phoenix crew lost on March 5, 1971, were returned to the United States for the tedious task of forensic identification. They were definitely from a Charlie Company, 158th Aviation Battalion, aircraft. The wedding band of the copilot, WO Ralph Moreira, was found with his name on the inside. Pictures of the crash site showed the exactness of the archaeological excavation. The area was cleared of brush, the dirt was sifted, and the bone fragments and teeth were returned. Then the remains were reviewed by numerous agencies so that multiple sources could provide their opinions. The process took a year.

Lt. Col. Mike Sloniker retired after twenty-three years of active duty on October 1, 1990. He continued to work out in the Pentagon Officers Athletic Center, and on October 2, he ran into Colonel Schlatter, who'd returned from a lengthy trip. Schlatter told Mike that a Phoenix crew was going to be buried at 10:00 A.M. on Friday the fifth. That one informal comment, among acquaintances in the Pentagon Officers Athletic Club, became a call to honor comrades missing for over nineteen years.

Forensic investigators had confirmed the remains. It was a C Company, 158th Assault Helicopter Battalion Phoenix flight crew. It had been shot down in Laos southeast of Landing Zone Sophia on March 5, 1971. Auction Lead Capt. David Nelson, aircraft commander, WO1

338

Ralph Moreira, pilot, Sp4. Joel Hatley, crew chief, and Sp4. Mike King, gunner, were finally coming home.

Having gotten to know Phoenix veterans in Chicago and New Orleans, Mike had a couple of phone calls to make. He immediately called Phoenix veterans Jack Glennon in Virginia Beach and Don Davis in Chicago. Their phone chain was so thorough that by 9:00 P.M. that evening, Mike had himself been called by at least two Phoenix to tell him about the pending services.

At 2:00 P.M., October 4, 1990, Jack Glennon called my Pensacola office from Norfolk, Virginia. Glennon asked me if I knew David Nelson and Ralph Moreira. I instantly responded, "Yes. My first CCN mission was with Nelson." He then told me of the burial ceremony scheduled at Arlington the next morning for Nelson, Moreira, Hatley, and King. The chill hit, hammering my body. My mind reeled back to the hot string extraction in North Vietnam with Nelson. Without a moment's hesitation, I told Glennon I would be there. I immediately called my travel agent to get an airline ticket from Pensacola, Florida, to Washington, D.C.

Mike Sloniker had remembered the Phoenix. With his two phone calls, Phoenix from across America assembled to honor one of their crews. He met them at 9:00 P.M. on October 4 at the Sheraton Hotel in Arlington, Virginia. Within forty-eight hours of notification, Dean Grau and family arrived from Minnesota. Ken Mayberry, traveling unaccompanied in a wheelchair, flew in from Nebraska. Bruce Updyke came from Indiana. Chuck Doty drove down from Maryland. After being notified at 2:00 P.M. that day, I flew in from Florida. Rick Scrugham flew in from Tennessee. He'd been notified at 10:00 A.M. that day. Don Davis from Chicago and Jack Glennon from Virginia were present. The next morning Tom Cullen would arrive from Connecticut.

Pat McKeaney could not make it from the west coast in time. But we all talked to him on the phone, very late that night.

The next morning, we assembled at breakfast and went in convoy to the National Cemetery, Arlington. We proceeded to a small chapel on the hill. At the entrance were the names of Hatley, King, Moreira, and Nelson, in alphabetical order without rank. A caisson pulled up a single flag-draped coffin which held the bone fragments excavated from the crash site in Laos. A formal U.S. Army color guard and marching band accompanied it. The coffin was carefully removed and carried into the sanctuary.

We filed inside and sat on the pews. Included among the mourners were several generals, senior officers, and numerous Special Forces and Ranger NCOs. A chaplain opened the service with an invocation. Eyes closed, I began thinking back to the service for Steve Hansen, and his father, a chaplain. We sang the National Hymn and were addressed by an army chaplain who introduced Mrs. Evelyn Hatley. Then her son, Joel Hatley, the crew chief on Nelson's ship, was remembered by his mother. She had written a poem. She explained how she came to writing it through her grief and sorrow.

The tone of the chapel service was set immediately by Joel Hatley's mother. She began telling us the exact hour and minute that Joel had been born, and paid tribute to the blessing of his short life by reading the poem that she had written. It had been her attempt to overcome grief. Although her voice remained steady throughout her reading, the emotion of the words gripped those who filled the chapel.

*A Picture, a Flag and a Gold Star Pin*

Evelyn Laton Hatley

In memory of
SP4. JOEL C. HATLEY
Co. C, 158th Avn Bn
101st Airborne Div.
APO San Francisco, CA 96383

That night I kissed my son Good-bye, and watched his plane soar to the sky.

Little did I know as he held my hand, that soon he'd lie in some strange land.

I still can see his smiling face, and feel his arms in last embrace.

His quiet voice and tender touch, his loving ways all meant so much.

He said, "Mother please don't cry tonight." I said, "I won't," I promised with throat so tight.

I held him close; I loved him so, and it hurt so much to see him go.

I'll be alright and I luv ya'll, were his last words going down the hall.

He waved good-bye going to the plane, and suddenly I felt so strange.

I thought—he's going where he's never been, tho 'Nam was his destination again.

I didn't know why—couldn't understand—but "Heaven" flashed through my mind then.

I felt we had really said good-bye, and he truly was gone to the sky.

I felt strange peace and calm within, and I felt I'd never see him again.

I watched his plane go out of sight, as he was lost in the still, dark night.

I love my son. Why must he go? My heart cried out,
now it ached so.

He went to 'Nam, but I soon learned, he really was lost,
never to return.


MISSING IN ACTION . . . the telegram read, but
inside I knew our Joel was dead.

He'd been shot down, the helicopter lost . . . Dear
Lord! My son! Oh, what a cost!

And then we wait and wait and pray, and hope we'll
hear that he's okay.

The time was short, tho it seemed long. The grief was
great but love was strong.

Each day seemed like a million years, as time was
washed away with tears.

At last word came, and what I knew within my heart,
was finally true.

KILLED IN ACTION . . . this telegram read, crashed
in flames . . . no survivors it said.

KILLED . . . NOT MISSING NOW it read, My Joel!
My Joel! Our Joel was dead!

Oh Lord! Oh Lord! Oh no, no please! And then I fell on
bended knee.

Dear God! I cried in unbelief, my heart exploded then
in grief.

The tears then like a river did flow; our Joel! Oh Lord!
What a way to go!


In crushed remembrance of his love, I bowed my head
to God above;

To thank Him for that life so sweet, and prayed
someday again we'd meet.

I felt his hand and tender touch, his last good-bye all
meant so much.

Just then I saw his face, his smile, and my heart raced
across the miles.

To join his heart in that last breath, to share his fate, to
    share his death.
To die with him in burning flames, to leave with me
    only his name.
There's no remains, no grave to be, nothing except
    sweet memories.
A picture of him is left instead, and a folded flag to
    show he's dead.
Always I'll look at the smiling face, of the picture I
    hold here in his place.
Always I'll hold in grief and strife, this flag as if it were
    my life.
Always a Gold Star Pin I'll wear, in memory of a life so
    sweet and fair.
A Picture, a Flag, and a Gold Star Pin, I'll always hold
    in the place of him.

After the memorial service, while families rode to the
burial site, the Phoenix veterans assembled behind the
horse-drawn caisson, army band, firing party, and funeral
detail. The soldiers were from the 3d Infantry Old Guard,
an army ceremonial unit, so visible at the Tombs of the
Unknown Soldiers at Arlington National Cemetery.

We watched as the coffin was gently placed back on the
horse-drawn caisson. Led by a formal honor guard and
military band, we walked behind the caisson as it was
drawn approximately a mile and a quarter down the hill to
the burial site. Ken Mayberry was in his wheelchair.
Halfway down the hill, he had a flat tire due to a National
Defense Service Medal falling off one of the soldiers in
the procession. It punctured his inner tube. Phoenix kept
jostling Dean Grau for the honor of assisting Mayberry
along, who now endured MS.

After the flag presentations to the families, Don Davis,
who'd rescued Dave Nelson off of Ranger South in February 1971, placed a pair of shined jump boots alongside
the casket in memory of Dave's being the only person

who could walk around Camp Evans in the monsoons without getting his highly shined boots muddy. Mike Sloniker had worn the boots in Vietnam during his first tour of duty with the 101st Airborne Division.

With TV cameras rolling, some family members present, and a large crowd of onlookers, Nelson, Moreira, Hatley, and King were finally laid to rest in the one coffin.

At the conclusion of the ceremony, Karla Carter, Dave Nelson's younger sister, walked over to the group of former pilots and tearfully asked, "Did you guys fly with my brother?" Don Davis responded that all the men present had flown with him. There were no dry eyes in the group. She then showed us all a cherished picture of her big brother, and pictures of his boots.

Afterward, we met briefly with the families at the reception hall of the hotel where they had stayed the night before. Dave Nelson's younger sister and brother were there, nice, genuine, Americans. Ralph Moreira's mother, Patsy, and her husband were there, along with Ralph Jr. I was in shock at seeing Angelo, Ralph's son. I couldn't even speak to him. He was a taller and heavier version of his dad. I related my memories of Ralph in the few minutes with Patsy and gave her a picture of him in the CCN deer hunt, southeast of Khe Sanh. Of course, she instantly picked him out in the unfocused photograph.

I listened as Rick Scrugham explained to Karla how he'd seen Dave's Huey explode in midair, confirming that there was no possibility of Nelson having survived the crash. At that point, I was finally relieved of the guilt I'd felt since 1978, when a retired major who'd been a POW erroneously reported that Nelson had been alive and died in Laos, in 1978.

When Karla asked, "How come the government didn't tell me about you guys?" we had no explanation. Words cannot describe the sadness and relief one sees in a family member's face, as an eyewitness tearfully recounts the aircraft exploding, like the *Challenger*. At that very moment, after nineteen years of prayerful waiting, the Nelson family finally knew and accepted Dave's death. Our meeting with the families was heartwarming but tense, and none of the families knew the others. Any of the family members present would have easily fit into a Marshall or Compton family reunion (my families) in Virginia. Ralph Moreira's son had a ponytail. My two sons had equally long hair and probably enjoyed the same music he did.

The family members were definitely surprised at our presence at the ceremony, and some suspected the Department of the Army had set it up. The families were still very resentful about their treatment, and they divided that resentment between the government and the news media, which had certainly not uncovered any additional facts, but continued to print credulous stories written in haste and carefully unconfirmed. The Department of the Army, with institutional, bureaucratic indifference, had not put any of the families in touch with the other families or with those of us the families unexpectedly encountered at the ceremony.

I left Washington with the feeling that I had come for Americans, friends, on the ground, in need.

## October 12, 1990, Arlington National Cemetery

One week, to the day, following the ceremony for Dave Nelson and his crew, a much larger procession of relatives, friends, and media followed another military funeral procession. A horse-drawn caisson carried the body, not of a military veteran but of a POW/MIA veteran.

Twenty-five years earlier, on April 29, 1965, Capt. Charles Shelton had been shot down over the skies of Laos. As there was no word of his death or survival, he was simply listed as missing in action, and Marian Shelton, his wife, returned from Okinawa to the United

States to raise the couple's five children. The youngest was just over a year old when Charles was shot down. Each year that passed, she lived in anticipation of a knock on the door that would bring word of her husband.

With the end of American involvement in the war in early 1973, Charles Shelton was not among the fewer than six hundred POWs returned. Even so Marian could not believe her husband dead. At this time the government began to take steps "converting" MIAs to KIAs, killed in action, with the classification "Presumptive finding of death." But Marian Shelton refused to accept a presumptive finding of death. She continued badgering the air force for more information.

She eventually learned from government reports that her husband had safely ejected from his crippled aircraft, parachuted to the ground, and radioed that he was in good condition, on the ground in Laos.

A villager later described the episode to U.S. authorities, stating that the airman had been captured alive by Pathet Lao (Communist) troops.

In 1973, Marian went to Indochina in search of her husband. There, she bribed a boatman to take her into Laos. After seven weeks in Laos and Thailand, she returned home with no new information. She would remain active in POW/MIA political issues across the nation.

For Mrs. Shelton, the mental torture created by her husband's absence never ended. Every alleged sighting kept her hopes alive. She had traveled from mountain villages in Laos to refugee camps in Afghanistan in her search for him. She took her story to top TV shows and podiums across the United States.

As a child, Marian Shelton had lost her older brother, missing in action, in World War II. Losing her husband to the unknown fate of missing, presumed dead, was a horrible coincidence. Adding to her suffering was the fact that because of her efforts the air force had changed her husband's status from "Presumed finding of death" to

"Missing in action" and ceremonially promoted him to colonel from captain. Colonel Shelton became the last MIA of the Vietnam era.

By September, 1990, Marian had finally reached the unhappy conclusion that her husband probably had died in captivity. At 11:00 P.M. on the night of October 4, 1990, in despair that her decades of searching and pain had been for nothing, she sat alone in the yard of her California home. She placed a .22-caliber pistol to her head and ended her life. At the very moment Marian Shelton took her life, Phoenix were in Washington, convening for the memorial ceremony for David Nelson, Ralph Moreira, Joel Hatley, and Mike King. Of those present at Arlington, only Elsie King could truly understand the pain of Marian Shelton.

The press would refer to Marian Shelton as the last casualty of the Vietnam War.

Four years later, on September 24, 1994, Col. Charles E. Shelton was finally declared killed in action. On October 4, 1995, the anniversary of Mrs. Shelton's suicide, a memorial service for Colonel Shelton was held at his wife's grave at Arlington National Cemetery.

In reporting the Shelton story, the *New York Times* said that the last name could finally be placed upon the Wall.

Veterans, however, knew that could not be so.

# 19

# The Price of Exit

### Hits Downed, Casualties, Veterans

After the ceremony at Arlington, Mike Sloniker graciously shared with me a copy of the LAM SON 719 after-action report that had been prepared for army archives. Dated April 24, 1971, the report was addressed to the commanding general, 101st Airborne Division. It had been declassified in 1989. The one hundred fifty–plus pages were filled with army acronyms, statistics, and statements regarding mission successes and reasonable aircraft and personnel losses.

I read the carefully couched descriptions of actions. The military language, acronyms, and contractions read like a foreign language. I initially took the vague references to successes and the reasonableness of losses as the grossest understatement and misstatement of results. Many pilots and crewmen I knew vehemently disagreed with the conclusions: there probably had been many successful accomplishments, but who determines an acceptable cost?

The military planners had hoped to repeat the success of the Cambodian invasion of 1970, in which American ground forces were used in conjunction with the ARVN, but the Laotian invasion differed from the outset; the Cooper-Church Amendment had prevented American ground troops' entering Laos. Even more important, American advisers, artillery observers, and forward air controllers were not permitted to accompany the ARVN units they had lived and fought with. These factors helped foster a lack of confidence in the operation that was magnified by communications problems with supporting U.S. aircraft and artillery. The stated goal of the invasion was to spend ninety days in Laos, destroying the enemy base areas 604 and 611. But American planners had not anticipated General Giap's October 1970 move of twenty heavy antiaircraft battalions to the area. The impact of tactical air strikes was reduced since the antiaircraft positions were heavily bunkered, and as at Dien Bien Phu in 1954, artillery positions had been tunneled into position. The helicopter crews suffered heavily from the misjudgments of the planners.

The planned ninety days ended after only forty-five days. Both South Vietnam and North Vietnam claimed victory.

The XXIV Corps after-action report claimed 19,360 North Vietnamese Army dead and inferred the permanently disabled casualties of 6,776. In all, this was roughly one-half of the fifty thousand enemy forces in the area.

The ARVNs reported 7,683 casualties, including 1,764 killed in action. *Newsweek* magazine, however, speculated on April 5, 1971, that 3,800 ARVNs were killed and 5,975 wounded, i.e., that *all* the ARVNs who participated in the initial 8,000-man thrust were wounded or killed!

In materiel, the North Vietnamese Army reportedly lost 2,001 trucks, 106 tanks, and 13 artillery pieces. The ARVN reported losing 211 trucks, 87 combat vehicles, 54 tanks, and 96 pieces of artillery. However, *15,000* North Vietnamese Army vehicles had been counted moving on just one day in December 1970, so very few had been destroyed.

The United States reported 108 helicopters destroyed and 618 damaged. The number was actually four times higher. In the approximately forty-five days of the Laotian invasion, 659 helicopters were employed in the operation; 444 helicopters were shot down by enemy fire.

Helicopters took serious antiaircraft hits on 1,072 total occasions, including those shot down or made unflyable until repaired.

The number of helicopters shot down exceeded the authorized inventory of the 101st Airborne Division. Of those, ninety-one were destroyed beyond recovery. Four more were destroyed in accidents.

On average, ten helicopters were shot down a day. On average, twenty-four times per day helicopters were struck by antiaircraft fire.

An amazing 267 aircraft were extracted in hopes of repair. Those were sling-loaded by Chinooks and Sky-crane helicopters from the battle scene to Phu Bai, where a major maintenance depot was located. However, 252 of these were determined not to be repairable and were DEROSed for salvage. Technically, as defined by the army, they were not destroyed by the enemy. Of course, if you talked to those who'd been flying them you'd get a different opinion. An additional sixty-two aircraft were flown back to their units, *then* DEROSed as salvage. Generally those aircraft were simply shot to hell, not flyable and not worth repairing. They, too, were destroyed by enemy action. The air force and navy lost seven fixed-wing aircraft. Forty-two fixed-wing aircraft took hits and returned to base.

Of 659 aircraft beginning the operation, a total of 1,072 aircraft, or 163 percent, had been seriously damaged by enemy fire, repaired, and returned to service. That meant *everybody* flying in the operation got hit seriously once. Nearly two-thirds of the pilots took serious battle damage more than once.

The fact that operations continued under such intense enemy opposition is a credit to the courage and skill of those who flew the missions. An even greater compliment to the pilots in the Khe Sanh and Laotian areas was the fact that only four aircraft were destroyed by accidents, i.e., accidents claimed less than .6 percent of the total inventory. There were only twenty-nine helicopters damaged by accidents, representing 4 percent of the inventory, even though pilots of 659 aircraft were operating twelve- to fourteen-hour days in an uncontrolled air traffic environment, and their piloting was aggravated by fatigue, low ceilings, fog, rain, and continuous exposure to enemy fire. They'd accomplished missions in a hostile environment in an unbelievably safe manner.

In the eyes of Gen. Creighton Abrams, then managing a congressionally mandated retreat from Vietnam, LAM SON 719 was a critical but necessary effort to buy time for training the South Vietnamese and accelerating the U.S. force withdrawal. Strategically, it was a test of the sustainability of helicopter operations in a midintensity antiaircraft environment of the kind which American and NATO forces faced in Europe.

LAM SON 719 was just the first draft of army helicopter history in a midintensity antiaircraft environment. And to this date, little has been written of the experiences pilots and crew members still hold in their minds.

After reading the 101st Airborne Division operational report and considering it in light of the Persian Gulf War, I realized that our military planners had finally gotten things right. General Berry returned to the States after Vietnam and successfully lobbied to have the army establish aviation as a combat arm.

Although many army and air force officers disagreed with the report's conclusions about losses in Laos, the differences stemmed from the definition of "acceptable" losses. What was acceptable loss to a general was totally unacceptable to the pilots, crewmen, and their families.

As a result of General Berry's efforts, as well as those of many other army officers, by 1990 army aviation had evolved into a well-organized and incredibly effective power, attaining a potential we couldn't even dream of in 1971.

I began to appreciate the career officers who remained in the army after Vietnam to refine airmobile tactics, procedures, and mission risk assessment. They had gotten the military's act together. Both militarily and politically, lessons had been learned from our experiences. Most important, the national will was firmly in support of the people who put their lives on the line. A newly grateful nation had blossomed with yellow ribbons for all who served in the Gulf War and before.

In 1991, a national spirit, empowered by the military institutions' ability to win, once again emerged in America.

# Epilogue

During the 1970s, I watched on television history unfolding. The fall of Vietnam, ending in the capture of Saigon, was widely televised. For most Americans, an even more serious event shadowed the history of the time. Vietnam fell in the aftermath of the Watergate debacle, which toppled Richard Nixon. There had been another Middle East war. U.S. forces remained in Europe, facing the Russian and Eastern Bloc threat. In January 1976, my son, Andrew, was born. My appraisal business was continuing to grow. In October 1978, my second son, Patrick, was born. During 1979, Stanley Karnow's excellent series on the Vietnam War was televised on PBS. To my mind, his was the first analytical, objective overview of the Vietnam War on television. Other than to "fight the spread of communism," most of us who'd served there really had had no true political understanding of why we were there. But I was profoundly disappointed that the Laotian invasion rated only a few paragraphs in history.

I began to expand my personal search for explanations, reading books and accounts arising from the era. I slowly became aware that the cause for the search was not something outside of me; I found myself on a deeply personal, introspective search for meaning, understanding, and peace. Studying the history, reviewing my personal experiences, and reading political studies of the war helped. But the major single step forward was reacquainting myself with members of the Vietnam Helicopter Pilots

Association (VHPA). The Chicago VHPA meeting was the beginning of a series of meetings, not to reenact or relive the experiences, but to honor the memory of all who had served. Affirming the experiences, successes, and hardships, as well as the memories of those lost. To us, the names on the Wall were *people*, people we had shared hard times and hard choices with. In those meetings, friendships, understanding, and appreciation were rekindled.

Not until the ceremony at Arlington in October 1990 were we able to share our grief, in the congregation of those who cared. Families and close friends were there due to love, the honor guard was there on duty, and a surprisingly large contingent of active-duty personnel was there by choice. Those present included Rangers and other servicemen from noncommissioned officers to generals. Crowded into the small chapel of the Stone Garden at Arlington National Cemetery, nine of us were pilots who'd flown with the dead. At that fateful juncture, in our minds, finally, we could put them to rest in a place of honor. No longer hovering souls, unanchored spirits in our memories, where they had been for nineteen and a half years.

While Evelyn Hatley read her poem, I regained a sense of appreciation of her sacrifice and of our national service. The honor of Americans as a people depends on those who serve at their call, aware of the demands that duty, honor, country place upon them. I then realized that history would weave those losses and wounds into the psychic fabric that comprises our national spirit and social conscience. As a nation, we now stand painfully aware of the sacrifices demanded of those in national service.

I have learned over the years that it's not just the veterans who are affected by the war and losses but the wives, children, parents, sisters, brothers, and extended families of those lost as well.

The most forgotten, least appreciated victims of the

tragedy remain the families of those lost. The bureaucracy in place during and just after the war years provided minimal acknowledgment of the families' losses. Little or no help was proffered, or interest expressed after the funerals: a short ceremony, a Purple Heart, a flag, and a Gold Star pin, and that was all. They were then left on their own, to grieve and reconcile their feelings.

Every generation's leaders and politicians should know the cost of a call to arms. War is godless, and the losses transcend generations. The leaders and politicians should also know that with each new generation there are those who seek the young warrior's challenges.

It is the military that implements the national resolve, whether right or wrong. It is the soldier's duty not to question the policy, merely to implement that policy by following orders. In commemorating those lost, we are mindful of liberty's cost.

During the past few years, I've frequently heard misstatements regarding the numbers of Americans who served and the number of casualties taken. *Achilles in Vietnam* was written by Dr. Jonathan Shay, a psychologist with the Veteran's Administration in New York State. Dr. Shay summarized the population and numbers of those served, wounded, and killed in the actions in Vietnam. I have taken the numbers provided by Dr. Shay and extended those for combatants and for the Warrant Officer Rotary Wing Aviator Classes 70-3/70-5. I have also included statistics for the infantry as found in *A Life in a Year*, by James R. Ebert. The results are in the following table.

It is no small measure of tribute to the courage of those who served in the army aircrews during the Vietnam war. The casualty rates were known to be high but did not equal the level of Special Forces units. Compared to all combatants, when casualties happened in a helicopter, there was a much higher fatality rate among helicopter pilots and crewmen than found in ground action. This was

| | Number | % Men's Population | % Who Served RVN | % All Combatants | % Infantry | WORWAC 70–5 # / % |
|---|---|---|---|---|---|---|
| U.S. Population | 53,100,000 | | | | | |
| U.S. Men | 26,800,000 | 100 | | | | |
| U.S. Military Personnel During Vietnam Era | 8,615,000 | 32 | | | | |
| U.S. Military Personnel Served in Vietnam | 3,145,000 | 12 | 100 | | | |
| U.S. Combatants in South Vietnam | 776,000 | 2.9 | 25 | 100 | 280,000 100 | 120/100% |
| U.S. Wounded in Action | 321,000 | 1.2 | 10 | 41 | 35 | 5/4% |
| U.S. Killed in Action | 58,000 | 0.2 | 1.8 | 7 | 3 | 36/30% |

evidenced by the 41 percent of all combatants who were wounded in action, with only 7 percent killed in action.

In my army aviator class, roughly 30 percent were killed in action. The two rotary wing aviator classes were representative of the broader experience during the later course of the war. Piloting a helicopter had four times the average combatant mortality rate.

It was in the reality of war's experiences that both those lost and the veterans who returned were consecrated as warriors and patriots.

The families should know . . . we lost them . . . too.

*We do have Prayers . . . you know . . .*

*Prayers . . . for forgiveness . . .*

*And the prayers trail after . . . trying to heal the wounds.*

> —Phoenix, the Charioteer,
> tutor and comrade to Achilles,
> in Homer, The Iliad, Book IX,
> c. 800 B.C., tr. by Robert Fagles

# Appendix

### Spanky's Gang Photograph

The Flight School photograph was taken in June 1969, at Fort Wolters, Texas. We referred to our Flight as Spanky's Gang, after the real Spanky: our respected tactical officer, CW2 Frankie Gilbert. We thought he was the best of the tac officers assigned to harass and eliminate candidates.

Candidate Jimmy Thornburgh spent five and a half years in Special Forces in Vietnam. When forced to leave, he became a warrant officer candidate, returning as a Cobra pilot, among the first to assault Tchepone, Laos, his dream come true.

Candidate Bruce Horton had served as a crew chief on a Huey in Vietnam. He died in an accident in North Carolina, several months after graduation. The author roomed with Horton and Thornburgh. Mr. Gilbert deposited Candidate Marshall upon them, obviously to keep them busy teaching proper military bearing, courtesies, shoe polishing, and display maintenance. Thornburgh and Horton were unrestrained hell-raisers.

Stan Struble wanted to serve his time and return home to become a ski bum in Colorado. He was killed by enemy fire in late November 1970, flying near An Khe.

Bruce Baer was badly injured in combat and returned to the States before his twelve-month tour of duty ended.

Doug Womack earned his place in history, a living example of determination and skill, at Landing Zone Lolo in Laos, March 1971. With the lead aircraft shot up badly, then watching the second aircraft shot down in the landing zone, he continued the assault. His aircraft was also shot up beyond use. He barely made it back to Khe Sanh. His young copilot was in such a state of shock he was replaced. Then Womack returned to Laos for more sorties in support of the South Vietnamese.

William Fitzgerald had one of the best views of the Ripcord evacuation in July 1970. Flying near the end of the green line of Huey helicopters, the Black Widows, he was among the last to extract troops under rocket, artillery, and small-arms fire.

Rick Lukens went on to Aviation Maintenance Officers Course, and became the maintenance officer for the Redskins, Cobra gunships at Camp Evans.

Ralph Moulton flew OH-6A Loaches for the combat engineers at Camp Eagle.

Richard Smith died in a helicopter accident after completing his tour.

Herb Nagel flew Cobra gunships with the 1st Air Cavalry Division.

Joseph Aiello flew with the 101st Airborne at Phu Bai.

Pete D'Agostino flew Hueys with the Lancers at Camp Evans.

# Sources

Adams, James. "Secret Armies." *U.S.* (April 1988).

Allcorn, Gary. Interviewed by author, January 1995.

Amos, Mike. Interviewed by author, January 1995.

Davidson, Phillip B. *Vietnam at War: The History, 1946–1975*. New York: Oxford, 1988.

Ebert, James R. *A Life in a Year*. Novato, California: Presidio Press, 1993.

"Final Report—Airmobile Operations in Support of Operation Lam Son 719, 24 April 1971." 101st Airborne Division (Airmobile), APO 96383.

"Into the History of Dewey Canyon II/LamSon-719." *Vietnam Helicopter Pilot's Yearbook* (1994).

Katz-Keating, Susan. *Prisoner of Hope*. New York: Random House, 1994.

Klose, Col. John A. G. U.S.A. (Ret.). "Nobody Knew His Name." *Military* (October 1990).

"Last Vietnam Era P.O.W. Declared Dead." *New York Times*, 25 September 1994.

Mihalko, John. "Into the Maelstrom." *Ripcord Report* (December 1994).

Nolan, Keith William. *Into Laos*. Novato, California: Presidio Press, 1986.

*Ripcord Report* (July 1985, December 1987, November 1994).

Rosenblum, Mort. "Vietnamese Supply Route Decided War's Outcome." *Pensacola News Journal*, 25 November 1994.

Seldes, George, comp. *The Great Thoughts*. New York: Ballantine, 1985.

Shay, Jonathan. *Achilles in Vietnam*. New York: MacMillan, 1994.

Stanton, Shelby L. *The Rise and Fall of an American Army*. New York: Dell, 1985.

Terry, Wallace. *Bloods: An Oral History of the Vietnam War*. New York: Ballantine, 1984.

Tilford, Earl H. "Search and Rescue in Southeast Asia, 1961–1975." Office of Air Force History, USAF, 1980.

Vietnam Helicopter Pilots Association, Membership Directory, 1993, 1994.

Walker, Greg. *At the Hurricane's Eye*. New York: Ballantine, 1994.

Yarborough, Col. Tom. *Da Nang Diary*. New York: St. Martin's, 1990.


Radio transcripts of CW2 Paul Stewart and Capt. David Nelson were provided in a videotape tribute to the Kingsmen by Joe Kline, a former helicopter crewman.


Additional radio tapes and transcripts made by Capt. Don Peterson were provided by Col. Mike Sloniker, U.S.A. (Ret.).

*They were the eyes and ears of the 1st Marine Division.*

# FIRST RECON—SECOND TO NONE

## A Marine Reconnaissance Battalion in Vietnam, 1967–68

# by Paul R. Young

Paul Young was a schoolteacher and former enlisted Marine whose only Recon experience had been as an unenthusiastic enlisted man in the late 1950s at Camp Pendleton. When the war in Vietnam heated up, he joined the Marines, earned a commission, and volunteered for duty in Vietnam as a grunt. But the day he got to Vietnam, 1st Recon Battalion was hit badly, and what the Marines needed was a Recon platoon leader. . . .

## FIRST RECON—SECOND TO NONE

# by Paul R. Young

Published by Ivy Books.
Available in bookstores everywhere.

CHAOS, HORROR, AND HEROISM

# SPECIAL MEN
# A LRP'S RECOLLECTIONS
## by Dennis Foley
### Author of *Long Range Patrol*

In five years, he went from private to captain,
from New Jersey to Vietnam.
But he always served with the best
the U.S. Army had to offer.

# SPECIAL MEN
# A LRP'S RECOLLECTIONS
## by Dennis Foley

Published by Ivy Books.
Available in your local bookstore.